This book may be

WRITING THE TECHNICAL REPORT

WRITING THE TECHNICAL REPORT

J. RALEIGH NELSON

*Professor Emeritus of English in the College of Engineering
University of Michigan*

THIRD EDITION

New York   Toronto   London

McGRAW-HILL BOOK COMPANY, INC.

1952

WRITING THE TECHNICAL REPORT

Library of Congress Catalog Card Number: 52-6546

IV

THE MAPLE PRESS COMPANY, YORK, PA.

To my students, the young men and women

who through the years sat with me

at the old oval table in "English 6"

this book is affectionately dedicated

Preface

Years ago, the editors of an encyclopedia asked me to prepare a statement of what I regarded as the essentials of a technical report. It was assumed that I would have some ideas on the subject since I was at the time teaching a course in report writing to senior and graduate students in engineering and was also editor of the Department of Engineering Research. It was specified that I limit myself to a statement of 150 words. A more searching test of how clearly I had come to see the fundamentals of my subject could hardly have been devised. The paragraph which I evolved at that time appears as the synopsis of this book (page xiii). After all these intervening years, it stands just as I wrote it, unchanged by a single word. It seems to me as simple and comprehensive a statement of the thesis of this book as I could possibly formulate. It defines a report as "a communication of information or counsel which is desired and which will be used by some one for some particular end." According to this definition the success of a report depends on its being so designed as to prove satisfactory under all the conditions under which it will ever be used. I was convinced that if one would always think of his report as a structure to be designed, like any structure, to carry its load, and to meet the definite requirements for its use, he would write with greater assurance and would escape the confusion that is often the result of his inexperience or of the very abundance of his material.

This emphasis on structural design still seems to me of supreme importance; every report must be planned for some particular use. For that reason my book is less concerned with incidentals of form and convention than with basic principles and basic procedures. The assimilation of these foundation principles would seem to be indispensable for advanced students preparing for professional practice and especially important for young men and women when they face the critical test of their first professional reports. In their early practice, to be sure, they will be relieved of responsibility, so far as the design of their reports is concerned, by the use of standard forms for standard procedures—test reports, progress reports, and other purely routine reports. For these they need only to be conscientious and reliable in securing their data and accurate in their computations and tabulations. But too long an apprenticeship in such routine, regimented reporting is apt to leave them quite helpless when, as is bound to happen, they are given the responsibility of organizing and designing a report independently and unaided by any prescribed form. When their first big day of opportunity arrives, they need somehow to have developed intelligence for grasping and evaluating the salient features of a problem and a high sense of responsibility for making their reports meet all possible requirements for use.

This book, in view of the needs of young or inexperienced writers in the various technological fields, lays a foundation of fundamentals; emphasizes the importance of right attitudes and sound judgments; suggests a method of approach to the task of organization and a method of production which are psychologically sound and which, intelligently followed, should give satisfactory results with the greatest possible economy of effort; sets up a few standards of criticism; and, finally, outlines certain simple critical procedures that a writer of a report can apply to his own work.

The book consists of five parts. The first deals with the design and composition of the report. The second gives specific directions for the setup of both long- and short-form reports. These are illustrated by several sample reports annotated for study. The third part of the book outlines a systematic procedure for the critical examination of a report, with a number of clinical studies of typical cases. The fourth, which is a summary of the fundamentals treated in the three preceding sections, provides a means of ready reference for both instructor and student. The fifth part presents a manual for a sixteen-week course in report writing which can be used as a basis for classroom purposes or as a guide for study for those in practice who wish to enlarge and clarify their appreciation of the fundamentals of report writing.

J. RALEIGH NELSON

ANN ARBOR, MICH.
June, 1952

Acknowledgments

It is more than forty years since I first sat down with five senior engineering students at the big oval table in the English conference room to discuss plans for a new course in report writing. I knew almost as little of report practice in those days as they did; but we were all somehow so desperately aware of the need for a course that should prepare our seniors for their professional writing that we agreed to work it out together. Between that day and the day of my retirement, nearly 3,000 students, according to a careful check of my old record books, sat with me at that same old, scarred oaken table to discuss the problems of their writing. They included graduate students and upperclassmen in engineering, in architecture, in forestry, and in military science; occasionally there were men from the Army, the Forestry Service, or the State Highway and Sanitary Engineering Departments. My greatest obligation is, I realize, to them. They made the course what it became, for they largely determined both its content and its method of approach. They certainly provided the dynamic of a perennial interest; no one could have failed to find their need and the diversity of their problems stimulating and inspiring.

I owe much also to my experience as editor of the Department of Engineering Research. When, in 1923, that department, then only three years old, reached the point where publications seemed warranted, I became chairman of the Publications Committee and editor of research publications. For thirteen years, I had the privilege of working with members of the engineering faculty, with the research staff, and with representatives of the cooperating industries for whom the department was conducting research projects. A more exciting task can hardly be imagined for one who was eager to observe the problems of technical writing. It rarely sank to the level of mere editing. My association with the research workers was quite personal: I followed the development of their major projects month by month, sometimes over periods of years; I saw the confusing mass of results accumulate; I saw them sifted and evaluated till only the essential results remained; I faced, with the investigators, the problems of organization and interpretation.

Very early in this experience, I came to view with apprehension the patron by whose money the project had been financed. My most important function was not inserting commas or revamping awkward sentences but helping the weary investigator plan the presentation of his results to meet the requirements of the man paying the bill. He was decidedly a major consideration when it came to the problem of writing the report. If the report did not suit his needs, it generally came back to be revised and rewritten.

To those years of planning how best to shape and organize research material for actual use I owe the conviction that became the central thesis of my course and is the most inescapable emphasis in my book, that a report must be designed for a specific purpose and that its success will depend largely on how well it is adapted for all the uses to which it is likely to be put.

Whatever generalizations I may have made as a result of these experiences as a teacher and as a coworker with a serious group of research investigators were put to a severe test in 1932–1933. In that year, The Detroit Edison Company engaged me to lecture on engineering reports once a week to a selected group of their men. I presented my lectures to this professional group every Monday and then met them in conference, hour after hour, over the problems of their departmental reports or of their individual reports on special projects. It was the supreme experience of my life so far as my study of report practice is concerned. I am sure I got more than I gave. At least, I was able to check my theory against their practice. Inevitably, there were points of disagreement, but my main thesis, which by this time I had come to regard almost as a declaration of faith, stood unchallenged; we were agreed that a report is no appropriate place for a parade of literary skill, but that it is a practical document made for use, which, like anything else made for use, must be planned to serve its purpose effectively.

I owe a great debt of gratitude to Alexander Dow, at that time president of The Detroit Edison Company; J. W. Parker, vice-president and general manager, and J. H. Walker, engineering assistant to the general manager, who made this profitable experience possible. I remember also with deep appreciation the courtesy and cooperation of the members of my lecture sections, many of them heads of the technical divisions of the company. I especially appreciate the permission of the company to use in this book material from the reports written as class assignments by these men. The company assumed no responsibility for the technical statements in these reports; it is understood that they are quoted merely as illustrations of my text.

Any attempt even to mention all the individuals who have contributed to the development of my course, and therefore to this book, is bound to fall short of a complete list. Such a list should certainly be headed by Dean Mortimer E. Cooley and Professor Henry E. Riggs, who first inspired the initiation of my course in report writing. Through the subsequent years, I relied repeatedly on their experience and counsel and that of many of my faculty friends, especially Dean Henry Anderson, Professors Louis A. Gram, Alfred H. White, William C. Hoad, John S. Worley, H. H. Higbie, and J. E. Emswiler. Professor A. E. White, director of the Department of Engineering Research, was for thirteen years the one to whom all my edited reports and other manuscripts had to be referred for final approval. It is impossible for me to say how much I owe to his friendly, but discriminating, criticism. Dean Herbert A. Sadler and Professor A. H. White were, for those thirteen years, the two members of my Publications Committee to whom all manuscripts were submitted and to whose final judgment I deferred on all matters of editorial policy. In the preparation of the revised editions of the original book I have profited by the experience of many of those who have used it in various ways.

In the spring of 1947, four years after my retirement from the university, I was notified by Karl V. Hawk, then head of the Personnel Division of the Department of Naval Research, that the second edition of this book had been adopted officially by the Navy. It was proposed to set up a training course in report writing in all of the experimental stations of Naval Research. Mr. Hawk requested me to design such a course, prepare a syllabus of day-by-day assignments, and plan a two-week indoctrination course to be given to a selected group of twenty-five men who were to serve as instructors in report writing in their respective stations. He wished me to prepare all the materials of instruction and come to Washington in August to conduct this pilot course in person.

I accepted the challenge of this alluring opportunity to stage a comeback—all but the personal appearance in Washington. Happily, I was able to secure competent representatives for that spectacular task. Professor Ivan Walton, who had been my associate for years on the English staff in the College of Engineering, and Assistant Professor Dorothy Greenwald, who had used my book in her course in Business Reports in the School of Business Administration, consented to undertake this sacrificial service in my stead. These two experienced teachers taught the pilot course with great success, despite the deadly heat of an August in Washington. I owe much to Karl Hawk for initiating this experiment in the teaching of report writing, and to him, Professor Walton, and Professor Greenwald for their suggestions and criticisms based on that summer's experience with an appallingly impressive group of highly trained technical men. Through the courtesy of Mr. Harder, the present head of the Personnel Division of the Office of Naval Research, I have been able to include here some of the material prepared for that experimental setup in Washington.

To all these friendly critics I owe most of what I have come to regard as essential in any consideration of report writing. But there are innumerable others, students, fellow teachers, technical investigators, authors of bulletins, even writers of routine reports, from whom I learned much. Perhaps the one thing I learned from them all—the one thing I should like to emphasize in my book—is that a report is generally an appallingly important document for somebody who needs it and will use it and that an appreciation of this fact should stimulate every man about to write a report to do his best to plan his report for every possible requirement of service.

Synopsis

Since a report is fundamentally the communication of information or counsel which is desired and which will be used by someone for a particular end, its success depends primarily on its being planned carefully to meet all the conditions under which it is to serve. The introduction should present a clear statement of the subject, of the purpose, and of the plan of organization of the material treated. It often also includes a brief statement of the conclusion, or recommendation, and sometimes a summary of results or findings. The conclusion should agree and balance logically with this introduction. The body of the report should be so written as to make evident the structural design announced in the introduction. Ideally a report should read coherently and smoothly, and should bear evidence of the writer's mastery of his subject matter in its larger aspects as well as in its minutest details.

Contents

PART III. THE CRITICISM OF THE REPORT

PART IV. SUMMARY OF BASIC PRINCIPLES

PART V. MANUAL FOR CLASS USE

PART I

THE DESIGN OF THE REPORT

The first part of this book will serve to review for the student much that, from his previous training in composition, will be more or less familiar to him. It is hoped that it will so simplify, unify, correlate, and apply what he has learned in a more or less fragmentary way over the period of his schooling, that it may give him a fundamental basis for his professional writing. For the man or woman already in practice, it may serve to recall, from their school days, many fundamental things now half forgotten. It is hoped that it will also stimulate a new interest in their professional writing and give them the confidence they often lack in the use of original methods of demonstration which they have developed as a result of their own experience.

Chapter One

Two Important Definitions

There is perhaps little to be gained by setting up a verbal definition of a report, to be memorized and used with slavish consistency throughout this book. It is important, however, that the reader and the author agree at the very outset on some fundamental conception of what a report is and how it differs from other types of composition. It will be readily recognized as a specialized form of exposition—a form of discourse distinguished from other forms in certain essential features. Description and narration enlist the imagination and even play upon the emotions; argumentation aims to convince the reader or to move him to action; exposition is concerned primarily with the communication of ideas in a form that the reader can understand and use. These are familiar distinctions.

As is often the case, one can get at the essential processes involved by regarding the derivation of the word "exposition" itself. *Exponere*, the Latin word from which it comes, means to put something out on display, presumably where it can be seen and understood. The Centennial in 1876, the World's Fair in 1893, the Century of Progress in 1933, the New York and San Francisco Expositions of 1939, and all the other great historic expositions, have been just that—great displays of objects of significance or of interest to the world at large. It is important to notice how carefully such large-scale expositions were organized in order to avoid creating confusion in the minds of observers and what pains were taken to give them the guidance they needed.

In attempting to arrive at a definition of exposition that will lay proper emphasis on its fundamental features, one might consider what would justify the inclusion of a display of concrete objects— incandescent bulbs, radio instruments, traffic signals, for example— as a part of any such great exposition. In the first place, such a display would need to be reasonably complete; otherwise, it would be both misleading and disappointing. It would purport to do something

3

that it failed to do adequately. For an exposition of electric bulbs, for example, it would be necessary to bring together samples of every significant type of incandescent bulb known. The mere mass of such material would be impressive, almost overwhelmingly so. It would also be most confusing, unless some plan could be made to display these thousands of bulbs in an orderly way. Nothing could result in greater confusion than to place them in their display cases just as they happened to arrive by express or post. If the exhibitor expected to create any impressions other than those of mass and confusion, he would have to decide what he hoped to accomplish by making such a display and then organize all details with strict reference to that objective. He might, for example, sort and arrange them according to their development, from the first crude experimental bulb to the very latest type of Mazda lamp, or he might group them according to their filaments. Whatever his purpose, it would determine the order and arrangement of the specimens in their display cases. Order and system would certainly be first considerations, but an order or system fitted to his underlying purpose.

There is still another requirement that would surely not be overlooked by any intelligent exhibitor. No matter how systematically his display might be organized, no matter how perfectly planned, it would lose much of its value for the general public unless it provided some means of interpretation and demonstration—signs, labels, booklets, guides, and demonstrators, all of them adapted to the various needs of the spectators. The demonstrators would have to be prepared to adapt their comments to the interests, the needs, and the limitations of experience of the drifting crowds. It would never do for them to estimate incorrectly the capacities of their listeners— to give a technical lecture to a group of high-school boys or an elementary demonstration to a technical expert.

The analogy is not inapt. In expository writing, one brings out from the mysterious chambers of his mind such ideas on his subject as he has assembled from a variety of sources; in presenting them, it is his purpose to create in the reader's mind a certain impression, to produce a certain effect, to serve him in a certain way. The writer must be always aware of his underlying purpose as the influence shaping and determining the form of his presentation; he must deliver his ideas in an orderly way; he must gauge his comment carefully and tactfully with reference to the limits of his reader's intellectual capacity so as to make it easy for him to get the ideas conveyed. As in the exposition of concrete objects, there must be a complete, orderly setting forth of all the ideas pertinent to the expositor's purpose.

The characteristics that must be embodied in any definition of exposition are, evidently, an orderliness of the presentation which results from its being made according to a preconceived plan perfectly adapted to carry out the purpose for which it is made, and a gauging of the amount and character of the interpretive comment to the readers' requirements. Exposition aims to economize the readers' attention to the utmost, to save him all possible confusion, and to give him such help as he needs in order to get quickly and easily the ideas presented without being burdened with superfluous comment. In its simplest and most fundamental terms exposition may, then, be defined as the systematic, orderly setting forth of ideas in accordance with a preconceived plan and a conscious unifying purpose, and with such explanatory comment as the reader needs.

Any working definition of the report as a special form of exposition will differ from this general definition only in the degree of emphasis with which the elements are weighed. The Latin verb *reportare*, from which the word "report" is derived, suggests a number of fundamental points of emphasis for any definition of a report. It means "to bring back." It implies that one goes out and gets something he is commissioned to get and bring back to the person or persons who have given him his commission. He needs to know exactly what is wanted, why it is wanted, and how it will be used when he brings it back. Those are points to be settled between him and his commissioner before he wastes time hunting around for something he does not quite understand and possibly "brings back" something that is not wanted at all. In the report, the objective is generally more definite and has a more imperative shaping effect than in any other form of exposition. As a form of writing, it is more consciously concerned with the practical use to be made of the ideas that are to be communicated. Everything about a report is determined by the requirements of those it is to serve—its length, its form, its style, the details of treatment. In length, it may range from a telegram, like Caesar's famous military dispatch, "I came, I saw, I conquered," to a great printed tome of a thousand pages or more, like the monumental Smoke Abatement Report in which a committee of engineers in Chicago in 1915 gathered together the results of a four-year study of the problem of the electrification of terminals. In form, it may be a purely tabular display of findings—"tables and labels"—with a half page of transmitting text; it may be an attractive brochure of architect's drawings with no text; it may be a cheap little pamphlet on "Garbage Treatment" printed for wide campaign distribution; or it may be a beautifully bound, beautifully illustrated prospectus designed to sell some project to susceptible readers. In every case, it will be evident that the way the report is to be used and the requirements of those who will use it determine everything about it.

It is just this emphasis on the use of the document that distinguishes a report most strikingly from other types of expository writing; it is prepared for a designated reader who wants specific information or counsel. In professional practice it should always be possible to determine exactly the requirements, preferences, and prejudices of such a reader and the uses he will make of the report. In classroom usage, it should be noted, the term "report" is used loosely to indicate course papers written with no such special consideration of a specified reader. In view of the limitation of experience of the average student and the importance of correlating his course in report writing with his technical work, it may occasionally be necessary to allow him to submit such general papers in order that he may learn how to apply the principles for the writing of reports developed in this book. It is highly important, however, that both student and teacher should recognize that such papers are not, in the strict sense of the word, reports at all; they are written without much thought of the practical use that a designated reader will make of them, and therefore without any very conscious shaping purpose.

In this book, the word "report" will signify a specialized form of exposition concerned with the communication of practical, useful information specifically called for by the person or persons to whom the report is submitted, in the form best qualified to meet their requirements and with such interpretative comment as they will need. This definition covers both the long-form report and the so-called "short-form" report; the former term will be somewhat arbitrarily used to refer to formal reports of six pages or more; the latter will be limited to reports of five pages or less, of both the formal and the informal type.

The emphasis in this definition on the ordering and interpreting of the ideas to be presented for the practical uses of those for whom the report is written rather than on the style of expression should be encouraging to the student or the young practitioner who is suffering from a secret inhibition, resulting from too persistent emphasis by his teachers on the way he says a thing rather than on the supreme importance of what he has to say.

If he accepts these definitions of exposition in general and of report writing in particular, with their common emphasis on writing with an absorbing purpose, he should find himself freed from his fear of not expressing his ideas effectively. He will appreciate the necessity of concentrating wholeheartedly on the ideas to be communicated and on the achievement of his purpose. The dynamic of his interest in his subject and his determination to make his presentation of it meet the requirements of those for whom he is writing should help him to forget himself and his inhibitions. Moreover, his training and experience, especially in any of the fields of technology, should have developed the habit of thinking a proposition through before attempting to discuss it with another. He is also accustomed to lay out in advance a carefully considered plan before undertaking any costly project. As he comes to realize the time and actual expense involved in the preparation of a report of any size, he will appreciate the economy of designing his reports as meticulously as he would any other structures qualified to carry their loads.

Here, then, is one kind of writing in which a student of technology should be able to succeed especially well. For poetic composition, he is apt to lack the requisite emotional sensibilities or to be temperamentally so constituted as to recognize or admit such sensibilities only reluctantly; for any form of fiction, he is apt to lack the type of creative imagination required; but for the organization and mobilization of his ideas for use, he is generally qualified, both by nature and training, to analyze a situation, to make up his mind what it demands, and then to make an orderly plan for accomplishing what must be done. In the report in particular, if he can learn to decide definitely before he begins to write what it is he is going to do, why he is doing it, and how best to do it, he should be able to succeed.

NOTE: It is suggested that the student read the chapter "For the Student" (page 315). The discussion of Assignments I, II, and III may well begin at once in connection with these first chapters (pages 316 to 327).

Chapter Two

Four Important Procedures

The preceding chapter has attempted to develop a fundamental conception of exposition as a kind of writing concerned with the orderly communication of ideas in accordance with a preconceived purpose and plan and of a report as a specialized form of exposition in which the use it is to serve determines almost everything—plan, scale, and method of treatment, and especially the amount of interpretative comment required. Having arrived at an understanding of what, essentially, this process of report writing is, we may well analyze it into the procedures involved. There are four distinct stages in the evolution of an idea, from the time when it is first conceived as a vague and uncertain possibility till the moment when it is ready to be submitted in a finished report. These processes in the organic growth of one's idea need to be understood; no one of them should be omitted or slighted; they should not be confused with each other; each should be allowed to make its natural contribution to the development of the idea to be presented.

First, there is the period of preliminary study. At this stage one is assembling and sorting his material. He is getting acquainted with its details, appraising it, determining its possibilities and its limitations; he is making up his own mind with reference to it and trying to decide what it means and what he can do with it. No one would, of course, think of omitting such a study as a necessary basis for writing; yet many people hurry or muddle their way through it, with the result that their work is superficial and their conclusions faulty, or they begin to write in a fragmentary way long before they see their proposition as a well-defined unit of thought or determine the purpose it is to serve. Ideally, this preliminary period should provide for an unhurried, unforced clearing away of all uncertainties and should dissipate all haze from one's own mind. Actually, it is often a rather long, painful period of confused groping. It should ultimately terminate, however, in an illuminating moment when one sees

8

clearly what his subject is and how he may give it direction toward some useful end.

Seeing his report project as a definite, limited proposition, the writer must then study the problem of communicating it to his reader. This second stage in the evolution of the report is a period of careful planning. The report, according to the thesis of this book, will be shaped largely by the purpose it is to serve; it will be judged by the degree to which it meets the necessities of those for whom it is written. One needs, therefore, to take the prospective reader's point of view, to keep constantly in mind the practical question of how he will use the report. On the basis of these fundamental considerations, one should organize, classify, arrange, order his material; he should, as a result of such detailed and analytical study, work out for his report the design that seems most logical, practical, and strategic. This second stage in the evolution of the idea reaches its satisfactory close when a structural plan has been developed that is perfectly adapted to realizing the purpose of the report.

The first two stages in the development of a report are evidently closely interrelated; one is synthetic, the other analytic, but taken together they provide an ideal preparation for the actual writing of the report. No injunction, at this point, is more imperative, especially for the inexperienced writer, than this: "In your effort to shape and pattern your material, don't begin to write too early. Don't even be in too much of a hurry to decide on the plan for presenting it." If one is wise, he will inhibit and restrain all impulses to write prematurely and fragmentarily. He should first strive to arrive at a clear conception of the limits of his material, the scope and scale of his treatment, the line of direction along which he will project it— in short, to get a conception of his project as a whole before he becomes confused by detail. Only then can one determine the shape, pattern, design, and plan of his report with proper appreciation of what it must do for his readers. These preliminary conceptions of his proposed task he needs in order that, as he begins to write and to deal with the confusing details of his subject matter, he may suffer no lapses into uncertainty as to precisely what he is doing, or why he is doing it, or how.

The actual writing of the report is the third, and in some ways, of course, the most critical, of the four stages in the production of the document. Many people create difficulty for themselves at this point by confusing the process of production with the process of criticism.

They view their own performance critically, either subconsciously all the time they are trying to write, or periodically as they stop to read over sentence by sentence or paragraph by paragraph what they have written. They are thus continually getting in their own way; they interrupt the flow of their ideas by shifting the focus of their attention from subject matter to the form of its expression. One should rather concentrate on his subject matter and write rapidly, impelled by the desire to get it all said, to reach the terminal. Ideally, one should do a piece of writing in a single, uninterrupted period of concentrated effort. By such a method, he achieves a unity of style and a proper proportion of parts that are impossible when he writes this today and that tomorrow.

Ideally, a report should be so written; practically, such a course is often impossible in view of the mass and complexity of the material. One should aim, however, to complete at least each of the longer unit sections in a period of creative effort. If he has exhausted his creative energies in such a period of strain, he may find relief in examining critically what he has written as a unit before he goes forward. Such critical examination should be concerned, however, not with the puttering details of sentence structure or of verbal usage, but with the way the ideas are being delivered, the clarity and effectiveness with which they are being presented, and the degree to which the unit section fits into the pattern of the whole.

As Chapter XIV on "The Rough Draft" points out, the inexperienced writer who follows the procedure outlined thus far will probably get a rough draft that is rough indeed. Written hastily, under pressure, with attention wholly concentrated on the ideas being presented, the first draft is apt to exhibit all the immaturities and defects of the writer's speech habits. But it should be a vital, unified, organic, and lucid exposition of the ideas presented. Obviously, few writers ever develop such facility of expression that they do not need to subject their first drafts to thorough criticism and revision. This period of self-criticism forms the fourth and final period in the production of a report.

For the young writer, such a program of procedure is indispensable. If he will follow it, not slighting any one of the stages or confusing any two of them, he will find that his reports will begin to give evidence of intelligent planning and will be qualified to do what is expected of them. Moreover, the habit of long, careful preparation and planning, followed by rapid composition performed with intensive concentration on the ideas conveyed, will develop a facility that may ultimately make his writing a pleasure. Meticulous care in the criticism of everything he writes will, at the same time, assure him the one indispensable condition for self-improvement. If he sets his standard high and refuses ever to be satisfied with a performance falling below that standard, he is bound to grow.

So important does some such program of procedure seem to the author that he has made it the basis of much that he has to say in the subsequent chapters. As his preface has stated and as his table of contents shows, he will devote the entire third part of the book to suggestions for the criticism of the report.

Chapter Three

Two Tests of Progress

Before attempting the long and often laborious task of writing a report, it is well to have some conclusive and specific tests which one may use to determine whether he has progressed far enough in the study of his material to be qualified to write. One must make sure that he sees his subject in its largest aspects and that he has discovered by analysis its logical component parts.

The first stage in the process of organizing one's ideas for some practical end has been shown to be that period in which the subject is evolving and taking shape by the natural processes of thought. One is defining in his own mind what his subject means, what it is and what it is not, trying to get an understanding of the reader or of the audience to whom he will present it, the effect he can hope to produce on them, and the way it can best be made to serve them.

When the inspired moment arrives and one feels sure that all uncertainties are cleared away, he should write out a brief, incisive statement of his proposition as he sees it. The attempt to make such a record is best accomplished by drafting a single comprehensive sentence that will test at this point the clearness and sharpness of one's understanding of his subject. Such a sentence, the so-called "thesis" sentence, is an attempt to record one's conception of his idea as a limited unit of thought and to define to himself the purpose for which it is to be used.

Having spent the time requisite to complete a piece of research, it is a reassuring experience to be able to say: "The series of tests run on X indicates that $a = b + c$"; or "The design for a new X to be installed at Y meets all the specified requirements for its performance"; or "A study of the operating record of X over a period of six months makes it evident that it should be discarded and replaced by a more efficient machine"; or "Of the three processes a, b, and c now available for making X, c is theoretically the most sound and is practically the best fitted to the conditions d, e, f in the factory at Y."

12

Such a sentence should serve to keep the writer from exceeding his limits, should help him to follow consistently the line of his objective, and may even suggest to him immediately the points to be included and the order of their sequence. It is a fairly reliable test of the synthesis of his material and his grasp of his subject as a whole. If it can be satisfactorily executed, it will indicate that he can proceed with the analysis and classification of the details of his subject matter without danger of becoming confused or inadvertently exceeding his limits. The thesis sentence is concrete evidence of how clearly and simply he sees his subject and, if kept before him as he begins to handle the details of his material, will often save him much confusion.

It should, of course, be admitted that such a test cannot always be applied. Some types of material lend themselves much more readily to such summation than others. A report that is largely descriptive, for example, may appear to resist stubbornly all effort to reduce it to such a synthesis. But even in cases where the use of the thesis statement seems impractical, it will usually clear one's mind of uncertainty if he will set down specifically his main objective or his most important emphasis.

Such a sentence is quite unlikely to appear anywhere in the text of the report. It is merely a working sketch which may be written on a card, to be carried in one's pocket or set up before one of his study tables as a constant reminder of what his project is, in its largest aspects. It is quite analogous to the lead sentence. The newspaper reporter has discovered by experience that he can save himself confusion in the rapid writing which falls to his lot by beginning his news column with a comprehensive sentence in which all the details are stated in brief form—an embryonic sentence which needs merely to be developed in detail to fill as many columns as are required.

It is analogous also to the working sketch, which is a common device helpful in the other arts. Leonardo da Vinci's notebooks are filled with such sketches—mere records of ideas conceived clearly by the artist but never worked out in detail into finished compositions. They are embryonic in the same sense as the lead sentence; they need only to be elaborated and developed to make complete compositions.

It cannot be too strongly emphasized that one should be sure he has in some such way achieved a clear, but simple, conception of his proposition as a whole before he attempts to develop any organic plan for dealing with details. Obviously, he should first have assembled all pertinent material bearing on his subject. He should have done all his reading, completed all his research, before he begins to consider the most effective plan for presenting his subject. Any plan made prematurely is apt not to comprehend the whole of the subject matter. It should also be evident that one cannot make a plan unless he is clear as to every condition his design must satisfy. The thesis sentence should have tested one's grasp of his proposition as a whole and one's sense of his own objective; but, before entering seriously upon the task of making a design for his report, one should be sure he is aware of every possible requirement of use it must meet. One should be determined to work out his plan always with reference to his prospective readers and their needs.

The processes involved in the first period are largely subjective— more or less a blend of conscious and subconscious forces as one gropes his way through the confusion of his accumulating material toward a unifying understanding of what it means and what can be done with it. But as he now passes into the second of the stages in the genesis of his idea, when he begins to plan definitely as to how he can most effectively deliver it to his prospective readers, he is entering into a period in which he must consciously and systematically exercise his power of analysis, must control and direct his thinking toward a definite objective. He must check details, determine their relative value, eliminate irrelevant material, add what he finds lacking; he must classify, order, and arrange. It is a period of detailed study which he should undertake without too definite a preconception as to form. The pattern of his exposition should take shape naturally and only after much free experimentation. He should not set up a pattern arbitrarily and then proceed to force his material into this mold; he should be striving always to discover a structural pattern inherent in his subject matter itself and perfectly fitted to the particular use to be made of it.

It is hardly necessary to point out that this method of developing a plan for a report by a process of progressive experimentation does not apply where one is forced to use standard forms. For such reports, the pattern is set arbitrarily, and one can only strive to organize each prescribed unit coherently. For that purpose, the analytic procedure recommended here does apply and may be found useful.

Possibly each person will have to make this analytic study of his material in his own way. It is difficult for one person to prescribe any analytic procedure for another, but it is an economy to go about the process of analysis systematically, consciously following a natural sequence of procedures. Whatever one's method, it should be flexible and should allow for errors of judgment, for constant criticism, for the abandoning of material found on second consideration to be superfluous or valueless. Finally, when, as a result of this open-minded, judicial consideration of his material, he arrives at what appears to be satisfactory analytic scheme for its organization, he should set that scheme up as a sort of experimental structure to be tested at every point before it is used as a basis for the design of the report.

For making such an analysis for a preliminary plan, the use of a loose-card system is recommended, especially for the beginner. As one gains experience, he may ultimately reach the point when he will be able to jot down immediately a plan that is organically correct. Swiftly and subconsciously, as he has worked, the proposition has taken form in his mind. But when the beginner writes out a plan for his report prematurely, he will rarely find it adequate for his purpose, although, having once written it down, he is likely to think of it as final. At least one type of young writer is inclined to combat every effort to tear down such a preliminary plan or to discover its weaknesses. The form has crystallized and set, and it is difficult for him to reshape it. If the writer whose design is under criticism is more tractable, he may be inclined to scratch up and work over the original copy till the page becomes a confused, tangled record of all the changes he has made. Often he himself can read it and interpret it only with difficulty. Confusion is thrice confounded.

Instead of attempting to set down at once on a sheet of paper any analytic scheme, the student will find it better practice first to write out on cards or slips of paper the topics he feels sure he must include in the treatment of his subject. He can then work with this objective material at his leisure till he arrives by progressive steps at a final plan of organization that seems to suit his purpose. Such a method allows one to let his mind play on the subject quite freely with the assurance that, no matter what errors of judgment he may make, he will be able to check them out at the proper moment. It is an experimental method which allows one to shift easily from one scheme of classification to another, to add, to subtract, combine, check in or out, arrange, and yet all the time be clearing and simplifying his conception of his proposition. It is critical; it is flexible; it results in the progressive elimination of erroneous first judgments. It terminates in an analytic scheme that has been tested at every point.

The directions for following such a procedure may be briefly outlined as follows:

1. With the proposition set up before you in the form of a thesis sentence, jot down on loose cards or slips of paper what appear to you to be the logical parts of this proposition, or at least the evident topics you must cover. Continue to do this till you feel that you have exhausted your subject matter. Do not be disturbed if at this stage you find that you have a confusing number of cards and can discover no plan of organization.

2. Test these cards with strict reference to the limits of your proposition and the purpose of your report, or the effect you have in mind to produce on your reader. Eliminate everything that does not belong strictly within the limits you have decided to observe or that does not further your main objective. Add anything that you discover you have omitted or overlooked.

You should at this point be reasonably sure that you have in hand all the material which must be treated in your report and that you have included nothing which will confuse you and cause you difficulty because it does not belong. Here is what you have to work with. That much is settled.

3. Now classify your cards.

Put together things that belong together. Be sure there is no overlapping and no confusion as to the relation of coordinate and subordinate points.

In each case, make a new single card for each major division with the subclassification noted on it. Keep your statement of points brief and simple, in a purely topical form.

By this process of elimination you should have reduced the number of your cards and greatly simplified your layout of material. You should begin to see the plan take shape.

4. Finally decide what is the most effective order in which to present the unit parts your analysis has disclosed. The loose-card system makes it easy to try out different arrangements by shifting the cards this way and that.

The decision as to the best order is much more critical than the young writer often realizes. It is almost never possible to say that one order is as good as another. There is one order, and only one, that will serve your purpose effectively. An illogical order of points will make it difficult to write the report; one will seem to be swimming against the current; he will find it hard to get from one part to another part or to make the structure hang together. A logical order will assure an easy, natural flow of ideas, so that the report will seem almost to write itself. One must decide at the outset on some principle of arrangement and observe it consistently. For this critical decision the character of the subject matter and the effect one has in mind to produce on the reader will be the determining considerations. The order may be determined by the time relationship, as in an exposition of a process, or by the spatial relations, as in a technical description, or by the development from the simple to the complex or from the familiar to the unfamiliar, or by the order of relative importance. In deciding the order of points, one should try as strategically as possible to follow the probable reactions of the reader's mind to the ideas presented. Nothing is perhaps so critical in the design as determining the most effective order.

When your cards are in the order you regard as final, number them before they slip into limbo again.

5. Having arrived at the point where the analysis is complete and your orderly scheme is clear to you, set it up on a sheet of paper, and throw your cards away. The pattern of your report has now evolved to the point where it is reasonably clear and is in a form to keep you, as you work, constantly aware of the relationship of part to part.

Provide in your setup for an introduction and a conclusion or final summary. These are functional units which are, of course, not a part of the analysis you have just made. They are, however, indispensable to the design of the report and should be included as integral elements.

Arrange the analytic scheme on the page so that it will instantly convey to the eye the relation of main and subordinate units. Use some consistent notation to indicate these relationships. The following are suggested: I, *a*, 1; or, if more than three orders are required, *A*, I, *a*, 1; or *A*, I, *a*, 1, (*a*), (1), etc.

Use parallel construction as far as possible for the statement of coordinate points.

Never indicate the division of a topic into subtopics unless there are at least two such subtopics. One subtopic under a major heading means that no division has taken place.

You will find that a simple outline is less confusing and easier to use than one that is very complex or detailed.

Time spent in perfecting the design of the report is time well spent.

The discovery and correction of defects of arrangement before one begins to write will minimize the labor of revision later. The plan should, of course, be structurally sound; it should represent a logical analysis and a sound classification of ideas. But it must be more; in consideration of the effect it must produce on the reader for whom it is designed, it must often assure you a presentation that will be tactful, diplomatic, even strategic. Keeping in mind the reader's personal prejudices, his likes and dislikes, one may build up one's arguments as effectively as he would in debate. But if a plan is strategic, it must be honest; anything that suggests propaganda, however concealed or camouflaged beneath the massing of facts, any effort of the writer to sell himself or his company to the reader, when he is supposed to be doing something else, will bring his report under suspicion. So subtly do such elements of propaganda creep into reports that when there is suspicion of any hidden purposes, they are often submitted to experienced analysts capable of discovering such elements. One company, at least, has been organized in recent years for this specific service.

This danger of carrying strategy beyond the pale of honesty is probably one against which the novice need not be specially warned. He will need only to make sure that his plan is so made that it will present his material in a logical, orderly way and to regard it with a keen eye as to the effect it will produce on his reader. It must be both structurally sound and strategically honest.

Note: It will be found helpful to study the examples of the thesis sentence and the outline plan given on the following pages.

EXAMPLE 1.
Title, Thesis Sentence, and Outline.

PROVISION

of

RESERVE GENERATING CAPACITY

Thesis Sentence: The method of providing reserve generating capacity should be governed by investment in system ties, system-tie capacities, and plant efficiencies.

PLAN

   I. Introduction
  II. Basis of Requirement for Reserve Capacity
 III. Methods of Providing Reserve
     a. Bulk method
     b. Duplicate-unit method
     c. Distributed method
     d. Compromise method
 IV. Limitations Imposed by Investment in System Ties
     a. Heavily tied radial system
     b. Loop system
  V. Conditions Determining System-tie Capacities
 VI. Effect of Plant Efficiencies
VII. Conclusions

EXAMPLE 2.
Title, Thesis Sentence, and Outline.

THE TYPE OF SPECIFICATION USED

for

LINE CONSTRUCTION

by

THE DETROIT EDISON COMPANY

Thesis Sentence: The elaborate specifications which The Detroit Edison Company has for line construction are justified by the results.

PLAN

   I. Introduction
  II. Development of Specifications
      a. Simple rules
      b. Semicomplete
      c. Complete
         1. Material tests
         2. Field trials
         3. Field suggestions
         4. Standardizing of material
         5. Approval
 III. Educational Program
      a. Division foremen
      b. Crew foremen
      c. Field estimators
      d. Planning engineers
 IV. Results
      a. Adequate strength
      b. Required clearance
      c. Reduced stock
      d. Improved appearance
      e. Lower cost
  V. Summary

EXAMPLE 3.
Title, Thesis Sentence, and Outline.

TWO SUGGESTIONS FOR IMPROVING DESIGN

of

WELDED-PIPING SYSTEMS

for

HIGH-TEMPERATURE SERVICE

Thesis Sentence: The method proposed for the design of welded-piping systems for high-temperature service provides for dividing the piping system into units so that connections between pipe and valves may be welded in the shop; it also includes a simple loose-sleeve guard for field-welded joints.

PLAN

I. Introduction
II. Development of Welding Unit
    a. Division of piping system into suitable units
    b. Shop welding of pipe to valves and fittings
        1. Preparation of valves for welding
        2. Welding
        3. Testing
        4. Annealing of complete unit
    c. Installation of welded unit
        1. Welding
        2. Testing
III. Protection of Field-welded Joints
    a. Design of loose-sleeve guard
    b. Fabrication of guard
    c. Application of guard to joint
IV. Summary

EXAMPLE 4.
Title, Thesis Sentence, and Plan.

THE BP-34 PLANE

Thesis Sentence: Considered from the point of view of its structure, its equipment, and its performance records, the BP-34 Plane seems to meet the demand for a high-performance pursuit plane.

PLAN

  I. Introduction
 II. The Structure
    a. Fuselage
    b. Wings
    c. Controlling surfaces
    d. Landing gear
III. The Equipment
    a. Instrument installation
    b. Armament
    c. Special instruments
 IV. The Performance
    a. Speed
    b. Rate of climb
    c. Vision
    d. Stability
    e. Range and endurance
  V. Conclusion

Chapter Four

Three Ways to Help the Reader

It has been shown that a writer faced with the task of delivering ideas can save himself time and waste motion by getting clearly in mind before he begins to write just what he is going to say, why he is going to say it, and how he can say it most effectively. It is equally true that the reader will be saved confusion and his time and effort be greatly economized if he is provided throughout the report with the help which these fundamental conceptions afford.

Before taking up a discussion of the actual writing of the report—the third of the four periods through which one passes in its preparation—it may be well to consider how one can help the reader to get the idea it conveys with the least effort. This is a very real obligation laid upon everyone who writes a report. It is his duty to make the reading of his report as easy as possible. How this can be accomplished can best be understood by analyzing the writing process with reference to the requirements of the reader. Such an analysis applies equally well to all forms of exposition; it is given here as preliminary to a series of chapters to follow on various techniques involved specifically in the writing of a report. It will show how in the introduction, in the body of an exposition, and in the terminal section, whatever its nature, the reader must never for a moment be allowed to become confused as to what the precise subject under discussion is, what the writer's underlying purpose, or what plan of organization the writer is using to give order to the development of his proposition.

The reader must at the very outset be given a clear, preliminary view of the subject matter as a whole. He must know the limits, the scope and scale of the proposed treatment in order to gauge in advance the demand to be made on his attention. He must understand what the writer wants him to get from the discussion of the subject. He can then at least meet him halfway. Moreover, if, before he is plunged into the discussion, he has a simple idea of the plan of presentation, he is much less apt to become confused by details. If the pattern of the whole is impressed on his mind in its simplest terms ($x = a + b + c + d$), he will be able to follow the discussion much more easily than he could otherwise do. The introduction should prepare the reader to receive the burden of the exposition by giving him in advance exactly these three fundamental concepts; the subject, the purpose, the plan.

One has only to recall his experiences with various lecturers to appreciate the value of a good beginning. The lecturer who makes a number of false starts before he gets under way confuses and discourages the student at the very beginning of the lecture hour by making it difficult to determine just what the subject for the day is. The lecturer is more helpful who indicates at the outset the limits of the material to be treated and the way it will be organized in order that it may all be presented in the hour available. "This hour," he says, "I am going to try to make clear to you how to determine the specific gravity of a liquid. I shall demonstrate the way one proceeds to determine the specific gravity of mercury, sulphuric acid, and water." The student is able immediately to focus and direct his attention properly and to decide the form his notes will take. With this forward look over the hour, he is able to get what the lecturer wishes him to get much more easily and to make a record much more coherently and intelligibly than he could otherwise do.

The introduction is so explicit a means of helping the reader to approach the task of reading the exposition that composing it is relatively simple compared with the task of handling masses of detail in the body of the document. One needs to develop every possible means for making it easy to follow through from part to part without losing one's feeling for the structural design. The pattern of the exposition must be made everywhere obvious by marking with unmistakable clearness the component units and their relation to each other and to the whole.

A piece of exposition is not cast *en bloc* in one great, undivided mass; it is broken up into subordinate units to accord with the analytic scheme that has resulted from the classification of the material. It looks, not like Figure 1, but like Figure 2 (page 25).

The scheme $x = a + b + c + d$ has been set up in the reader's mind by the introduction as a fundamental pattern that is to determine the order of treatment to be followed. It must be made easy for the reader, as he proceeds, to recognize these component units. They will be given distinctness by initial emphasis on the topic each presents. This is the psychological basis for the topic sentences at the beginning of paragraph units or of topic paragraphs at the beginning of sections or larger units. This is shown graphically in Figure 3 (page 26), in which the topic sentences are represented by the crosshatching.

This initial emphasis on the topic alone, though it would define the component units sharply from each other, would give too disjunctive an effect if at the points of transition the relation of part to part were not also indicated. One must create a coherent structure in

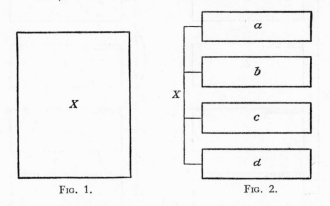

FIG. 1. FIG. 2.

which each member is a functional part. Figure 4 is an attempt to represent this graphically. The arrows represent lines of reference at points of transition from one component unit to another, showing their essential relationships.

A simple illustration may make this clear. If x in Figures 3 and 4 represents an investigation to determine why production has fallen off in a factory and to suggest remedial measures, a might cover the statement of the conditions disclosed by the investigation, b, the effect of these conditions on production, c, a temporary, but immediate, measure of relief, d, a permanent and adequate remedy. The plan is evidently represented by the formula

$$x = a + b + c + d$$

It will be assumed that the scale of development warrants a paragraph treatment of each component unit in this plan.

There are two ways of introducing topic *b*. One may say simply: "The production in this factory has fallen off seriously in the past year." This use of the topic sentence, illustrated in Figure 3, does notify the reader that he is through with topic *a*, which reviews conditions found to exist, and that he is passing to a consideration of topic *b*, the decline in production; but it fails to indicate also the logical relation between *a* and *b*. One might say: "These conditions disclosed by the investigation have caused a serious decrease in production in the past year." This backward reference, represented

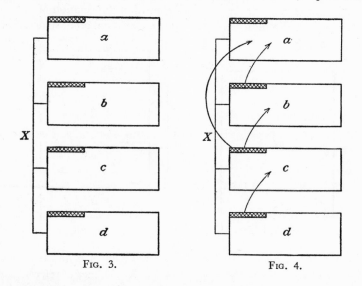

Fig. 3.   Fig. 4.

by the arrow at the beginning of *b*, Figure 4, indicates a relation of cause and effect existing between *a* and *b*.

In the beginning topic *c*, one might, similarly, say: "Temporary relief might be afforded by putting all the machinery in better condition." Although this would emphasize the new topic *c*, it would again fail to relate it in a coherent way to the other structural units. This might easily be effected by saying: "The decline in production, which has resulted from the unsatisfactory conditions in the factory, might be temporarily relieved by putting the present machinery in better repair." As is shown in Figure 4, topic *c* is at this point shown to be related to both *a* and *b*.

At the beginning of topic *d*, one might say: "Complete revision of the entire mechanical equipment of this factory is the only permanent relief that can be afforded." He might indicate the relation between *c* and *d*, as a relation of temporary and permanent relief, with something like this: "The conditioning of the present equipment of the factory will afford only temporary relief; permanent relief can be assured only by installing new machinery at a number of places in the production line."

The use of such transitional comment in conjunction with the topic sentence makes the units in the structural design stand out distinctly from the level of the page, without, however, making the treatment of these units too disjunctive. It is a second means of keeping the reader constantly and continuously aware of what the writer is doing at those points in the structural plan where it is possible to become confused as to what has been done and what is about to be done. It is important that the reader should be thus oriented and constantly guarded against confusion.

The terminal section may also be used effectively for a final checkup to make sure that the reader has understood what the writer has intended, that he has understood the essential emphasis, that he has not overlooked some important point, that he has followed through without confusion from beginning to end. The terminal section is, like the introduction, a rather more intimate comment of the writer to the reader regarding the performance that is contained in the body of the paper itself. It is a third means of keeping the reader conscious of the structural pattern ($x = a + b + c + d$).

By these three means the writer's effort from beginning to end is directed to keeping his reader constantly aware of the limits within which he is working, of his motive, and of the design that he is following as a means of giving order to his treatment of the details of his subject matter and structural soundness to the whole.

A better summary and restatement of these fundamental considerations which have so largely determined the conscious development of the technique of expository writing can hardly be found than in the classical remark of Mrs. Royce, wife of the famous Professor Josiah Royce of Harvard, a characterization of his lecture method that has frequently been quoted. She said whimsically:

"Oh, Professor Royce's method of lecturing is quite simple. He always tells his students at the beginning of the hour just what he is going to tell them, and how he is going to tell it to them; then he tells them exactly what he told them he would tell them in exactly the way he told them he would tell them; then, at the end of his lecture hour, he always takes time to tell them that he has told them what he told them he would tell them."

The study of an article on "Activated-Sludge Sewage Treatment" which appeared in the *Engineering News-Record* in June, 1916, will illustrate how these three means are used to keep the reader aware of the writer's purpose and plan. This article is presented in full, with marginal comment and a graphical analysis of essential functions, on pages 30 to 34. The introduction begins by pointing out that the activated-sludge treatment of sewage is a comparatively new method which is growing rapidly in favor and that it has been tried in various places with apparently increasing success. The question naturally has arisen whether this method has sufficient merit to warrant its general adoption. Such an appraisal can be made only by considering first the unsolved problems in the use of this method and then the advantages that this method would have over other methods if the problems were solved. The subject X is revealed by the title, Activated-Sludge Sewage Treatment. The purpose is indicated by the idea of the appraisal represented in the graph, Figure 5, by the arrow; it is desired to determine whether this is a good method or not. The plan of treatment is to consider the unsolved problems and then the advantages. X clearly equals $A + B$.

The paper falls into two parts, A and B. The section giving the unsolved problems begins with a brief introductory paragraph which is represented by the formula $A = a + b + c + d$. The unsolved problems are four: the winter-weather problem, the water problem, the problem of odors, and the cost problem. To each of these problems one paragraph is devoted.

The unsolved problems and the possibility of their solution having been considered, there appears a brief transition paragraph which may be paraphrased as follows:

If it be assumed that all of these problems may ultimately be solved, that the winter weather will not prohibitively affect the biological forces involved, that the water problem will be solved, that the odors will ultimately be eliminated, and that the cost will be satisfactorily reduced, one may reasonably ask what are the advantages of this method over other methods.

Clearly this paragraph does nothing more than ensure that the reader has the four problems and their probable solution clearly in mind before he goes forward to consider the advantages of this method. The paragraph is purely transitional.

The section dealing with the advantages, like that dealing with problems, begins with a brief introductory paragraph which might

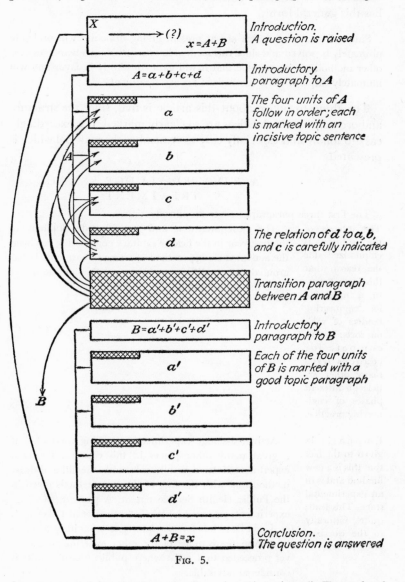

FIG. 5.

be represented by the formula $B = a' + b' + c' + d'$. To each of these advantages a paragraph is given.

Since the purpose of the article is to answer the question, "How valuable is X?" a brief conclusion is added to the discussion which has this general form:

Since all problems which are at present giving difficulty will probably ultimately be solved and since this method has such evident advantages over other methods, it is probable that it will gain constantly in favor and will ultimately displace other methods of sewage treatment.

The thing to notice about this article is that, since the structure and organization of the ideas are so clearly marked, it is exceedingly easy to follow and especially easy to remember the material which is presented.

ACTIVATED-SLUDGE SEWAGE TREATMENT[1]

The first three paragraphs cover the introduction x.

The interest of the subject is emphasized for the reason that this is an article in a magazine for engineering readers of various sorts; it must compete for readers with many other articles on different phases of engineering practice.

The most interesting and promising development of the past year in the field of sanitary engineering has been the activated-sludge method of sewage treatment. It has aroused more enthusiasm than any other development since the Imhoff tank.

Emphasis is given to the fact that this is a new method and is in an experimental stage. This leads quite naturally to the question of its value.

Activated-sludge experiments are being conducted at a great many other places in this country. Brooklyn experimented on a small scale with the fill-and-draw method and with the first of the two methods given in the Public Health Service patent. A paper upon these experiments was read by W. T. Carpenter at Lakewood, N. J., on Dec. 3, before the New Jersey Sanitary Association. Apparently none of the other experiments has as yet proceeded to a point where publication of results is considered advisable.

---

[1] *Engineering News-Record*, 73: 5, January–June, 1916.

This paragraph is purely functional. It exhibits all three of the functions of an introduction; the subject, an appraisal of this new method of sewage treatment; the purpose, an attempt to appraise its value; and the plan, a consideration of the unsolved problems and the advantages.

A judicial appraisal of the process at the present time is not easy. There are too many unsolved problems involved. However, an appraisal will be attempted by discussing: first, the unsolved problems, and second, the advantages of the method if these problems be solved.

This is the topic paragraph of section A.
$$A = a + b + c + d.$$

The unsolved problems include: (1) the winter-weather problem; (2) the plant-supervision problem; (3) the sludge problem; (4) the cost problem.

Note how in the series of paragraphs on the four problems the similarity of form—the parallel construction of the topic sentences—emphasizes the fact that one is dealing with a series of similar points.

The winter-weather problem may resolve itself in one of two ways: It may prove that the process will be economically possible in any part of this country, or that it will be applicable only for cities where the sewage throughout the year remains above a certain critical temperature. In this connection it should be stated that the temperature of the sewage itself will be likely to be a greater controlling factor than the temperature of the air introduced, as the air can probably be heated sufficiently at a low cost. The nearer the outfall sewer is to the center of population, the more likely will the sewage be to remain throughout the year above the critical temperature, and hence the more likely will it be that the activated-sludge process will be possible for that city.

The plant-supervision problem is an almost entirely unknown quantity for the new method. The lack of intelligent supervision of sewage-treatment plants in general has often been discussed in engineering periodicals and in textbooks, and it is unfortunately an extremely pertinent subject for discussion. It seems probable, from the nature of the activated-sludge process, that it will require more intelligent supervision than most processes that have hitherto been in use. This is so, primarily, because of the comparative ease with which the sludge tends to lose its "activated" properties. The neglect of any one of a number of factors, such as air supply, sludge percentage, or detention period, will cause this loss of "activation." Should the process come into general use, it seems probable that in any plant where a sufficiently high standard of supervision does not obtain poor operation will at times occur and the effluent be below the required standard. In general, therefore, it is probably true that the successful application of this new process for such higher standard should be viewed by communities as a distinct advantage rather than as an evil, as it will help to keep that part of the public works above the influence of the political element.

The sludge problem cannot as yet be said to be definitely solved. It has been demonstrated that activated sludge has a higher fertilizing value than ordinary sewage sludge, and this fact has caused such firms as Armour & Company and Sulzberger & Sons Company to begin an active investigation of the process. The cost of realizing this fertilizer value, however, depends largely upon the cost of removing the moisture, and this is the feature regarding which no final figures are yet available.

Here the relation of the problem presented in this paragraph to the three preceding problems needs to be indicated and its closer dependence on the air problem. The graph attempts to indicate how this first sentence serves by this reference backward and forward to tie the structure to-

The cost problem is obviously related to each of the three foregoing problems, but it is related much more intimately to the air problem. The greater portion of the cost of the activated-sludge process, exclusive of sludge handling, lies in the cost of air compression. Probably at least $3 of the $5 cost figure given by Mr. Hatton refers to air cost. If this cost estimate is based on power at $\frac{3}{4}$ cent or less per kilowatt-hour it is obvious that for a great many communities which are not able to secure power at less than $1\frac{1}{2}$ cents the cost of sewage treatment by the activated-sludge method will be $8 or more per million gallons, exclusive of sludge-handling costs. It is highly desirable, therefore, that the cost of the process be reduced still further, and the most fruitful point of attack would seem offhand to be the air cost.

gether at this point.

This is the transition paragraph between sections *A* and *B*. Note that the transition is effected by first a backward reference in the form of a summary and then a forward reference to section *B*.

Here is the topic paragraph for section *B*.

The following four paragraphs develop the four topics *a'*, *b'*, *c'*, and *d'*.

If it be assumed now, for purposes of discussion, that all of the problems above will be solved—that winter weather will not prohibitively retard the biologic forces involved, that adequate supervision will be provided, that the sludge problem will be successfully solved, that the total cost of treatment is brought within the means of the average community—it is pertinent to consider the advantages of the new method compared with others.

The following will probably be its most important advantages: (1) ability to control the quality of the effluent; (2) lack of odor development; (3) small plant area; (4) low first cost.

If we assume that the plant has adequately intelligent supervision and that it is designed with a sufficiently flexible air supply, it will be comparatively easy to regulate the quality of the effluent to current requirements. This is not so true of a plant composed of Imhoff tanks and sprinkling filters. In the latter case the sprinkling filters must be designed sufficiently large to be capable of delivering the highest quality of effluent that will be required at any time. The cost of flexibility in such a plant is therefore first cost, which is a constant expense. In the activated-sludge method the cost of flexibility is principally operation cost, since the quality of the effluent may be largely controlled by varying the rate of air introduction. This advantage of the new method is more important than may appear at first sight. There are many communities for which the sewage-treatment problem involves simply nuisance prevention. For such communities it will be unnecessary to deliver as pure an effluent in cold weather as in warm weather, and for them the ability to regulate the quality of the effluent by means of a variable operating expense (which is never more than is actually required), rather than by means of a constant first-cost expense (which is for part of the year excessive), will be an unmistakable advantage.

The new method does not appear to develop objectionable odors in any part of the process, if we make a slight reservation in the matter of sludge treatment, regarding whose odor characteristics we are not as yet finally informed.

It is definitely established that the new method will require much less plant area than present methods delivering a corresponding quality of effluent. This will reduce the cost of land per unit of sewage flow to a much lower plane of importance and will make it possible to select sites nearer the center of population, thus reducing the length of outfall and increasing the freshness of the sewage.

The relatively low first cost of the method is primarily due to the fact that its "cubic performance" (for definition of term see *Engineering News-Record*, Dec. 18, 1915, page 751) is much higher than, for example, that of sedimentation and sprinkling filtration. The daily cubic performance of the activated-sludge method will probably be about two or three volumes of sewage per daily cubic performance of only about 0.5 to 0.7 volume of sewage per volume of device. Other factors such as the lessened land area and the lessened length of outfall sewer also help to reduce the first cost. Low first cost is important, because, for a great many communities the economic limit is not determined by annual cost but rather by bond issue, and for such cities it will be financially easier to install a "low-first-cost—high-operating-cost" system than a "high-first-cost—low-operating-cost" system.

This brief terminal section answers, on the basis of the discussion, the question raised in the introduction by the word "appraisal." The words "evidently, then," mark it as terminal in character.

Evidently, then, the process deserves the most painstaking investigation. Its possibilities appear to be very large. If the present difficulties can be overcome, we shall have added to engineering knowledge a valuable, if not the most valuable, method of disposing of liquid wastes.

NOTE: It will be found helpful to make a similar analysis of the reports on pages 165 to 187 and 188 to 217.

Chapter Five

The Three Primary Functions of the Introduction

In proceeding to discuss in more detail the various means which a writer has available for helping his reader, one naturally considers the introduction first, not only because it occurs first in the setup of a report, but because to the reader it is more important than any other part, unless it may possibly be the terminal summary or conclusion. In report writing, in particular, there is an increasing demand that the first page or two shall provide a comprehensive idea of the whole report.

A busy executive at the head of an industrial organization often has no time to devote to a detailed reading of a long report. He wants to be able to get the answer to the question in his mind or the solution proposed for his problem quickly and immediately without the necessity of hunting for it through long pages of text. The introduction is most useful to him in this first hasty examination of the report if in a page, or less, it gives him the whole story at a glance. He needs to know what the proposition is, how the writer proceeded to investigate it, what he found out, what he concluded, what he recommended, and how he plans to organize the details of his report.

If such a reader needs to reinforce his first impression thus gained, he is apt to turn to the final page and read the conclusions, the summary, or the recommendations in their final, and often more substantial, form. Even the more deliberate reader, setting out to read a long report in all its details, finds by experience that his reading is greatly expedited and his chances of becoming confused greatly reduced if, before he plunges into the reading of the body of the report, he is given a clear, and greatly simplified, understanding of the whole task before him.

The young writer will find that, if he can learn to write a satisfactory introduction and to check carefully against it as he proceeds with his writing, especially to check his conclusions when his report is finished, his danger of becoming muddled as he attempts to handle masses of detail will be greatly lessened. He will be more easily able to discover digressions in the body of his report and bring the whole structure into better alignment with his main objective.

In all forms of exposition, and especially in report writing, the introduction is a critical part of the performance: it seems important therefore to understand at the outset the functions it may perform. Stated most simply the essential functions of any introduction are three: (1) to make clear to the reader the precise subject to be considered; (2) to indicate the writer's attitude toward this subject; (3) to lay out the plan for its treatment. The introduction may be thought of as a preliminary conference in which the writer and the prospective reader "go into a huddle" and agree in advance on the exact limits of their subject, the terms in which it will be discussed, the angle from which to attack it, and the plan of treatment which will be most convenient for them both. What one is attempting to do is to focus the reader's attention sharply, exactly, and immediately on the subject to be treated. Naturally, because of the great variation in the character of subject matter and the wide diversity in the capacity and experience of readers, all three of these simple functions show many variations.

In popular exposition, where there may be some question as to whether the reader will be interested, it is often expedient to emphasize the value of the subject or its inherent interest for the class of readers to which it is being presented. Bulletins, such as are issued by experiment stations or departments of engineering research, offer good examples of this. Professor George Granger Brown in his bulletin on "The Relation of Motor Fuel Characteristics to Engine Performance,"[1] says in his introduction:

The relation of the volatility of motor fuels to the performance of the engine is a matter of concern not only to every man who owns and operates an automobile, but is a matter of vital importance to all producers of motor fuels and even to automobile manufacturers who must adjust the development of their motors so as to use the available fuel oils with the greatest economy and efficiency. Accurate knowledge of the volatility of motor fuels as affecting engine performance is, therefore, of prime importance for all who are concerned in the production or use of motor fuel.

[1] G. G. Brown, The Relation of Motor Fuel Characteristics to Engine Performance, *University of Michigan, Engineering Research Bulletin* 7, May, 1927.

In popular exposition, and often in technical or scientific exposition, it may also be necessary on occasion to define what one means by his subject. This is especially the case if the phrasing of the subject is likely to be misunderstood or if one proposes to use a term in a slightly new or unusual sense. For example, in his bulletin already referred to on "The Relation of Motor Fuel Characteristics to Engine Performance," Professor Brown used the term "volatility" to include a quantitative concept that it had not generally had in similar discussions up to that time. Had he not defined his term "volatility," there would have been a lack of agreement between him and his readers. He would have been talking of one thing while they thought of another. He takes great pains, therefore, in his introduction to define volatility as including the degree to which a fuel will vaporize as well as its tendency to vaporize under equilibrium conditions.

Sometimes, it is possible that a subject as announced may be confused with subjects that are cognate or similar. Exposition, for example, is similar in some particulars to argumentation, to description, to narration; yet essentially it is different. It is concerned with making ideas clear as well as convincing, and, though in form it is often somewhat like description or narration, it deals with generalizations rather than with the visualization of particular objects or of particular events. In the introduction to a book on exposition, one might very well make an effort to clear up these relationships so that the reader would be spared confusion as to the exact conception of exposition the writer had in mind. Certainly, the reader and the writer must be thinking of the same subject and not of subjects only somewhat similar.

These three forms of comment, made in the interests of fixing with precision in the mind of the reader the subject for discussion, are very seldom called for in the writing of a report; they are more apt to be needed for the popular or academic paper. One does not need to popularize his report or to convince the reader that it has value for him. Nor does one often need to enter into definition of terms in a report, especially in a report on a practical problem, or into any elaborate warning against confusing the subject of investigation with others that parallel it. The reader of a report, having requested it himself, is generally eagerly awaiting its arrival and is aware of what it purports to treat before he opens the covers and begins to read.

There are, however, certain variations of this first function, having to do with establishing the subject of discussion in the reader's mind, that are quite likely to be needed in report writing: comment must frequently be made on the scope or scale of treatment or on the necessary limits of the investigation or of the contents of the report. To guard against any misunderstanding, one must often point emphatically to some condition that has limited the report in certain of its aspects. If, for example, after one has been directed to make a certain investigation, he finds his facilities too limited to permit the investigation on the scale originally proposed, he will need to explain this limitation and indicate the scope of treatment that was finally considered feasible. If one were commissioned to investigate the performance of some metal at temperatures as high as 2500 degrees Fahrenheit and found his laboratory equipment allowing tests only as high as 1500 degrees Fahrenheit, his introduction would need to state why the investigation had been so limited. Otherwise, his patron would be disappointed at only a partial fulfillment of his commission. If one needs to forestall criticism or even question as to exclusions or inclusions, the introduction is the most appropriate place to make clear exactly what the reader may expect to find in the report so that he may be neither surprised nor disappointed at what he actually finds when he reads it.

The first function of an introduction is, then, to make clear as immediately and unmistakably as possible the exact subject as a limited unit of thought. The second function is to indicate the unifying principle that is to shape it for use. Every type of exposition is made what it is by some underlying objective or purpose of the writer or by some consistent emphasis or point of view which makes it distinctly different from any other report or paper on the same subject. It is most important for a writer always to think of the report or paper he is about to write as having a definite work to perform; it is to do something for somebody whose necessities are always to be the determining consideration. If one conceives his writing in this way, he will not be shooting aimlessly into the air and exhausting himself in making a big noise. He will be learning to aim accurately and to shoot to kill.

Two of Professor Schneidewind's publications on chromium plating[1] illustrate how a difference in objective demands a difference in treatment. His *Bulletin* 10, "A Study of Chromium Plating," pre-

[1] R. Schneidewind, A Study of Chromium Plating, *University of Michigan,*

pared for the use of electrochemists, gives them the details of the technique of the plating process as well as the theoretical basis for its use. It was written for technically trained men. *Circular* 3, "Commercial Chromium Plating," is a rewritten edition of practically the same material for the more limited and practical use of manufacturers and platers, men presumably with little technical or theoretical background. This difference in objective gives the two publications their distinct character.

In his introduction to this circular, Professor Schneidewind points out this difference in purpose:

The present circular has been prepared as a contribution to the development of the practical side of chromium plating. Although little new material of a scientific nature is presented, it is hoped that it may be of assistance to manufacturers of materials requiring a plated finish, in determining whether to adopt chromium plate instead of some other form of plating and to give sufficient details regarding equipment, process, and costs to help them in their decision. It has also been thought that such a circular might be of real service to the practical plater who has no need for any elaborate or technical account of the process, but who does need information regarding the equipment used and come understanding of the basic principles of the process simply told.

Sometimes, especially in papers of a general character, the unifying, shaping influence is less explicit—only a common emphasis or interpretation given to all the facts, or a common point of view. The process of manufacturing breakfast food, for example, may be explained in an article in *Good Housekeeping* to a group of housewives in such a way as to convince them that the product is safe because produced under sanitary conditions. In such a case the account of each stage in the process will be demonstrated with emphasis on how, by the use of automatic machinery, all possible contamination of the materials is eliminated. Another article on the same manufacturing process written for mechanical engineers, an article, for example, in a semi-popular magazine, *Popular Mechanics*, would go into detail regarding the automatic mechanisms employed. Such unifying considerations are often explicitly stated in the introduction; they will almost always be indicated in one way or another.

Engineering Research Bulletin 10, May, 1910.

R. Schneidewind, Commercial Chromium Plating, *University of Michigan, Engineering Research Circular* 3, January, 1930.

If, before he begins a paper, a reader understands what the writer proposes to do for him, what emphasis he expects to maintain consistently throughout, what point of view he is planning to assume with reference to the material, the reader can get what he is supposed to get with much less effort than if he gropes his way through a maze of material with no preliminary notion of whither he is being led. Also, he has an important basis for judging the writer's performance. Having committed himself to a definite task, has the writer accomplished that task satisfactorily? Has he done completely and adequately what he intended to do? After all, that is the one great criterion of his success or failure.

It is even more important of the report than of the more general expository paper that the reader understand from first to last why the report was written. As was emphasized in Chapter I, in report writing the unifying purpose is likely to be more consciously employed to give the report direction to an end than in any other form of exposition. The investigation is made with a view to determining why certain difficulties have been experienced in a certain process, or an examination is made of all possible devices for doing a certain type of work with a view to recommending the one that will best satisfy the requirements of the person for whom the report is written. Such objectives are usually explicitly stated in the introduction to the report.

The third and last function of an introduction is to lay out the plan of treatment and so to give the reader a forward look over the whole area mapped out for treatment. Any guide knows that, if he is to conduct observers through the confusion of a factory, he needs to give them a preliminary idea of what they will see and an orderly impression of the plan of the departments through which he is to guide them. A printed program, followed without too many confusing encores, saves an orchestra program from becoming a jumble of sounds. Even the unmusical listener can understand what he hears much better if he knows which number on the program he is supposed to be listening to at any one moment. An impression of the order and arrangement of what is to be received, a preconception of the pattern to be fashioned, an itinerary to be followed, given in advance, help one beforehand to approach his task of listening or reading or observing with the assurance that he can get what it is intended he should get. Since in report writing the writer is under a moral obligation to make the reading and handling of the report as easy and as little confusing as possible, he will be wise if he gives a statement of the plan of organization he will use a conspicuous place at the end of the introduction to a report.

Sometimes this statement of plan is given in considerable detail. Professor W. C. Hoad in his report[1] on waterworks improvements for Fort Wayne, Ind., says: "In this report upon the water-supply problem with which the City of Fort Wayne is now grappling, the engineering data and recommendations pertinent to the situation are set forth under seven chapter headings."

He then lays out in advance the seven chapters in a brief and concise statement of their content. In this particular case, this was a very helpful thing to do, for thus each reader could, and probably would, choose those chapters within his special range of interest.

In another of his reports on a similar subject for Flint, Mich.,[2] Professor Hoad merely outlines his general lines of treatment. It is less diagrammatic but more comprehensive—the emphasis is on the large purpose behind the plan of treatment, rather than on its actual form.

The general plan of waterworks strengthening and improvement outlined in this report not only covers those things which are needful to be done at once if the water supply service is to be brought up to the level of the city's present and immediate future requirements; but also points out the way of making well-integrated expansions and enlargements in future, so that for many years to come the orderly growth of the water plant may keep step with the growth of the city itself in population and industry.

No one introduction will of course need to exhibit all these variations of the three essential functions. The character of the reader and the character of the subject matter will determine what sort of comment will be most helpful in preparing the reader to follow with intelligent interest and without confusion the thing one has to write. But here is evidently the first problem to consider as one begins to think of writing his report. What are the needs of the reader? Which of the fundamental functions must the introduction perform?

[1] W. C. Hoad, Report on Waterwork Improvements, Fort Wayne, September, 1930.

[2] W. C. Hoad, Report on Waterwork Improvements for the Test of Flint, November, 1929.

NOTE: Reference may to advantage be made, at this point, to pages 162 to 230 and 237 to 253.

Chapter Six

The Important First Focus of Attention

In general, as has been shown, the introduction to any exposition serves to prepare the reader to receive, with the greatest economy of effort, what the writer has to give him. It affords the reader his first contact with the subject, indicates the writer's intent with reference to it, and previsions his general plan of procedure in presenting it. Actually, the writing of a good introduction is not so simple as this would seem to indicate.

It is apparently hard for some writers even to get started without a good deal of waste motion. They fail to appreciate how important the first focus of the reader's attention is. In all expository papers there is need for the utmost directness in establishing the initial contact between the reader and the subject. The first sentence, or at least the first paragraph, is critical; for deftly, decisively, and immediately it must focus the attention on the precise subject to be treated and indicate something of the method of approach. The rambling, indirect approach to the subject that reminds one of a plane circling over an uncertain area looking for a spot suitable for a forced landing is wasteful of the reader's initial interest. Readers of reports, at least, will not tolerate the sort of introduction that begins with a series of general statements which give the reader only the most vague notion of what the specific subject is to be and that succeeds in providing the focal point of attention only after a half page or more of successively narrowing circles. For reports the introduction must be as brief and direct as possible.

For all forms of exposition, one needs to learn how to write initial sentences that provide immediately the correct focus of attention. In the case of a general expository paper, the reader is less concerned with the use to be made of the paper or its relation to his prac‧

tical problems than he is with its subject as a subject. The initial sentence is, however, still critical and should still aim at the utmost directness. The subject should be stated at once with such definitions and comments as are needed to establish it in the reader's mind exactly and clearly. The historical background of the subject or the theoretical basis for discussing it are often important points to be developed in the introduction. The reader should then be told what the paper proposes to do with this subject, what conclusions have been reached, and what the plan of treatment is.

The following introduction to a student paper on "The Fessenden Oscillator" is typical.

Subject	The Fessenden oscillator as a producer of sound is one of the latest and most scientific devices for transmitting messages under water.
Background	The idea is not a new one by any means as is shown by the fact that a German by the name of Berger conducted experiments in 1910 which have a direct relationship to this latest invention. He conducted his work in the Danube River, using a submerged piano wire 2 millimeters in diameter. The wire was excited by friction of a hand-driven wheel and it was found that a clear-toned note was produced capable of being propagated in the dots and dashes of the Morse code through a distance of about 4 kilometers.
The relation of the subject to this background of experimentation	The latest development of the principle established by Berger is the electrical oscillator designed in 1915 by Professor R. A. Fessenden, who at that time was at the head of the research department of the Boston Light and Signal Company. His purpose in designing the oscillator was to provide a means of pushing the water backward and forward with great rapidity.
	Generally speaking, the distance the vibrations will travel is dependent upon two factors: first, the area the water pushed backward and forward; second, the distance through which the area moves. The metal diaphragm that Professor Fessenden uses in his oscillator presents a surface area to the water many times greater than the piano wire used in Berger's apparatus, and the results were that sound was transmitted by water vibrations a distance of about 30 miles.
Purpose, scope, and plan	The present paper will give a detailed account of the Fessenden oscillator and comment fully on its application to a number of uses very important in the equipment of naval vessels and submarines.

The initial sentence in this general paper represents the utmost economy of the reader's attention. The subject is thrust forward to the very first point of attention; the predicate seems to define the subject in terms of its functions, to stimulate interest by emphasis on its scientific character, and to suggest by the words "the latest" that it has a historical development. The introduction gives briefly that historical background in its account of the evolution of the idea of the oscillator. No mention is made of what is to be done with this subject until the very last paragraph of the introduction. Then, the purpose and plan of the paper are very simply indicated by the final sentence: "The present paper will give a detailed account of the Fessenden oscillator and comment fully on its application to a number of uses very important in the equipment of naval vessels and submarines."

In a report the questions with which the reader, as he glances at the first page, is subconsciously charged are somewhat more practical in character than are those with which he approaches the reading of a general exposition: What is this report about? How did it come to be written? Who authorized it? Is it part of the routine of the company's report system, or is it a special study that will be of use to me in my special work? What does it propose to do? How is it related to my interests? How can I use it? The writer should not fail to take advantage of this initial moment when, in establishing contact between the reader and the report, the reader is thus interested in questions that concern its use. A deftly constructed initial sentence can do much to satisfy the reader's subconscious requirements; one should learn how to write such sentences.

Each of the following examples illustrates how the emphasis of the sentence may be so directed as to answer the reader's most urgent question, while incidentally also giving him the other information about the report he needs at once. It will be noted that the subject matter in the five reports is practically identical but that in each report it will be given a different treatment because of the different purpose it is to serve.

1. This report, which has been prepared at the suggestion of Mr. Blank, proposes to study the effect of x on y, with a view to providing Department B with the data needed for improving their present methods of production.

2. The investigation of the effect of x on y, which is the subject of this report, was undertaken two years ago at the request of Mr. Blank, who felt

that the company needed, for use in Department *B*, a larger body of well-classified data as a basis for studies leading to improved production methods.

3. This is the third in a series of progress reports on a study of the effect of *x* on *y* which is being made at the request of Mr. Blank with the idea of providing data for Department *B* as a basis for improving their methods of production.

4. This report, which was requested by Department *B* for use in *C*, proposes to review the experience of this department in installing *x* on *y*.

5. The problem of securing satisfactory *xyz's* has given Department *A* trouble for the past five years.

The reader of a report is likely to want first to get his bearings with reference to the purpose of the investigation or the use that is to be made of it. One begins, therefore, with the focus on objectives; follows with the necessary definition and explanation of the situation, the investigation, or proposition with which the report deals; and ends with an indication of the plan of treatment.

The introduction to a report[1] on "Human Tolerance to Horizontal Acceleration in Electric Streetcars" written by E. L. Eriksen and R. T. Liddicoat for the Electric Railway President's Conference Committee illustrates this approach. It begins with the initial focus of attention on the purpose of the investigation, and therefore of the report. The statement of the problem, the method of investigation, the results, and the plan follow after this initial emphasis or purpose.

Authorization The investigation which forms the subject of this report was undertaken at the request of Mr. C. F. Hirshfeld, Chief Engineer of the Electric Railway Presidents' Conference Committee, and was conducted by the Department of Engineering Research at the University of Michigan. Its

Purpose purpose was to determine how acceleration affects the standing passengers in an electric streetcar and what is the best way of accelerating such vehicles.

Method of The problem involved the study of the effect on the pas-
investigation senger of building up the accelerating forces in starting the car. Test conditions were secured closely similar to those experienced by passengers in an electric streetcar. Passengers stood in a position chosen as standard, on a test platform which made possible a record of comparable data as to the acceleration obtained before the chosen unit of discomfort

[1] E. L. Eriksen and R. T. Liddicoat, Final Report on Human Tolerance to Horizontal Acceleration in Electric Streetcars, *Department of Engineering Research*, University of Michigan, February, 1932.

was reached. Several variations were used in the application of the accelerating forces: the car was accelerated suddenly, uniformly, progressively, or with a sudden jerk, according to the nature of the test.

Results

The investigation showed that it is difficult for a standing passenger to maintain his equilibrium in a position oblique with respect to the vertical and also made evident the importance of not increasing this difficulty by subjecting the platform of the car to horizontal motions that are not integral parts of the acceleration.

Interpretation of results

The results of the tests led to the conclusion that a car can be accelerated at starting with the least inconvenience to the standing passengers and also with the minimum sacrifice of operating time if the acceleration is built up uniformly from zero to its full value at a maximum rate of increase that should never be larger than 7 feet per second per second.

Supplementary tests

In order to provide data showing how the results taken with the passengers in a standard position would be affected if they stood in other positions, another series of tests was run. These tests indicated that the stability of the standing passengers was decreased if they stood facing backward, or if they wore heels of a height to which they were unaccustomed; stability, on the other hand, was materially increased when passengers were supported by straps and especially by stanchions.

Plan

For the convenience of those readers who may want to examine the results and conclusions without going into the details of experimental procedure, the report has been presented in two parts. Part I gives the analysis of the problem, a summary of results, the conclusions, and certain technical deductions from the tests which, while they are not strictly integral to the discussion, throw considerable light on the report. Part II presents an account of the equipment, the conditions of the tests, the procedure, the results, the method of checking the data, and the consideration of possible errors.

One can learn to make his first sentence do a great deal for the reader. One should observe how experienced writers get the reader's attention and direct it to the subject of discussion both in written reports and oral demonstrations. First sentences should be simple, direct, easy to grasp; they should not be periodic or too complicated in structure, nor should they be too long. So far as is possible without sacrificing the desirable qualities of directness and incisiveness, they should exhibit sufficient variety of phrasing to avoid monotony of effect. Initial sentences may well begin with the subject and be built from that. The predicate should be significant and should agree perfectly with the main emphasis or main line of development in the report. For example, if an initial statement is made that a thermostat is a *simple* device for controlling temperature, it is disappointing to find that it is actually highly complex. If a problem under consultation can be easily solved by controlling a certain factor, the initial sentence should not emphasize how difficult it is to find a solution; the emphasis should be on how simple the solution is. It may be helpful to examine carefully a few examples of introductory sentences taken from a set of reports written by the author's class in report writing at The Detroit Edison Company.

INITIAL SENTENCES

1. The Detroit Edison Company has recently installed zone-stoker air controls at two of its plants which have proved to be an improvement over the conventional manually operated butterfly or louver damper control.

2. The purpose of this report is to present a summary of work done to date by this department in carrying out the program for the examination of lead sheaths of cables that failed in service.

3. An instrument for furnishing a continuous record from which actual heating values can be determined is a necessity for the Trenton Channel Powerhouse of The Detroit Edison Company because of the fact that at this powerhouse the refinery gas is purchased on a contract that includes a penalty-bonus clause based on the variation of the lower heating value of the gas from a specified value.

4. This report summarizes, for the information of the Bailey Meter Company, the results of a series of tests conducted on Boiler 13 at the Trenton Channel Powerhouse of The Detroit Edison Company.

5. The study of air conditioning or comfort cooling for the home and small commercial buildings which is presented in this report was instituted at the request of Mr. J. W. Parker in order that The Detroit Edison Company might gather information on this subject which would be useful in promoting the more extensive use of comfort cooling in this territory.

6. Slime in the condensers in Delray Powerhouses 2 and 3 has been controlled by three methods; the baking of the condensers, the plugging of the condensers, and chlorination. Slime is usually defined as a conglomeration of inorganic matter. Its formation presents a serious problem in condenser operation.

7. The problem of substituting the services of The Detroit Edison Company for those provided by privately owned industrial power plants is extremely perplexing.

8. This report develops a statistical method for the comparison of power-house operating data.

9. The investigation which forms the subject of this report was initiated by The Detroit Edison Company in 1929. The original purpose was to analyze failures of distribution transformers, but in 1931 was extended to include transformer outage due to the blowing of primary fuses, in order to gain a wider knowledge of these failures and determine what could be done to reduce them.

Example of How to Throw Initial Emphasis on the Topic Idea.

The ability to construct a topic sentence so as to throw the initial emphasis on the topic to be treated in the paragraph is important. The following sentences illustrate how much more effective a sentence is if the topic idea is given a point of initial attention:

INCORRECT	CORRECT
A six-cylinder motor supplies the *power* in the Buick car.	The *power* in the Buick car is supplied by a six-cylinder motor.
The draft and the quality and size of fuel will determine the *thickness* of the fire.	The *thickness* of the fire is determined by the draft and by the quality and size of fuel.
The accumulation of ash makes it necessary to *clear* the fire at intervals.	*Clearing* the fire at frequent intervals is necessary because of the accumulation of ash.

Example of Value of Initial Emphasis on the Topic Idea.

CLOSED FEED-WATER HEATERS

Construction.

The closed feed-water heater is built up of a steel-plate shell, etc.

Operation. [N.B. Need of emphasis on *operation.*]

The water is admitted to the tubes from the water supply, etc.

[Corrected: *In the operation* of a closed feed-water heater, the water is admitted, etc.]

Efficiency.

In the closed heater the heat must be transmitted through a metal wall to a mass of water. In the course of time, scale accumulates on the inside of the tubes, and grease from the steam collects on the outside, so that *the heat conductivity* becomes very poor. [N.B. The topic idea of *efficiency* is not apparent till the reader reaches the italicized words in this sentence.]

[Corrected: *The efficiency* of the closed heater is not very high. In these heaters, the heat must be transmitted, etc.]

It has (x) been shown by recent investigation that air in feed water encourages corrosion. [N.B. Need of a transition word to mark the beginning of a new point. Insert at (x) "also."]

(x) Electrolysis is liable to take place. [N.B. Same as above. Insert at (x) "Then, too."]

Economy.

(x) In the closed heater, the hot condensed steam is wasted. [N.B. Need of a topic sentence emphasizing the topic idea of economy. Insert at (x): *The economy* of the closed heater is also quite unsatisfactory, both because of its wasteful use of steam and water, and because of the high initial cost and upkeep. In the closed heater, the hot condensed steam is wasted.]

(x) The steam condensed in heating the water must be thrown away, etc. [N.B. Need of a transition word to mark a new point. Insert at (x) "Moreover."]

(x) The tubes are subjected to the extremes of hot and cold, a condition which has a tendency to work them loose in the heaters, in which event water under full boiler pressure *escapes* into the steam space and is wasted with the condensed steam. [N.B. The reader has no clue to the topic idea of leakage until he reaches the word "escapes." Insert at (x): *The leakage* in these heaters is also considerable.]

(x) The closed heater *costs* more in the first place than the open heater. [N.B. The paragraph has two parts: (*a*) initial cost; (*b*) upkeep. There is need of a topic sentence to make the design of the paragraph clear at the beginning. Insert at (x): The initial cost and the upkeep of these heaters are both high.]

NOTE: It is suggested that further study be made of the initial sentences in the Annotated Reports (pages 162 to 230).

Chapter Seven

Some Special Problems in Introductions to Reports

In the development of any introductory text the question of what comments on the subject need to be elaborated must, of course, be determined by considering what the reader will require in order to prepare him for his task of reading what is to follow. The introduction to a report often involves certain specific problems that require special consideration.

1. One of the first things to consider in writing an introduction to a report is how much of an analysis of the situation, or problem, with which it deals is needed. It is not safe to depend on the assumption that the reader understands the problem clearly, just because he has asked one to investigate it. At least, he has a right to expect that after one has studied it and is ready to report on his solution, he will be able to set up an analysis of its salient factors as a basis for that solution. Moreover, following the fundamental thesis already laid down that a report should be so written as to be perfectly qualified for all the uses to be made of it, it seems reasonable to require that the introduction shall be a self-contained, self-explanatory section. For even though it is written specifically for someone familiar with the problem to be treated, it is highly probable that he will expect it to be read by others less familiar than he, to whom it must be intelligible without his having always to be at hand to explain what it is all about. His board of directors, his foreman, his other associates to whom he may pass it on for consideration should be able to read and understand it even though they lack any collateral knowledge of the particular situation with which it deals. One can always so word his statements as to indicate that he is aware he is setting up more or less familiar facts in the interest of a complete understanding of the problem.

This is a report on an investigation of trouble experienced with the boiler installed in our Plant *A* last August. *It will be recalled* that this boiler has given trouble on several occasions. In August, ... A week ago, ... Again in October, ... It was the last failure that led to the present investigation.

Then might follow a brief review of this final failure of the boiler.

The situation with which this report deals is in its general features *familiar* to most of the executives of the company. There are some features involved, however, that need to be reviewed as a basis for considering the recommendations made.

These features would then be briefly sketched.

Sometimes a carefully worded initial sentence or two will be sufficient, but frequently a paragraph, or even several paragraphs, may be required to give an adequate analysis of the situation or the background of the problem to be discussed in the report. If it is at all complex, even one of the main sections in the report may be required. Certainly one should consider carefully whether he has set up his problem or his proposition fully enough to be understood by all who may have occasion to use the report.

2. A report on a design problem demands a careful and exact statement of the requirements that the design must satisfy. The same is true of a report concerned with making a choice of some one unit from a group of units by a process of comparison.

The design for *X*, which is presented in this report, has been made with due consideration of all the requirements for a thoroughly modern plant for the treatment of *Y*.

In selecting a method of reduction for this type of ore, it must be kept in mind that . . . , that . . . , and that. . . .

How much these requirements or determining conditions will be elaborated must, of course, be contingent on the character of the problem itself. One sentence may do it, but in a long-form report a half page or more is often needed; sometimes an entire section will be used. Even whole pages of specifications may be required, in which case the appendix may be called on to relieve the introduction and then only the most general features of the specified requirements will be included in the introduction itself.

The specifications for this design have been appended to this report. It will be noted that, in general, they provide for an *X* which is sturdy, operates automatically, and records, in a way easy to read, all measurements made.

3. If a report is dependent on the reader's being familiar with fundamental theory, it is usually good policy to review that theory briefly for the benefit of readers who may require such help. If the statement of the basic theory can be made brief and simple enough, it may be an integral part of the introduction, where it really belongs, since the reader needs it to understand what follows.

This process is based on the theory that. . . .
It may be well to recall the fundamental theory involved in this process.
Of the several theories to account for this action of X, the one most generally accepted now is. . . .

In highly technical reports, especially in reports on research, this review of basic theory is so important and so difficult to present that it must be treated in the body of the report, often as a major section.

4. Having set up the problem and having elaborated such material as is basic for considering it, one should indicate how he proceeded to attack it. If his method of investigation was in no way original or unusual, little need be said about it; but if it did vary in any important particular from the stock method familiar to the prospective readers, the method of investigation should be explained in such detail as seems necessary. This may vary from a sentence or two in the introduction to a major section in the body of the report.

In running these tests, the necessity for securing accurate and thoroughly reliable results seemed so imperative that a new thermostatic control of X was purchased and installed on all units.
The method used in making these traffic studies was so entirely new and proved so satisfactory in securing significant data that it will be explained in full in the report. Briefly, it was an original photographic method by which a moving picture made a record of the traffic passing a given point.

5. The inclusion of results or findings or of recommendations in the introduction is another important problem in writing the introduction of a report. Such an inclusion is apt to be overlooked or overdone. As was pointed out in the general discussion of the functions of the introduction in Chapter V, the person most concerned in the report is apt to want to know as quickly as possible, and with as little reading as possible, the answer to his question or the results of the investigation he has ordered. The statement of results would seem to be an integral part of any introductory text that purports to be complete. There is, however, no time or space in the introduction

for anything but the briefest, most compact, but most incisive statement. The complete and elaborate summary of results or the fuller setup of recommendations will be found in the terminal section. In the introduction the ideal should be to meet the inquiry of the reader as to the results but to do it with the utmost brevity.

The investigation showed that nothing short of a complete redesign of the production line will be of any use. It is therefore recommended that such a redesign be provided for at once.

The results of the tests showed that two of the specimens, *A* and *B*, were not up to specifications, but that the other three *C*, *D*, and *E* were fully qualified to meet requirements of service.

The examination of the property in question leads to the conclusion that it would prove a profitable investment if it can be purchased for not more than $10,000.

6. The necessity of elaborating some one of these elements in the make-up of the introduction to a report will often result in an introduction that is evidently too long and too heavy. It throws the whole report out of balance. There is, of course, no law governing the length of introductions; but one's sense of proportion will indicate that even for a long-form report not more than two or three pages at most can be given to introductory comment. Instinctively one will realize, too, that no reader wants to be kept waiting too long for the actual delivery of material to begin. One should carefully check his introduction to make sure it has not exceeded the necessary functions of an introduction, that it has been strictly concerned with preparing the reader to follow the report with the least possible danger of confusion, and that it has not inadvertently developed ideas in detail that should be presented in the report proper. Then one should condense and condense till the introduction is reduced to the briefest form compatible with completeness. If, after these revisions, the introduction is evidently too long, one has, fortunately, in the so-called "preliminary section," a useful means available for relieving it of the overburden.

It frequently happens, as was intimated in the previous chapter, that the analysis of the situation or the problem to be considered, the specification of requirements, the review of fundamental theory, the account of previous research, the summary of findings must be fully treated as a preliminary to the reading of the report. Ideally, if these functions can be performed by the introduction, they should be made an integral part of that section. If, however, they need fuller development, they may be made the first main section of the report. Such a section should, in the mind of the writer, be always recognized as strictly preliminary—a part of his effort to prepare the reader for his task.

It should be recognized as such by the reader also. In announcing the plan of the report, it may be indicated as one of the preliminaries. If one thinks of the formula for his report design as

$$x = a + b + c + d,$$

he must relate this preliminary section to that formula in some such phrasing as:

After a brief review of the theory on which this method of operation is based, the report will treat in turn a, b, c, and d.

After a survey of previous research on this problem, an account will be given of the test apparatus developed specially for the present study, the procedures followed, and the results that have thus far been obtained.

Or, without such mention of the preliminary section in one's announcement of his plan, he may mark such a section as preliminary in its initial sentence.

A brief review of the generally accepted theory of X seems advisable before proceeding to the consideration of the methods to be considered in this report.

Before considering the various machines available for such an installation, it is important to understand the exact conditions that must be met and satisfied.

The most common example of a preliminary section that is not a part of the analytic pattern but that is preliminary to it is the summary of results, or summary of conclusions. In many report forms, this thrusting of the conclusions or results forward to a position ahead of the a, b, c, d, of the report proper is mandatory. Such an arrangement is quite in accord with the ideal of this book to plan the report for the convenient use of those who must handle it. Often the most important reader whose requirements the report must serve has little interest in the detailed report and little time to devote to a detailed reading of it. He may scan the introductory page or two to get his bearings and his perspective, but he will seize upon the section marked conspicuously " Summary of Conclusions" as the one thing of vital import. It seems important always to regard such a section as a part of the preliminaries, as one would if it were brief enough to include as an integral part of the introduction. It should be treated always as a preliminary summary and not in the detail in which the same material would be presented in the terminal section of the report. Presumably the terminal section will be read only after one has followed the development of the conclusions through the detailed account in the body of the report. Nor should it be assumed that such a thrusting forward of the conclusions or results into a position of first attention in the setup of the report will necessarily leave the report with no terminal section. As will be shown in the chapter on terminal sections, there is, even in this type of report, usually need for an appropriate and effective ending.

The inexperienced writer should be warned that it often takes a nice balancing of arguments and a considerable amount of experimentation to determine whether to keep all the preliminary comment in a coherent, self-contained introductory section or whether to use this device of the preliminary section for such elements as need more elaboration than the limited space allowable for an introduction will permit. One may always try out such a scheme and, if he finds it failing to justify itself by falling too far short of the mass that a reasonable proportioning of major sections would seem to make desirable, he can abandon it. He should then condense it to the lowest possible terms and throw it back into the introduction. In doing so, he should be careful to find the most logical point in the introductory text at which to place it and should, if necessary, rewrite his entire introduction to provide a final perfect integration of all the preliminary considerations.

The recourse to a preliminary section will be found very useful in attempting to maintain a balance between the introductory and terminal sections of a report. One can relieve the apparent length of his introduction, even though he actually is not abbreviating necessary preliminary considerations. He can give the reader what he needs and must know in order to prepare him to read the report proper, without appearing to keep him waiting too long for the action of the piece to begin. In the case of very long reports, the main body of the document, in which the supporting data and the detailed interpretation of their significance and use are massed in impressive display, is often preceded by a complete, but abbreviated, account of the whole report. This is the so-called "short report" and is quite analogous to the preliminary section. It is prepared for the convenience of readers interested in the general procedure and specific results but not in the details of the supporting data.

The ideal introduction is one which is a complete epitome of the whole report, which may be read independently of the detailed report that follows, or which, regarded as an integral part of it, will provide an adequate preparation for the most careful and critical examination of the report itself. This ideal kept constantly in mind will guide one in determining wisely what his report introduction must include and which of the essential introductory functions it must perform.

The study of the following examples of how some of these problems in writing the introductions to reports are handled can, to advantage be supplemented by examination of the introductions to the Annotated Reports (pages 162 to 230) and to "A Study of Introductions" (pages 237 to 253).

Example 1. *Introduction to a Report on a Research Problem.*

Subject

Purpose

Inclusion of a brief summary of findings. These are more fully summarized in the terminal section

Limits of the material. Plan of the report.

This investigation of the standard phenolphthalein methyl orange, barium chloride, and direct-absorption methods of analysis for the determination of hydroxide and carbonate was undertaken with the view of determining their accuracy in solutions containing moderate concentrations of hydroxide, varying from 100 to 500 parts per million of OH, and low concentrations of carbonate, ranging from 0 to 80 parts per million of CO_3. Considerable experimentation in the analysis of experimental boiler-water solutions falling within these concentration limits had given rise to the feeling that the standard methods left much to be desired in the way of an analysis which would give accurate reproducible values, especially for the carbonate. This feeling was also confirmed by data from tests made by other investigators on actual boilers in operation.

In general, the results of this investigation show that the phenolphthalein methyl orange and the barium chloride methods of titration, which have been standard practice in boiler-water control, both yield seriously inaccurate values for low concentrations of carbonate in the presence of hydroxide concentrations such as are normally found in boiler waters. The direct-absorption method developed by the writers give good accuracy in the determination of total combined carbon dioxide, which for most alkaline boiler waters may be assumed to be present almost entirely as carbonate. Since either of the standard titration methods has been found to give a sufficiently exact value for hydroxide, a combination of one of these titrations with the direct-absorption method is indicated as necessary where both hydroxide and carbonate must be accurately known for control purposes.

The experimental work described in this report includes tests on both pure solutions and actual boiler waters. The report is divided into three main parts, the first two dealing with laboratory investigations on pure solutions made up to known concentrations of carbonate and hydroxide. The tests described in the first part were made with a rather complicated apparatus developed for use in a laboratory study of the sulphate-carbonate ratio in boiler waters, while those in the second part were carried out with a simplified apparatus adopted for plant-control work. The third part of the report describes a series of plant tests in which carbonate concentrations indicated by this simplified absorption apparatus were compared with those obtained by various routine analytical methods.

CONCLUSIONS

The conclusions derived from this investigation may be stated as follows:

1. Neither the phenolphthalein methyl orange titration nor the barium chloride method for the determination of carbonate is to be relied upon in waters containing high concentrations of hydroxide and low concentrations of carbonate.

2. The direct-absorption method for the determination of carbonate will give very accurate results in solutions of even very low carbonate concentration and is not affected by most impurities found in boiler waters. Many of the other methods of analysis are seriously affected by such impurities.

3. The direct-absorption method has been simplified so that the apparatus does not have to be operated by a chemist. About 20 minutes is required for the analysis of each sample.

4. Either the phenolphthalein methyl orange or the barium chloride methods of analysis will give results of fair accuracy for the hydroxide.

5. Unless the sample is handled correctly after it is taken from the boiler, no method of analysis can give accurate results. Since filtering the sample in the air in the laboratory may introduce serious errors, this practice should be prohibited. The best method of taking the sample requires that it be filtered at boiler temperature, cooled under boiler pressure, and passed into the sampling flask without contact with the air. A method for doing this without undue expense and trouble has been developed and applied with satisfactory results.

6. As a result of the errors introduced by varying procedure in filtering boiler-water samples and by the use of inaccurate standard methods for the determination of carbonate, it seems necessary to regard all carbonate analyses previously reported for boiler waters in the technical literature as approximate values which may be high by as much as several hundred per cent.

NOTE: The terminal section is included in this case in order that the student may study the relation of the summary of conclusions that are an integral part of the introduction to the more detailed summary of these same conclusions given here.

Example 2. Introduction to a Report on a Research Problem.

Subject

     The design of a fractionating column is aimed to secure the necessary intimate contact between liquid and vapor. The following report is written with this fundamental idea in mind. It is evidently possible to increase the efficiency and capacity of a column if more intimate contact between the

Purpose

liquid and the vapor can be secured. The report which is based on research carried on by the Universal Oil Products Company will aim to show that this can be done.

Controlling conditions

     The research has made it evident that there are several important considerations to be taken into account because they directly affect the liquid-vapor contact. The number of plates in the column and the column diameter are two very important factors in design. These two factors lead to the second fundamental consideration. Entrainment is the limiting factor on the allowable vapor velocity in the column and since efficiency is directly proportional to the entrainment any design that produces a minimum of entrainment is desirable. The third factor influencing design is the vapor velocity through the column. Columns designed for high vapor velocities are in general more efficient than columns designed for low velocities regardless of the operating velocity. The fourth important design factor to be considered is the pressure drop over the column. The pressure is the driving force that determines the vapor velocity through the column.

Conclusions

     In all probability, it would not be economical to alter the design of the columns which are now operating satisfactorily. However, the alterations which would produce greater capacity and efficiency in the proposed columns of the Universal Oil Products Company can be incorporated in the design plans and built at a cost which would be repaid by savings during the first six months' operation. These altera-

Plan

tions are a direct result of a careful study of the liquid-vapor contact, entrainment, vapor velocity, and over-all pressure drop in bubble-cap fractionating columns.

Example 3. *Introduction to a Report on Choice of Machinery.*

<table>
<tr><td>

Subject

Purpose
</td><td>

The purpose of this report is to recommend, on the basis of an analysis of all the factors involved, the most satisfactory type of propelling machinery to be employed in a proposed cargo vessel for the Rawdon Transportation Company.

Before such an analysis can be made, it is necessary that definite specifications for the general requirements of the vessel be made clear. These specifications, as laid down by the Rawdon Company, are as follows:
</td></tr>
</table>

Requirements

```
Deadweight capacity. .20,000 tons
Speed.............16 knots
Shaft horsepower.....6,000
Cargo.............Moderate to high density, bulk
Route.............New York City to San Pedro, via
                      the Panama Canal
```

No specification for gross tonnage was made because the higher density cargoes which will be carried make the space-requirement factor of minor importance. The relatively high speed was considered necessary in order to compete with other modern cargo boats now being put into service. The dead-weight specified is the minimum acceptable for the given speed and power. Although the latter two factors, cargo and route followed, are usually considered to be variable, the solution to the particular problem in hand is so highly dependent upon these factors that they must be considered fixed. The principal reason for this is found in the highly varying differential in the prices of Diesel and boiler oils, and the cost of labor, between the United States and foreign countries, which means that a separate analysis would have to be prepared in case a foreign port were available for fueling.

Plan   The first part of the report will be a general consideration of the various types of propulsion equipment available and a decision as to the two types best suited for the case under consideration. The remainder of the report will then be a detailed analysis of these two types, concluding with recommendations as to which will be the more satisfactory to employ.

Example 4. *Introduction to a Report on a Technical Question.*

Subject and purpose   This report is the result of an investigation to determine the practicability of producing an alcohol-gasoline mixture, containing 15 per cent of alcohol, which will compete with gasoline as a fuel for motor vehicles. The report has been

Authorization   requested by Mr. C. L. Wyeth, Chairman of the Board of Directors of the Standard Oil Company of Ohio, who desires

Use   information regarding this type of fuel mixture with a view to maintaining the present volume of motor fuel in spite of the decreasing supply of petroleum.

Background   Due to the abundant petroleum resources of this country, very little has been done toward producing a mixed fuel. Recently, however, the Bailor Manufacturing Company has set up a plant at Atchison, Kans., and is producing alcohol at the rate of 10,000 gallons per day. Their product is blended with gasoline and sold as Argol 5, 10, and 15, the numerals referring to the per cent of Argol fluid, 78 per cent of which is absolute alcohol.

Results   The investigation showed that a mixture containing 15 per cent alcohol blended with gasoline gave very satisfactory engine performance. When using the mixed fuel, improvement was noted in acceleration, power output, smoothness, and maintenance costs. Against this may be weighed poorer starting performance and greater fuel consumption.

Production of alcohol from corn, Jerusalem artichoke, molasses, and acetylene is now possible since these raw materials are available in sufficient quantities to support a very large industry. It appears advisable to produce alcohol from corn at present and to encourage the growing of artichokes to furnish a cheaper raw material in the future.

Plan   In determining the practicability of the alcohol-gasoline mixture as a fuel for motor vehicles, the investigation was carried out in three stages. The sources of raw materials were first studied to discover costs and quantities available. The costs and methods of manufacturing alcohol were then investigated together with the methods of blending alcohol and gasoline. Test results were finally studied in order to compare the performance of motor vehicles operating on mixed fuel with the performance of those operating on pure gasoline.

Example 5. Introduction with Emphasis on Careful Definition of an Unfamiliar Term.

Definition of term

Prequalification in its broadest sense is the determination of an applicant's qualifications for a given responsibility before entrusting him with that responsibility. Applied to construction, it is the determination of a contractor's competency and responsibility to complete a given structure project satisfactorily before he submits a bid.

Its relation to the limited subject

There is nothing new or mysterious in prequalification except in connection with public contracts. Private corporations, architects, railroads, public utilities, and others have always required it. They limit bidders for their work to contractors whom they believe to be financially responsible, to have experience for the particular work, and to have a suitable plant or means with which to secure such a plant. It is only within recent years, however, that prequalification has come into use on public works.

Distinction between prequalification and qualification simultaneously with opening of bids

For a long time, it has been admitted that in awarding public contracts, the successful contractor shall be the responsible contractor with the lowest bid. But determination of responsibility after bidding has often been troublesome. The solution of a difficult problem is by prequalification reduced to the solution of two much simpler problems. With actual prequalification, a group of qualified bidders is established in advance of the opening of bids and as a separate act. The opening of bids then merely determines from this qualified group which one is the low bidder. Determination of the qualifications of the bidder simultaneously with the opening of his bid, or subsequent to the opening of his bid, is not real prequalification.

Purpose

So far it has been the association of contractors that have had to wage the battle for predetermined competency of bidders and to carry conviction of its importance to the association of engineers. This paper has been prepared to put in definite form material on this subject which will be of assistance in encouraging the wider application of this

Plan

practice. It will give in detail the procedure to be followed and will consider both the advantages of the plan and the objections which are sometimes raised regarding it.

Example 6. An Introduction and Preliminary Section.

Subject

This report is a compendium of facts and theories held by those responsible for boiler-water conditions in the Central Heating Department relative to the use of zeolites in feed-water treatment. It gives the results of several tests conducted both in the laboratory and in the plants with zeolite materials, and brief discussions of major operating experiences. It is

Purpose and use

intended as a reference work for those members of the department personnel who find it periodically necessary to reacquaint themselves with certain data and theories related to the operation of the zeolite-acid treating systems in both the Beacon Street and Congress Street heating plants. The data may also be of interest to others not particularly familiar with the arrangement of these zeolite softeners and the allied treating equipment. It should be remembered by them that the data and discussions apply primarily to that equip-

Limitations

ment and may therefore not be directly applicable to zeolite softeners located elsewhere because of differences in design.

Plan (the preliminary section is announced as an integral unit section in this plan)

The report is divided into: (*a*) a discussion of certain preliminary considerations, (*b*) a statement of the results of experiments conducted with different zeolitic materials, and (*c*) a narration of important operating experiences at the Beacon Street and Congress Street heating plants.

PRELIMINARY CONSIDERATIONS

Beginning of preliminary section

In order to orient the reader with reference to the general subject of zeolite softening, it has been thought advisable to preface the main body of the report by a discussion of a general and introductory nature. Accordingly the discussion which follows considers first the constitution and reactions of zeolite materials and secondly reviews the reasons why zeolite materials were initially considered for use in feed-water treatment in the Central Heating Department.

The Reactions and Constitution of Zeolites.

The name "zeolite" is applied to a class of mineral of very complex chemical constitution, containing principally sodium, aluminum, and silica.

NOTE: The student may supplement these brief examples by referring to the Annotated Reports (pages 162 to 230). In these he will find illustrated many of the typical problems of report introductions.

Chapter Eight

The Paragraph as an Evidence of Design

It has seemed necessary to go into so much detail regarding the important functions of the introduction that it may be well to recall that the general subject under discussion is how, by every available means, to economize the reader's time and attention. Emphasis has been placed on the necessity of discovering by analysis a plan of organization that will take into account all the details of the subject matter and all the conditions under which the report will be used. Evidence of design gives a reader assurance that the writer "knows his stuff," has made up his mind with reference to it, and has carefully considered the reader's convenience. This is true of all expository papers; it is especially important of reports that the analytic scheme determining the structural pattern of the document be sufficiently evident to facilitate its use. It is therefore imperative that one develop every possible means of marking the organic structure of one's report. The reader may thus be kept aware of this structural pattern throughout the report and can rely on it to direct him through the maze of the discussion without confusion; thus safeguarded, he may devote his entire energies to grasping the ideas presented.

It has been shown that one of the functions of the introduction is to set up such a pattern in the mind of the reader, to provide a framework on which he may assemble the details of the subject matter as they are delivered to him through the body of the report. That is easy enough to do. What is really difficult is to use that pattern consistently as one proceeds to handle the mass of one's material; it is even more difficult to keep the reader constantly aware of it. Some forms of exposition, reports in particular, as will be shown later, use explicit means to mark the unit sections in such a structural scheme; but for all types of exposition, including the report, the paragraph, properly conceived and consistently used, is one's surest and most reliable means of demonstrating his analysis. It seems imperative, therefore, to clear away at the very outset all uncertainty as to why the paragraph is used, what determines its length or mass, what its characteristic features are, and how it is related to one's analytic plan. This should make it possible for one to use the paragraph with greater precision as an evidence of the plan that lies beneath the surface and serves to give structural soundness and coherence to his writing.

To appreciate why he requires the aid of some paragraph system, the student needs only to consider his probable reactions if, in one of his more technical courses, his textbook were printed without paragraphs—page after page of unbroken text. The strain on his attention would be enormously increased. He would, in fact, be forced to analyze such a text for himself into its components, in order either to get the ideas presented without undue effort or to be able to remember them. Unless he were quite experienced in dealing with the particular subject matter treated, he would have small chance of making such an analysis satisfactorily. The fact that the pages are broken up into the paragraphs is evidence that the writer, who presumably understood his subject and the limitations of the student's experience, has made the analysis for him and presented the ideas in units that he can comprehend. Evidently, the paragraph is at least an attempt on the writer's part to make the text easier for the student to read—to conserve his mental energy for the task of assimilating the ideas presented and to relieve him of the necessity of discovering, by a painful analytic process, the pattern being used to present those ideas.

The second question that often gives the young writer much concern until he has a clear conception of the psychology of the paragraph is how long a paragraph should be. He is apt to imagine vaguely that there is some rule of thumb that will determine this delicate adjustment. Many an inexperienced writer lets his ideas run along comfortably till he passes the half-page mark, when he slows down suspiciously and says to himself: "Well, I guess that's about enough for one paragraph." By a sort of imitative process, he camouflages his uncertainty as to the proper length of the paragraph and merely aims to make his page look like the printed page with which he is familiar. He may approach somewhat nearer a sensible means of determining the length of his paragraph by writing till he somehow feels that he has encountered a new topic, which necessitates his switching to a new paragraph. He is correct at least in his appreciation of the fact that each paragraph must be a unit and must develop about a single topic in the general setup of topics. Unfortunately his application of this idea is largely a matter of guesswork; he guesses his way through the entire composition of his paper and, unless he is an unusually keen guesser, is liable to make many mistakes.

There is clearly a need here for some really fundamental consideration to determine the length or mass of the paragraph. If the student will examine his own instinctive reactions to paragraphs of various lengths, he may find the answer written in the constitution of his own mind. He should study how he is affected when he opens two texts on the same subject and glances over the pages in a cursory fashion. In one, the average paragraph runs to two pages or more; in the other, few paragraphs exceed a half page. If both texts have been recommended as equally authoritative, there can be little question as to his choice. Instinctively, he realizes that the text with the shorter paragraphs will be easier to read; it looks, he says, "more interesting." He feels the other text will be "heavy," difficult, taxing. And he is correct. He has found, without realizing it, the really sound consideration that must determine the length of a paragraph. The massive, solid paragraphs will demand a greater and more continuous strain on his attention than the smaller units. It is obvious that the length of the paragraph is to be determined largely by considering the natural limits of the reader's attention, and that this depends on his familiarity and experience with the subject matter under consideration. Evidently the paragraph provides a simple means for using the reader's attention economically.

The habit of observing sharply the way a skillful and experienced speaker attracts, directs, controls, and economizes the attention of his listeners will soon give the student the clue to the psychological basis of the paragraph. He will discover that the speaker's procedure, very simply stated, consists in requiring of the audience successive periods of concentrated attention, involving a certain amount of mental strain, and then allowing them brief, but definitely indicated, moments of rest. Having introduced his subject and prepared his audience for their task of listening, he focuses their attention sharply on the first topic in his order of topics, as, for example,

The new process is based on a somewhat familiar theory.

He then aims to hold the unbroken and concentrated attention of his listeners on that focus till he can get over to them all that he must say on that topic. As he approaches the end of his presentation of that topic, he will indicate by his voice, his manner, even by the structure of his sentences, that he is about through. He slows down; his voice is apt to take on a deeper, lower tone; there is the effect of a cadence falling to a close. And when he is at the end, he pauses for a moment with unmistakable evidence of having finished with topic 1. The listeners shift in their seats, take a long breath, relax the strain of their attention quite unconsciously for a moment. But it is only for a moment; the speaker comes back at them with another topic in his scheme of topics, and again he sharply focuses their attention on that.

The process involves three quite simple operations.

While he sees all faces lifted with interest, he sketches his treatment of this part of his subject. But instinctively he will manage to get it all said before he observes any evidence of wandering attention or waning interest.

Thus he proceeds to deliver the list of topics that cover his subject. If he senses the capacity of his audience for this sort of subject matter correctly, he will send them away at the end of his lecture informed, entertained, but not fatigued. He has used, but not abused, their available attention.

Repeated observation of this everyday experience as a listener will soon make clear to the student why paragraphs are a necessity in presenting ideas, what is a sound basis for determining their effective length, and what are the characteristics of a good paragraph considered from the viewpoint of the reader's or listener's needs. Possibly he may then arrive at a definition of a paragraph as the best evidence of a design based on an analysis and classification of one's ideas. The following basic conclusions appear to emerge from such a study.

1. There is a limit to the period of attention normal for every reader or listener. One cannot exceed this or attempt to hold the attention beyond this natural limit without overtaxing or fatiguing the listener or reader and probably losing him altogether. In other words in either listening or reading, when one reaches his natural fatigue point, he will stop listening or reading, at least, effectively.

2. The period of attention differs with age and experience and even in individuals of the same age and experience. Little children have a period of attention measured only in the fraction of a minute. For adolescents, this period is considerably lengthened; for adults, it approaches a norm within each range of ideas, depending on one's mental discipline and intellectual development. The student can illustrate this for himself by considering how he would organize three different talks on how radio works, one for a class of junior boy scouts, one for a senior-high-school group, and one for his Tau Beta Pi initiation thesis. One might well study in this connection Professor Huxley's lectures on highly scientific subjects given to the workmen in the Manchester industries. They are beautiful examples of skillful gauging of the useful attention of an audience by considering its limited experience and its consequently limited interest in and attention to difficult and unfamiliar subject matter.

3. The period of useful attention differs greatly also with the character of the subject matter. A textbook in history or in economics will exhibit discursive paragraphs a page or more in length; a text in mechanics or in many other technical subjects in engineering may exhibit paragraphs of four or five lines only. A page or two of the sensational doings of Mary Queen of Scots will actually tax the reader's attention less than reading the four lines describing a complex mechanism. The latter will involve a reference to a line diagram and require moments of tense consideration if the complicated thing is to be understood at all. Evidently one can present some types of material in much longer portions than others without danger of exceeding the normal period of attention of his reader.

4. The skillful writer or speaker either consciously or instinctively takes into account this fact of the natural limit of attention inherent in the mind of his reader or listener and the difficulties involved in his subject matter for that reader or listener. In planning to present his subject matter, he will analyze it beforehand into units of a weight or size that will not be too taxing. And he will provide moments of rest where his instinct or his insight indicates that the reader or listener is likely to reach a fatigue point. He will provide pauses where he and the reader will at least agree to stop and recover themselves from the strain of concentrated effort.

It is, of course, fatal to the coherence of an exposition to have the reader weary and stop except at the logical pauses in the structural plan. Every student has had the experience of attacking a long, solid-looking paragraph in a badly written textbook—attacking it with determination to concentrate and get through it somehow. His determination, and possibly his interest, carry him half or two-thirds through, when he finds his attention flagging. Finally he lays his book down, and his mind, released from the strain, shoots off somewhere into space where it rehearses last summer's trip into the Canadian wilderness or refreshes itself with dreams of a happy future. When the little diversion is over, he will pick up his text and again attack the difficult paragraph. If he is a conscientious student, he will go back to the beginning of the paragraph, take a running start, and with still greater determination rush through the paragraph in the hope of, this time, making the end. If he is a somewhat indifferent student, he will take a chance and give that particular paragraph up; he is thus probably left with no knowledge of the ideas presented in the latter third of the paragraph. Incidentally, he is likely to be quizzed on this part which he "skipped" and is discredited as having not prepared himself properly. Evidently no writer should risk having his reader pause in the middle of a period in which continuous, concentrated attention on a topic is required. His paragraphs must never so overtax the reader that he will have to make any such break in order to rest. They must be carefully planned.

5. In presenting one of the component units of an analytic scheme, the reader's attention must be focused sharply and as immediately as possible on the topic to be treated. This provision of an initial focal point of attention is the function of the so-called "topic sentence." It serves to mark each paragraph unit so unmistakably as to make it easy for the reader to identify the subject matter almost at a glance.

6. Having caught and directed the reader's attention to the topic for discussion, the writer must hold it without releasing it till he has said all that needs to be said. There must be no break in the current of thought. Each unit must be coherently planned and must exhibit a logical sequence of ideas that will hold the attention of the reader and never allow it to lapse till he reaches the end.

7. Some means is usually employed to let the reader or listener know at the end of each unit that he has reached a natural rest period during which he may relax and recover from the strain put upon him, the demand for unbroken attention placed on him by the reading of the paragraph.

The student needs to keep these observations on the characteristics of the paragraph well in mind. Evidently paragraphs are indispensable. They are a necessary concession to the limits of human attention. Their length is determined only by a careful and sympathetic consideration of how difficult one's subject matter is and how limited the reader's experience. The three ideals to be achieved by a paragraph are to focus the attention as immediately as possible on the idea that makes it a component unit of the whole, to hold the attention by an unbroken sequence of sentences developing that idea, from beginning to end, and to indicate the end when that point is reached.

The paragraph has usually been defined as a coherent treatment of a single topic which is generally one of the component units of a large whole. That definition includes many of the points developed in this chapter. A much more fundamental definition, however, so far as this book is concerned, is this:

The paragraph is an adjustment of the amount of material to be delivered during any one moment of concentrated attention to the capacity of the reader for such attention.

It should be kept in mind that the skillful writer or speaker, often unconsciously and instinctively, takes into account the difficulty of his subject and the limits of his reader's experience with the subject matter. He gauges the adjustment of the one to the other with intelligent precision and aims never to overtax the attention of those to whom he is presenting his subject matter. The student is urged to think of the paragraph as an adjustment necessary for the economizing of the reader's attention, for this conception of its function is fundamental for our further consideration of how the paragraph can be used with precision as an indication of the structural pattern of an exposition.

NOTE: It is important, in studying this chapter and the three following, to examine the paragraphing of the Annotated Reports (pages 162 to 230).

Chapter Nine

The Relation of the Paragraph to the Plan

The paragraph does not often occur as the isolated, unrelated exposition of a single idea. Even the old-fashioned editorial paragraph, which 50 years ago or more was a heavy, closely organized, single-paragraph discussion of editorial opinion, is today split up into a half dozen or more "snappy" paragraphs. It looks more intriguing so and is easier to read. The paragraph more frequently occurs in a complex structure of which it is merely a component part. One needs, therefore, to be able not only to use the paragraph consistently as a coherent, unified treatment of a single topic, but also to indicate accurately and deftly its relationships within the paragraph system of which it is a unit part. Used in this way, it is a writer's surest and most valuable means of demonstrating to his reader that he has a plan and is using it consciously.

It has been shown that the paragraph is always an attempt to adjust the amount of material to be delivered during any one period of concentration to the natural limits of the reader's attention. Its relation to the plan depends on the scale on which that plan is to be developed. This can best be understood by taking a specific case. A comparison of the paragraph scheme in a 300-, a 1,000- and a 3,000-word exposition of the same subject will make it evident that the paragraphs always represent those units in the analytic plan which are not too long or too heavy for the reader to negotiate easily. They are framed with consideration of the reader's natural period of attention.

Here is the outline for a demonstration of the superiority of the electric locomotive over the steam locomotive; as an outline it is structurally so perfect that it could be used no matter what scale of development were required. Its perfection as a design is due to the fact that it represents the analysis of the typical paragraph quoted below. This paragraph is taken from Watt and McDonald's "Composition of Technical Papers,"[1] to which the reader is referred for an unusually clear and helpful treatment of this whole subject of paragraphing.

I. Introduction
II. Comparison of Efficiencies
    a. The electric locomotive
      1. Design
      2. Maintenance
      3. Inspection
    b. The steam locomotive
      1. Design
      2. Maintenance
      3. Inspection
III. Comparison of Economies
    a. The electric locomotive
      1. Time
      2. Fuel
    b. The steam locomotive
      1. Time
      2. Fuel
IV. Comparison of Braking Systems
    a. The electric brake
    b. The automatic air brake
V. Conclusion

The thesis sentence is evidently: The electric locomotive is superior to the steam locomotive in three particulars: it is more efficient, it is more economical, and it has a better braking system. In a 300-word treatment of this thesis, Scale 1, Figure 6, a single coherent paragraph would be sufficient and would not impose any unreasonable tax on the reader's attention. Such a paragraph treatment would be about a page long; it would read as follows:[2]

When a railroad company considers the electrification of its road, the first and most important question to arise is: Do electric locomotives give better service than steam locomotives? The evidence shows that in nearly every case where electrification has been tried, they do give better service. In the first place, in spite of the fact that they are still in their infancy as compared with steam locomotives, they are much more efficient in opera-

[1] H. A. Watt and P. B. McDonald, Composition of Technical Papers, McGraw-Hill Book Company, Inc., New York, 1925.
[2] *Ibid.*

tion. The best types are now operated at 92-per-cent efficiency from third rail to rim of drivers they are, moreover, maintained in their original operating condition at a cost of only 3 cents per mile; and they need inspection only after 1,200 miles of operation. Steam locomotives, on the other hand, in spite of the fact that superheaters, stokers, and other mechanical devices are gradually increasing their efficiency, are not nearly so efficient;

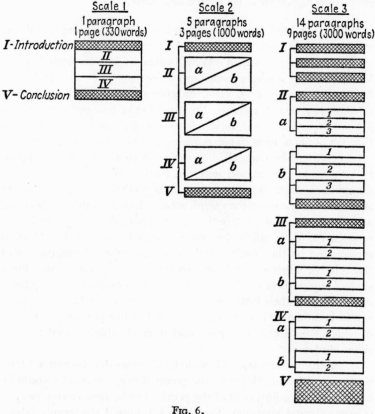

Fɪɢ. 6.

moreover, they have to be continually overhauled and repaired; and they need very frequent inspection. In economy, as well as in mechanical efficiency, the electric locomotive is superior to the steam locomotive. The electric locomotive is a timesaver in that it does not, like the steam locomotive, require coaling, taking on of water, and changing of engines. It is economical also in fuel saved. The steam locomotive, because unlike the electric locomotive it is an independent generator of energy, actually uses in moving its trains only about 10 per cent of the total coal which it consumes; the rest is used in firing up and banking, and while the locomotive is standing idle on sidings or in the roundhouse, or is coasting down grades. The electric locomotive has another advantage in its use of the electric brake instead of the automatic airbrake, since the latter results in frequent overheating of the car-wheel rims from the friction caused by the brake shoes. Under actual operating conditions, therefore, there can be little doubt of the decided superiority of the electric locomotive.

If one increased the scale of development by adding detail and additional supporting facts, so that his exposition was expanded into a 1,000-word paper, which was not broken up into its analytic parts, he would have a single paragraph three pages or more in length. Such a solid mass of material, unbroken by logical pauses, would make too great a demand on the attention of any ordinary reader. He would instinctively shrink from the task of making his way through such a formidable paragraph and would either skim it superficially or be compelled to subject it to a painstaking analysis to be sure he understood how the thesis was demonstrated. Evidently the writer should perform this analysis for the reader in advance and use some paragraph scheme based on this analysis and adapted to the reader's capacity for attention. As is shown in Figure 6, page 73, there might be one short paragraph of introduction represented by the crosshatched section, one for the comparison of the relative efficiencies of the two types of locomotive, one for a similar comparison of their relative economies, and another for a comparison of their braking systems; a brief concluding paragraph would be added. This would give a total of five paragraphs no one of which would exceed a page and most of which would be considerably less.

If, again, one increased his scale by three so that he had a 3,000-word exposition of this thesis, the group of five paragraphs would be an inadequate adjustment of the portions to be read during periods of concentrated attention. The more substantial paragraphs which were a page in length would again stretch out to a three-page limit. Making another adjustment, as is shown in Figure 6, the writer would need to make his paragraphs represent the subordinate units in the analytic plan. The introduction would be elaborated somewhat, probably into a group of three paragraphs. The comparison of efficiencies would require a brief introductory paragraph, one for the efficiencies of the electric locomotive, one for the efficiencies of the steam locomotive, and a brief concluding paragraph comparing the two. This would be a total of four paragraphs. Similarly, four paragraphs, including introductory and concluding text, would be required for the comparison of economies. Possibly two paragraphs would do for the consideration of the braking systems. With a concluding paragraph the nine pages would thus be broken up into 14 paragraphs. Presumably no one would need to be more than a page in length—the maximum norm set by the original one-paragraph treatment of the thesis.

The thing to note in this study is that the paragraph is always being used consistently to represent a component unit in an analytic scheme of units. Whether it is a major or a minor unit is determined by the scale on which the plan is being developed. It should be noted that such an adjustment is very flexible—that, because in Sections II and III, for example, the amount of detail required the addition of introductory and concluding text, such functional text was not needed in the case of Section IV. Moreover, it is quite possible that in Section III the massing of detailed data might require a group of three paragraphs representing 1, 2, and 3 under both *a* and *b*. This would give eight shorter paragraphs in this section, whereas in Section IV possibly only two would still be needed. These adjustments would be decided always with consideration of the reader's ability to handle this type of subject matter, but also, always, with reference to the pattern of the paper. The paragraph, to repeat, is thus always an effort to adjust the amount of material to the period of concentrated, unbroken attention that one may reasonably expect from his prospective reader.

Experience, the development of intelligent and sympathetic insight into the capacities of the reader's mind, and a generous consideration of the difficulties of one's subject matter are needed to make these adjustments with unfailing skill. It does help, however, to adopt as a definite part of one's procedure in preparing to write, a consideration of the question of scale of treatment before he actually begins to write. If one would always consider the possible, desirable, or necessary scale of development for the exposition he has outlined, he would ultimately write with a more conscious feeling for the proper proportioning of parts and would apportion his material to his paragraph units with consistent regard for the ease with which his reader will receive what he has to give.

An outline with the notation of a tentative scheme for using the paragraph would look like this.

I. Introduction (3 paragraphs)
II. Comparison of Efficiencies (1 introductory paragraph)
    a. The electric locomotive (3 paragraphs, one for each subtopic)
       1. Design
       2. Maintenance
       3. Inspection
    b. The steam locomotive (3 paragraphs, one for each subtopic)
       1. Design
       2. Maintenance
       3. Inspection
III. Comparison of Economies (1 introductory paragraph)
    a. The electric locomotive (2 paragraphs)
       1. Time
       2. Fuel
    b. The steam locomotive (2 paragraphs)
       1. Time
       2. Fuel
IV. Comparison of Braking Systems (2 paragraphs)
    a. The electric brake
    b. The automatic air brake
V. Conclusion (1 paragraph)
   Total of 18 paragraphs

No exact forecast can be made by the inexperienced writer, but there is no better way for him to learn to use the paragraph with some precision as an evidence of careful planning than by spending always at least a half hour in considering this problem of the scale of development and the consequent distribution of the subject matter to the paragraphs.

Chapter Ten

Coherence within the Paragraph System

Since, as has been shown in the preceding chapter, one is usually employing the paragraphs in groups, it is necessary to be able to

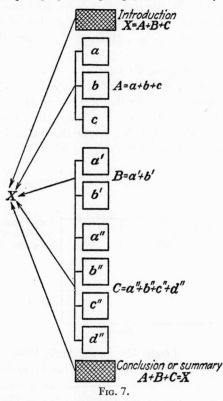

Fig. 7.

indicate the relation of paragraphs to each other and to make clear their part in the development of the subject as a whole. One needs to learn to tie paragraphs, as it were, into bundles, to make evident the close inherent relationship between the members of a group in their performance of their common function, as well as the larger relationships to other groups. Figure 7 suggests graphically what is meant. The subject, *X*, is given in three major sections, *A*, *B*, and *C*, each of which is broken down into its component parts. There is also the usual introduction and conclusion or other terminal section, represented by the crosshatched section.

When one stops to consider how many different relationships may exist between paragraphs or between groups of paragraphs, it is evident that here is a technique not easy to acquire. Paragraphs may be in a series; they may be related as contrasting units; they may be involved in a comparison; they may be related as cause and effect; they may be in any one of a dozen or more relationships which need to be indicated by transition devices of various sorts. Fundamentally, however, the technique of marking the transition points is quite simple.

1. The initial emphasis on the topic idea of each paragraph, which is accomplished by the use of a simple, but incisive, topic sentence, is sufficient to notify the reader that a new unit of thought is being introduced and therefore that a transition point in the scheme of topics has been reached. It is important that he be kept aware of what is *a* and what is *b* and of the point at which he passes from one to the other.

Graphically represented, such a transition would look something like Figure 8:

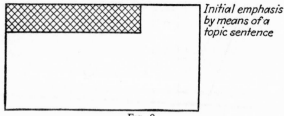

Initial emphasis
by means of a
topic sentence

FIG. 8.

In an article in the *Atlantic Monthly* for April, 1938, on "Radio in Europe," the transitions from part to part are so marked.

Let us begin our survey with Great Britain, the first European country to organize its broadcasting on a national scale.

In Germany there is no freedom of speech except as the government dictates.

If Italian radio has less popular influence, it is because, owing to a low standard of living and the high price of receivers, there are proportionately fewer radios in Italy than in any other European country.

Within their geographical limits and their comparatively small resources, the smaller European democracies—Switzerland, Belgium, Holland, and the Scandinavian countries—have in many ways the ideal broadcasting service.

2. Often, in a well-developed paragraph of considerable length, the topic that gives the paragraph unity is stressed not only at the beginning but also at the end. This makes it still more obviously a rounded-out unit of the whole. Such a paragraph might be represented graphically as in Figure 9:

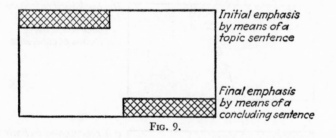

Initial emphasis by means of a topic sentence

Final emphasis by means of a concluding sentence

Fig. 9.

Two examples of paragraphs so marked by both initial and final emphasis will make this more clear.

1.   It will be seen that the norm is only slightly above the normal amount of 2 parts of carbon monoxide to 1,000,000 of air.

. . . .

These investigations seem to be the only ones of this kind. They confirm the common assumption that carbon monoxide, if present in the atmosphere, is in amounts too small to be easily detected.

2.   With natural zeolites an increase in capacity can be obtained by increasing the amount of salt used up to a certain point; beyond this, there is no noticeable increase.

. . . .

Thus it will be seen that, by using abnormally large amounts of salt, extremely high capacities can be obtained but that these are of no practical significance because they are uneconomical.

3. Often a more explicit means is used to mark the critical points of transition from part to part. A word or phrase may be injected into the topic sentence as a means of marking the place of the paragraph in a series or its relation to the preceding paragraph or to the

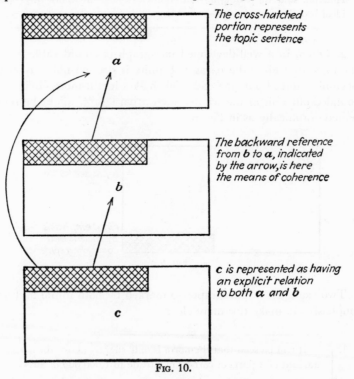

The cross-hatched portion represents the topic sentence

The backward reference from *b* to *a*, indicated by the arrow, is here the means of coherence

c is represented as having an explicit relation to both *a* and *b*

FIG. 10.

paragraphs in the group. Such words as "this," "these," "first," "second," "finally" and such phrases as "as a result of," "in consequence," "in spite of," which effect a backward reference, have a great functional value as indicating the kind of transition being made. Such words and phrases are naturally known as "transition" words or phrases. **Figure 10** shows graphically three paragraphs so related.

Two examples of a group of paragraphs where the relations are indicated by single words or single phrases which are integral parts of the topic sentence may be sufficient to illustrate this very common technique. The transitional means are italicized.

Example 1.

a.
There are *two limiting factors* that must be considered in preparing fuels having high volatility at low temperatures, yet not excessive volatility at high temperatures, to meet the wide range in operating temperatures.

b.
The *first of these* is indicated by dew point, which must be sufficiently low to prevent excessive condensation on the cylinder walls.

c.
The second condition limits the degree of volatility that should be possessed by the fuel at low temperatures.

Example 2.

a.
Among the factors in the problem the significance of which has not commonly been recognized are four worthy of especial notice. The *first* concerns the character of the source of smoke.

b.
The *second significant fact* disclosed by the researches of the committee is that which emphasizes the relatively great importance of the solid constituents of smoke.

c.
The significance of the solids in smoke as agencies suggests the *third* important fact disclosed by the researches, namely that. . . .

d.
The *fourth significant fact* is to be found in the obvious tendency of all sources of atmospheric pollution to increase. . . .

4. Often a phrase, clause, or even an entire sentence, sometimes two or three sentences, summarizing the substance of the preceding paragraph, or paragraphs, will precede the topic sentence. Such a transition will be necessary only when there is danger that the reader may lose an important connection. This is illustrated graphically in Figure 11. If the crosshatched portion of Figure 11 is understood to represent the topic sentence, the blank space preceding the crosshatching might be a transitional text preceding it.

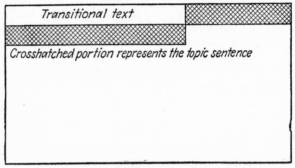

Fig. 11.

In each of the following examples, the topic idea is italicized. The backward reference precedes it.

1. Having completed the survey and determined the reasons why the plan has thus far been a failure, it will *next be necessary to consider whether it can still be made to work.*

2. All these facts would seem to justify the objections of our clients, *which will now be taken up in detail.*

3. Two of the methods have been shown not to be ill-adapted to the conditions in this plant; *the third is, as will be shown, much more likely to give satisfaction.*

5. Sometimes such explicit words, or phrases, or clauses of transition are used as parts of the final sentence of a paragraph, pointing forward to the succeeding paragraph and indicating its relation to the paragraph just completed. Such a forward reference as a means of transition is to be used sparingly. If used too frequently, it gives the reader no "full stop" for rest or reflection. Also, it is apt to rob

the following paragraph of its legitimate topic sentence. Figures 12 and 13 illustrate both the forward and the backward reference.

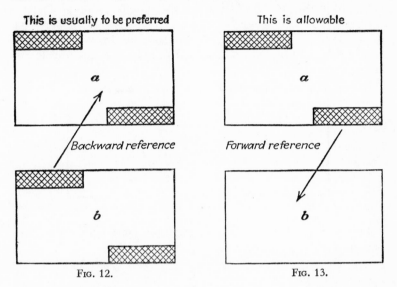

FIG. 12.   FIG. 13.

The following are three typical examples of forward reference; the sentences are, in each case, the final sentences in their respective paragraphs. They would have been more effective if, in each case, they had been used as the topic sentence in the paragraph that follows.

1. All the processes considered so far in the report are applied to the treatment of feed water before it enters the boilers. *A number of systems of scale prevention are intended to operate within the boiler.*

2. Not only are nonstandard forms unnecessary, but, owing to the waste of stock and the excess of labor involved in printing them, *they are decidedly uneconomical.*

3. As was pointed out before, the 5-week period once a year during which the diplomas are printed requires the complete attention of a compositor and a pressman, who must be taken away from their regular work. *Two suggestions are made to take care of this irregularity in the routine.*

6. When the plan is at all involved or when the discussion has proceeded so far that the reader is in danger of being confused as to the point in the plan reached, a brief transition paragraph may be inserted. The sole function of such a paragraph is to point back over the territory traversed and to point forward to the area still left to cross. Such a paragraph is like a road sign saying to the traveler, in effect:

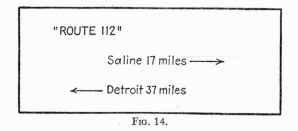

FIG. 14.

In Figure 15, the crosshatched paragraph represents the transition paragraph.

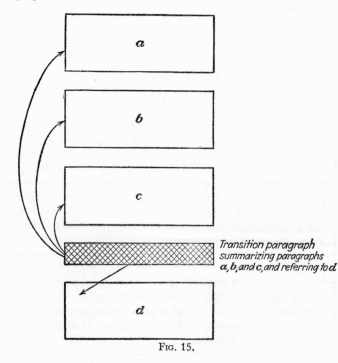

FIG. 15.

The following are examples of the transition paragraph taken from three different reports:

1:    In the preceding section of this report an effort has been made to describe some facts learned through experimentation with different zeolite materials. Many of these have direct application in the operation of the systems actually installed. *How some of these principles have been found to apply in the operation of these systems will be shown in the following section of the report.*

2.   Since, therefore, no laboratory test for measuring the volatility of motor fuels has been described which can be directly interpreted in terms of engine performance, it was necessary, before the relative values of different motor fuels could be determined with any degree of precision, *to make careful tests on a number of representative engines.*

3.   Now these are the facts in the case. There is the fact of the growth of the yeast plant, and there is the fact of the splitting up of the sugar. *What relation have these two facts to each other?*

The function of all such means of marking the points of transition in the structure of a paper is to orient the reader—to tell him, in other words, which way is east—at the critical point when he is passing from one component unit of the plan to another.

NOTE: It is suggested that the student reread the illustrative examples pages 25 to 27, and examine again the article on activated sludge on pages 30 to 34. He will also find some illuminating examples of problems in transition in "Studies in Coherence" (pages 265 to 277).

Chapter Eleven

Sectional Headings as Evidence of Design

The paragraph, as has been shown, is the most useful and natural means a writer has for making the structural pattern of a composition evident as a guide to the reader. He should think of it always as a means of marking the analysis and organization of his material made in the interests of utilizing the attention of his reader most economically and effectively. He should diversify his transitional devices till his finished work shows a coherent handling of paragraphs which is so natural and unobtrusive that the reader is quite unaware of how it has been effected.

As evidence of organization, no substitute can be as satisfactory as an orderly, coherent paragraph scheme. In reports, however, where everything must be done to expedite both a rapid first reading and a ready use of the text for frequent reference reading, there have developed in the course of years other still more obvious means of marking the plan of organization. It was stated in Chapter X that one way of keeping the reader from getting lost in the maze of detail in the body of one's exposition is to mark the unit parts distinctly so that he is always aware of what is a and what is b and what is the point at which he passes from a to b. It has been shown that the topic sentences, with the various explicit transition words and phrases and transition sentences, or paragraphs as the case demands, are intended to do just that. But in a report the route must be charted even more obviously. There is need for additional safeguards to assure even the most cursory reader against confusion. Headings marking the various sections are such supplementary means—almost mechanical and quite foolproof. It might be said, rather crudely, that in a report, the unit sections are taken apart and actually labeled for the reader's convenience. One might, perhaps still more crudely, say that the reader of a report is provided with road signs; in the headings he has a means of making his way through the report without getting lost and with the assurance that he will reach his destination safely.

There has been, and still is, no perfect agreement as to any one system of headings. It is a usage that has not yet been entirely standardized, although each year has seen a nearer approach to uniformity; certainly there is beginning to be a more conscious use of such headings as a means of marking the plan of a report; they are no longer used, as often was the case years ago, merely to call attention to some one part that needed emphasis. The system that this book suggests seems soundly based on the theory that the headings have value only as they help the reader find his way about in a report and expedite his handling of it. It seems to meet the requirements for a system that can always be relied on to represent the structural plan of the report, which agrees perfectly with the table of contents, and which indicates always and consistently the relation of main and subordinate units in such a plan. Moreover, it is flexible enough so that it can be applied, according to one's best judgment and experience, as it is needed. One section, where the coherent flow of ideas must be uninterrupted, may be marked by a single main heading, whereas in another section of the same report, where it is important to stress sharply the subordinate units, second- or even third-order headings may be used. It is the system that the author employed in editing the hundreds of typed reports that passed through his office monthly during his years as editor of the Department of Engineering Research and with slight modification to the published bulletins and circulars. It seems consistent and practical.

The specifications for this system as applied to the typing of both the long-form and the short-form report should be studied with reference to the illustrative examples that follow:

1. In the long-form report the main headings are displayed in capital letters in the center of the page. They are underscored to mark them as distinct from the text. In single-spaced text, three spaces before and two after the headings, in a double-spaced text, four spaces before and three after are recommended.

2. The second-order headings in such reports are displayed at the margin in a line above the text they introduce. Capital and lower-case letters are used, and the headings are underscored. A period usually follows such headings. The text begins on the line below. The spacing is increased by one space preceding the heading but is kept the same following it.

3. The third-order heading in the long-form reports is like the second-order; it is displayed in capital and lower-case letters underscored. As an inset at the beginning of the first paragraph in the section it marks and is followed by a colon and a double space preceding the text, which follows in the same line with the heading.

4. The short-form reports omit from the series of headings the heavy, all-capital headings; they use the second-order headings as main headings and the third-order headings of the long-form reports as their second-order headings. Short-form reports are usually single-spaced.

5. The headings, the outline, and the table of contents should agree as to relation of parts.

Example 1. *Two Orders of Headings in a Single-spaced Long-form Report.*

Main heading   PRESENT PRINTING SYSTEM

                After the character of the work has been simplified and made as uniform as possible by means of the foregoing suggestions, the printing department itself should be considered with the end in view of making any necessary changes to cut the cost of producing that work. In order that the reader may have a clear picture of the routine of the plant as it now operates, a brief description is necessary.

Second-order Job Ticket.
heading   The first step in the execution of a printing order is the making out of the job ticket. These are made from requisitions coming from the Purchasing Department, through which office all orders in the university must come. The job ticket itself consists of a manila envelope, printed on one side with a form calling for all information concerning the job and with sufficient room inside for all samples, proofs, and special instruments which should be kept with the job. This job envelope, or ''ticket'' as it is usually called, never leaves the job but follows it through the shop to completion. When the job is completed, the ticket is taken into the office; and after certain information required for billing the job is taken from it, it is filed.

Second-order Composition.
heading   With the ticket made out and the samples of printed material inside it, the job is now ready for composition, the first operation in printing. The office manager takes the ticket to the compositor who, after inspecting the samples, determines from his files whether or not the form is standing.

Example 2. Second- and Third-order Headings in a Single-spaced Long-form Report.

Second-order heading
A good example of a transition and introductory paragraph to a section

Profitable Enterprise.

So far we have not considered the opportunities that the present situation presents, and we have been inclined to stress the dependence of these opportunities on the solution of the problem of legislation. Yet past experience shows that, even without such legislation, flying operations of a commercial nature may be carried on with profit. Already, a variety of enterprises have proved successful. These include not only passenger and freight carrying, but such specialized work as photographing and aerial advertising by what is known as ''skywriting.''

Third-order heading

Passenger Carrying: The first field of aerial activity capable of commercial exploitation was that of carrying passengers on short flights. This enterprise found immediate favor at the close of the war and offered an opportunity to the individual flying his own plane as well as to the organized company. It served also to acquaint more people with aircraft and helped to break down the attitude of skepticism and prejudice. This field still offers considerable opportunity, and it will be found that a reputable concern operating near a large city can do $300 or $400 worth of business on Sundays and holidays.

Third-order heading

Freight Carrying: As the gradual demands for passenger service between cities and towns led companies of a more permanent nature to establish scheduled intercity service, it was natural that freight transportation should enter in as an auxiliary. The expense connected with such shipments limited the scope of this work, and, in general, it was found that only with goods of perishable nature was the gain in speed able to make up for the advance in cost.

During the past year, however, the newspapers have begun to use aircraft for rapid transmission of photographs of exceptional events. By means of aircraft, photographs of the Dempsey-Firpo prize fight which left New York shortly before midnight were in Chicago in time for the morning editions, and similar service has been rendered for other prize fights and such national calamities as the earthquake in Japan.

At present, this field offers but few, and irregular, opportunities; but there are many indications that it may yet assume the proportions of a major enterprise and is one that is capable of yielding large profits.

Example 3. *Sketch of an Entire Short-form Report, Showing the Slightly Different Use of Headings.*

OPERATING COSTS FOR AIR–CONDITIONING SYSTEMS
USING SILICA GEL AND ELECTRIC REFRIGERATION

Air-conditioning systems using silica gel, electric refrigeration, or both together are compared in this report to show the relative operating costs of each with different types of cooling loads. The report was requested by Mr. J. H. Walker to set forth the effect of moisture removal on the operating costs of air conditioning with different types of system. Four different systems are considered. These are, a commercial silica gel unit using deep–well water for cooling, a modified silica gel unit using city water and rehumidification for cooling, an electric–refrigeration unit using city water for condensing, and a combination electric–refrigeration and silica gel unit using city water and heat to reactivation of the gel beds for condensing. These units are outlined in the diagrams on Plate 1. They are compared with particular regard to costs and conditions in the residential area of metropolitan Detroit.

Effect of the Moisture Load.
A discussion of the effect of the moisture load may be helpful in correlating the cost characteristics of the different systems. [This topic is developed in seven paragraphs.]

Assumed Operating Conditions.
Since the degree of comfort in a room is determined by the effective temperature, the four cases considered are computed for a common effective temperature of 71° Fahrenheit. [There follow three paragraphs.]

Conclusions.
The operating costs shown on Plate 2 and previously summarized indicate that the units using silica gel do not have much to recommend them. Their operating costs are higher in most cases and they are probably more expensive than an electric–refrigeration unit. The combination unit, which has the most favorable operating cost, is certainly much more expensive. Simplicity in the control mechanism also should not be overlooked. The electric–refrigeration system has fewer distinct processes to control and would therefore have a much simpler and more dependable control mechanism. Of the four cases considered, it is probable that the electric–refrigeration unit offers the lowest over–all cost for air conditioning. This conclusion is only slightly affected by the magnitude of the moisture load as may be seen from Plate 2.

Example 4. Sketch Showing the Relation of Headings to the Outline Plan.

THE USE OF HEADINGS IN DOUBLE–SPACED TEXT

I. Introduction

II. Development of Welding Unit

    a. Division of piping system into suitable units

    b. Shop welding of pipe to valves and fittings

        1. Preparation of valves for welding

        2.

        3.

        4.

    c.

        1.

        2.

III. Protection of Field–welded Joints

    a.

    b.

    c.

IV. Summary

THE USE OF HEADINGS IN DOUBLE-SPACED TEXT

This sketch will illustrate the use of the headings through part of the first section of the student long-form report outlined on the opposite page. The text of the introduction will follow the display of the title on the first page without the display of the word ''Introduction'' as a heading; such a display is superfluous. Four to six spaces will be allowed between the title and the text.

DEVELOPMENT OF WELDING UNIT

This is the first main heading. Four spaces precede this display, and three follow the text it introduces. It is in capital letters followed by no period; it is underscored.

Division of Welding Unit.

This is a second-order heading. Capital and lower-case letters are used as shown, followed by a period; it is underscored; three spaces before and two after this heading. The text follows, as in this example, on the line two spaces below the heading.

Shop Welding of Pipe into Suitable Units.

Text in the line below, as in the paragraph above.

Preparation of Valves for Welding: This is a third-order heading. It is displayed in capital and lower-case letters, as shown, aligned with the paragraph indentions. It is followed by a colon, and, after 1 space, by the text in the same line.

Example 5. Sketch Showing the Relation of the Headings to the Table of Contents

TABLE OF CONTENTS

Page

NOTE: The introductory text will follow the display of the title, without any heading marking it. Its introductory character is sufficiently evident from its position preceding the first main heading, which marks the beginning of the body of the report.

DEVELOPMENT OF SPECIFICATIONS

Simple Rules.

Semicomplete.

Complete.

    Material Tests:

    Field Trials:

    Field Recommendations:

    Standardizing of Material:

    Approval:

TRAINING OF USERS

Division Foremen.

Crew Foremen.

Field Estimators.

Planning Engineers.

RESULTS

Adequate Strength.

Reduced Stock.

Required Clearance.

Improved Appearance.

Lower Cost.

SUMMARY

NOTE: The headings in this sketch are displayed in the exact relation to each other and are placed on the page in the precise way they will be used in the text. One will be saved many a slip if he will translate his outline plan in the form just shown on page 93 to that shown on this page.

Chapter Twelve

Special Types of Paragraph

In any report complex enough to require the use of sectional headings special functional paragraphs (topic paragraphs, concluding paragraphs, transition paragraphs) are apt to be developed in order to provide a coherent, readable text without undue dependence on the headings themselves.

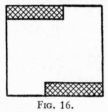

Fig. 16.

The first striking feature of a paragraph unit, Figure 16, has been shown to be the focusing of attention sharply on the topic idea in the initial moments of the paragraph. The focus is generally established within a sentence or two. For a unit so limited as a paragraph, this can be effected by a single sentence. If, however, one is setting up for discussion a topic that will engage the attention of the reader, not for a page or less, but for three, four, possibly five or six pages, a single sentence is usually not adequate. The reader must be given an intimation that for a considerable space he is now to consider in some detail one of the major parts of the whole report. He must often be prepared for the task by being given a forward look over the next few pages which must be taken together if they are to be understood. If such introductory comment were an integral part of the paragraph developing the first component of the section, it could easily be mistaken at first glance for the topic sentence or sentences of that paragraph. To give it evident importance as a functional paragraph not concerned with delivering ideas but with orienting the reader at a critical point of attack, it has come to be split off from the section that it introduces. It is an introduction in miniature which performs for the section such of the normal introductory functions as seem needed. It serves the section as a topic paragraph just as the topic sentence served the smaller paragraph unit. This is shown in graphically in Figure 17; the topic paragraph is represented by the crosshatched portion marked $x = a + b + c$.

It has also been noted in considering the characteristics of the paragraph that the end is often marked in some explicit way as the terminal point. In paragraphs used in groups, this function is, of course, often entirely lacking. In a section such as that under consideration, however, it is often necessary to mark sharply by a brief functional paragraph the moment when one has arrived at the terminal point; the reader needs, after following through pages of detailed discussion, to know that "that is that." Such a paragraph is like an order to stop and take account of what has now been actually done. The brief summary is characteristic of this function. In the graph, Figure 17, the terminal section is so represented by the formula $a + b + c = x$, al-

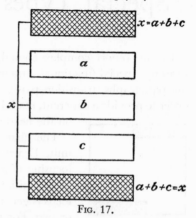

Fig. 17.

though it actually is quite as apt to take other forms. As was the case with the topic paragraph, such terminal comment is best split off from the last paragraph in the section and displayed as a brief independent paragraph, since evidently, from its very brevity as compared with the paragraphs representing the component units of the section, it has some special vital function to perform. It may or may not be marked with a subordinate heading indicating its function, as "Summary," "Conclusions Drawn from This Experiment," "Importance of These First Findings." Usually, except in very elaborate reports, it is displayed without such headings.

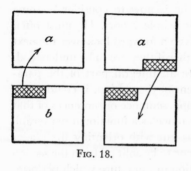

Fig. 18.

In Chapter X in considering how the relations of paragraph to paragraph were indicated it was pointed out that most frequently the transitions were effected by a backward reference from the topic sentence of one paragraph to the substance of the previous paragraph or paragraphs. It was also noted that a forward reference is sometimes used from the terminal sentence of one paragraph to the topic of the following paragraph. This is represented graphically in Figures 18, 19, and 20. By analogy, one can see that naturally both the topic paragraphs and terminal paragraphs in sectional units take on important transitional functions. An attempt is made to show this analogy in Figures 19 and 20. In Figure 19 the arrow represents the reference from the introductory paragraph—the "topic paragraph"—of section y to the terminal paragraph of section x. In Figure 20, the transition is effected by a forward reference from the terminal section of x to the introduction paragraph of y.

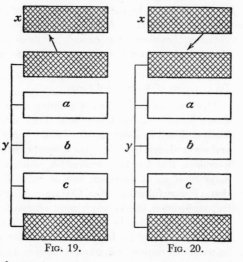

FIG. 19.   FIG. 20.

It is much better in most cases to use the introductory text to a section—the topic paragraph or paragraphs—rather than the terminal text—as a means of transition. Only rarely would one need to use both in the same section. The backward reference as a means of transition is practically always to be preferred to the forward reference. The latter is definitely to be avoided or is to be used as little as possible. The transition paragraph having no introductory or concluding functions, which has been explained in Chapter X, is to be used where needed within the body of such a section to establish the relations of parts in the structure of the section itself.

These special types of functional paragraph, having little to do with the development of the subject but being of such vital importance in keeping the structure of the report sound and coherent, are illustrated in the following examples:

Example 1. Topic Paragraph to a Section.

STANDARDIZATION OF FORMS

The definition of a term having here a special meaning
The importance of the topic
How far this importance has been recognized by the university

The term "standardized" is used in connection with printed matter to mean that a limited number of kinds and sizes of paper, styles of type, and arrangements of the type on the paper have been settled upon as those which are to be used. The advantages incumbent upon standardization of printed forms are chiefly the lower cost of the forms and the improvement of the general appearance of the printed matter due to the increased uniformity. That the university appreciates this is shown by the fact that its printed forms are about 65-per-cent standard. A survey of the nonstandard forms indicates, however, that enough of them could easily be changed to standard to bring the total up to between 95 and 98 per cent.

Disadvantages of Nonstandard Forms.

What this section is to do, and what it contributes to the general report on desirable changes.
The subtopics are then presented in order

That nonstandard pieces of printing are not necessary is shown by an examination of them. They are, in most cases, forms designed in great haste to fulfill a sudden requirement and never altered because of the natural reluctance to change something that has been reasonably satisfactory. The great majority of them, however, can so easily be standardized that it is wasteful not to do so. Certain large forms for tabulating, registration blanks which must necessarily be large and odd-sized, and certain labels which must withstand submersion in alcohol for long periods are examples of printed material that cannot be of standard sizes and standard papers, but these are in the minority. There is no real objection to almost complete standardization.

Example 2. Use of Both Introductory and Concluding Paragraphs in a Long Section.

DUTIES OF EACH EMPLOYEE

The topic is carefully introduced

Because of changes in the volume and character of the work required of the printing department that inevitably occur from time to time, it is necessary periodically to make adjustments in the duties of the employees. The most recent major change in the work done by the department was the cessation of printing in the library cards, formerly quite a large standing order. This, as well as other smaller variations, has resulted in an uneven distribution of load among the employees, which has not been adequately compensated for up to the present time.

Its relation to the purpose of the entire report, which is to outline needed changes, is well indicated

Before considering the proposed changes in the administration of the plant to remedy this defect, it will be well to summarize the duties of each employee to show up this inequality.

Office Employees.

[One paragraph, one page in length.]

Plant Employees.

[Six paragraphs, one for each group of plant employees.]

. . . .

Concluding* paragraph for this same section. This is an example of a concluding paragraph that is largely concerned with the transition to the next section. It is a good example of the successful and proper use of the forward reference as a means of transition. The first sentence seems to summarize the section. The rest of the paragraph points forward to the next section

The loads on the 12 employees have now been examined and in 5 cases out of the 12 are seen to be unsatisfactory. By a consideration of certain changes which seem advisable at this time in the equipment of the plant and in the character and amount of work allotted each employee, it will be shown that the efficiency of the department can be substantially increased by more evenly distributing the load per employee, by eliminating some employees and thereby reducing the pay roll, and by improving the quality of the printed material produced.

*The leaders represent the omitted text.

Example 3. *Sketch of an Entire Student Long-form Report, Single-spaced, Showing the Use of Headings, Introductory Paragraphs, Transitional Devices, and a Concluding Section.*

<u>A NEW BALANCING PROCEDURE</u>
for
<u>INTERNATIONAL RADIO RECEIVERS</u>

Limitation of subject matter   This report deals with only three production systems for testing and balancing, or phasing, radio receivers. Two of these are being used at present in several of the more important manufactories in Chicago, Ill., and the third is the one proposed by the writer of this report for the International Radio Corporation. By eliminating the inadequacies of the other two systems, the new routine allows more receivers to be balanced and tested than are being handled at present with the same number of employees and the same area of floor space. Furthermore, the cost of testing per unit will be substantially less. For these reasons, it is urged that the proposed changes be made.

Purpose   The primary purpose of this report is to set forth in some detail the changes that are necessary to put the International plant into operation on the new schedule with an increased output. Since electrical equipment that is both rugged and accurate enough for continuous duty on production is expensive, the changes advised have been carefully scrutinized with regard to the size of the investment they will entail. It is important to note that the proposals taken as a whole do not entail as great an expense as would renting added floor space to continue the present system with the increased future production.

Plan   In order that the changes to be made may be completed with a minimum of delay and requirement for readjustment, the faults of the present systems will be displayed for the guidance of those who will install the new equipment and those in charge of the operation of the equipment. The second major portion of the report will cover the modifications necessary to prepare the purchased equipment for installation, changes of location in present equipment, assembly and installation of new apparatus by the maintenance department, and revisions required in the sequence of operations to use the new apparatus and schedule. Finally, estimates will be given of the decrease in cost and increase in output.

First main heading

DISADVANTAGES OF PRESENT BALANCING SYSTEMS

Introductory paragraph to the first main section

Two systems are commonly used for balancing radio receivers in production, but each leaves something to be desired. They differ mainly in the method of generating the test signals, but they differ also in other important details. Since one lacks flexibility and compactness and the other accuracy, reliability, and low cost, neither system gives complete satisfaction.

Second-order heading (Note the relation of the headings to the topic sentences)

International Radio Corporation System.

The International Radio Corporation is using a system which has been developed by additions here and there as the plant grew and which, therefore, does not represent the latest in testing and balancing technique.

Third-order heading

Signal Generation: The first point on which the International system fails to meet the requirements of a good balancing procedure is the matter of test-signal generation.

. . . .*

Third-order heading

Frequency and Signal-strength Adjustments: Another consideration, which is of importance since it occupies most of the time of the balancer, is the question of frequency and signal strength adjustments.

. . . .

Third-order heading

Sequence of Operations: The last point of weakness of the International system lies in the duplication of motions by the peakers, balancers, and final testers.

. . . .

Second-order heading

Continental Radio Company System.

The Continental system incorporates many newer practices in the line of testing and balancing receivers, but it, too, has disadvantages. Its weak points are those affecting the strength of the signal output and the checking of performance by audible means.

Third-order heading

Output Measurements: Difficulties arise at first in the Continental system with the method of measuring receiver output.

. . . .

Third-order heading

Audible Performance Checks: A second drawback of the Continental system is the use of loudspeakers to check the performance of the set.

. . . .

Concluding paragraph marking the close of the first main section

It is easily seen that both the systems in common use are inadequate since they contain many points of failure each of which alone is not very serious but which taken together represent a sizeable drawback to the system. However, recognition of these inadequacies is a long step

---

* When the body of a paragraph is omitted, as it is in all developing paragraphs, the omission of the text is indicated by a row of leaders.

toward their elimination and indicates the changes required to establish a system that makes for the greatest efficiency at the least cost.

The second main heading

CHANGES REQUIRED BY THE NEW BALANCING SYSTEM

Introductory paragraph to the second main section

It is evident from the numerous weaknesses of the present systems that more than a few omissions, additions, and substitutions must be made in the existing equipment and procedures in the International plant. Since this proposed plan is in practice in no factory, the instruments and apparatus that are manufactured at present by radio—instrument companies are designed not for this system but for those already in use. Consequently, both items to be acquired will need slight modifications to operate satisfactorily in the proposed scheme. The changes to be made involve new, purchased equipment, location of old equipment, apparatus to be made by the maintenance department, and the sequence of operations used in balancing a radio receiver.

Second-order heading

Changes to Be Made on Purchased Equipment.

The new equipment to be purchased consists of two kinds of apparatus: Monarch Manufacturing Company multivibrators, and Yaxley anticapacity switches.

. . . .

Second-order heading

Changes in Old Equipment Location.

Several changes in the location of the old equipment are to be made, also.

. . . .

Second-order heading

Assembly and Installation of New Equipment by the Maintenance Department.

The two major functions of the maintenance department in the proposed alterations are: (1) the assembly and calibration of signal generators of the type known as the ''Ferris microvolter''; (2) the mounting of all new equipment in the proper location at the balancer's position.

. . . .

Second-order heading

Changes in the Sequence of Operations.

The changed equipment will, of course, mean that some changes in the routine operations will be required.

Third-order heading

Effect on Other Departments:

The inspection department will be most affected by the proposed changes, but the repair department and cabinet department will be slightly affected also.

. . . .

Third-order heading   <u>Changes in Personnel:</u> No employees will be discharged as a result of the changes to be made; the net effect will be to increase output with the same number of employees owing in part to a redistribution of tasks among them.

Third main heading

ESTIMATES OF OUTPUT AND COST

The topic sentence for the section   The adoption of the proposed system will give the plant a greater output with no increase in floor space or cost.

CONCLUSION

This is really largely a summary   It has been shown that the present commonly used balancing procedures are inadequate on many counts. They fail on such points as signal generation, frequency and signal strength adjustment, output measurement, audible performance check, and the operations involved. Of particular interest to the International Radio Corporation is the failure of their system to balance the number of radio receivers required on the floor space available for balancing equipment. It can be shown that, by a revision in the series of operations and the apparatus used, the required number of sets can be produced with no increase in floor space and the additional benefit of a decreased cost per unit.

TABLE I

	New plan	Old plan	
	Balancing-peaking	Peaking	Balancing
Number of men required per line......	15	6	9
Total sets put out per ten-hour day....	900	765	
		$30.00	$58.50
Total balancing cost per ten-hour day..	$97.50	$88.50	
Testing cost, per set.................	$ 0.108	$ 0.116	

NOTE: The number of units representing full output is slightly less than 900 per ten-hour day.

Recommendation   Table I presents the results of calculations that show conclusively that with the same number of men (hence, same floor space) the new plan produces the required number of units at a reduced cost. Since the new plan fulfills the urgent needs of the International Radio Corporation and reduces operating costs in addition, it is recommended that the proposed plan be adopted at an early date.

Chapter Thirteen

The Terminal Section

Before considering how best the terminal section may be made to serve the reader, it should again be emphasized that every reasonable and legitimate means should be employed throughout the report to make it easy for the reader to get what one wants him to get. In the general discussion of such means in Chapter IV and in subsequent chapters on the functions of the introduction, it was shown that the introduction should set up in the mind of the reader, before he actually begins to read the body of the report, a clear conception of the subject to be presented, of the purpose of the writer, and of the plan of treatment. It was also emphasized that the plan announced must be followed consistently and must be made sufficiently evident to guide the reader through the maze of detail in the body of the report. The paragraph and the sectional heading were demonstrated as the most obvious and effective means of making the analytic pattern easy to follow.

Now, it must be admitted that no matter how perfectly all these means may be used, a reader may find himself, at the end of a long, complicated report, confused by the massing of details. He may, in the multitude of facts and supporting data, have lost the sharp impression of the outline of points to be covered, as announced in the introduction, or even the underlying purpose of the writer. If only, before one dismisses his reader, he will in some way lift the essential things out of this welter of detail and display them strikingly as the things to be remembered, he can often leave a final impression of having completed his task effectively and according to his preconceived plan. As the introduction may be thought of as a preliminary conference in which reader and writer make sure they understand the subject and the terms and method of presenting it, so the "conclusion," or, to use what seems a more exact term, the "terminal section," is a final conference in which the writer of the report checks up to make sure his reader has got the essential idea and has understood the writer's purpose in presenting it. Because such a checkup often takes the form of a summarized restatement of the points covered, it often reinforces the impression of the pattern of the report and thus provides the reader a ready means of remembering the details by providing him a framework on which to hang them. The terminal section is, thus, the third, and last, means to be considered for aiding the reader to get and retain the impression of the subject, the purpose, and the plan of a report.

The decision as to how to conclude a report is often critical, for many an otherwise satisfactory performance may be rendered ineffective by an inappropriate final comment or may seem merely to stop short without reaching any goal. An effective final comment is, of course, evidently more needed in general expository papers than in reports; yet even in reports one needs to regard the total effect of his treatment of his subject. At least, one needs to give the impression that he has completed what he essayed to do and that he has reached a certain objective which he set out to reach.

To conclude a paper of any type with just the right touch requires a delicate sense of the final effect one wants to leave in the mind of his reader—just how he wants his reader to feel about the subject treated, how to react as he lays the document down. There is in each case just exactly one right concluding comment to make, but it is not always easy to determine what it is. It is almost a distinct and individual problem in each case and one about which it is difficult to generalize; certainly it will be necessary here to limit any generalizations that may be ventured to the terminal sections of reports only.

There are, however, some requirements that one might well keep in mind in planning such a section of a report. It must, in the first place, not seem perfunctory but must add definitely to the value of the report. It must seem to be an indispensable, organic part without which the report would seem incomplete. Otherwise it is better omitted. Then, it must not develop new material, except to reinforce the conclusions drawn or the recommendations made. In the third place, it must give the impression of a completed performance. The introduction raised a question; here is the final answer. The investigation that forms the subject of the report was made to determine the cause of a certain phenomenon; here it is. The report was to survey a certain field of practice; here, in brief, is the whole area, mapped in simple perspective. It has attempted to evaluate a system or a procedure; here is the writer's final judgment regarding it. A final and very important requirement is that it should agree with the introduction on all vital points. In so far as the limits of the report or the underlying purpose or the plan of organization may need final comment, it should reinforce the impression of these functions given by the introduction. It is well always to write one's terminal section with special consideration of the commitments made in the introduction.

That determination of what is the most appropriate and effective terminal section for a report cannot be settled by any rule of thumb. Yet, since the terminal section does represent the achievement of the objective that one set out to achieve, it is often helpful in deciding how to end a report to consider what that objective is.

A classification of possible objectives like the following is of necessity loosely made, and the categories are not mutually exclusive as they should be; there will be all sorts of combinations and shades of purpose possible in actual cases. But some such classification may be found suggestive and helpful to one trying to decide upon the most appropriate final comment for his report. In general, it may be said that one's purpose is to inform one's reader, to give him one's critical judgment, or to advise him what to do; reports are, in other words, factual, critical, or advisory.

1. Factual.

If a report is concerned with giving a survey of a limited subject matter, the reader at the end is often most served by having the confusing details reduced to a simplified, but comprehensive, summary so that he can take with him from the reading of the document its essential substance in a concentrated form.

If it is an account of a research or an investigation, there is need for a summary of findings, results, or conclusions. If such a summary has been given either as a part of the introduction or as a preliminary section (see pages 53 to 56), the terminal summary should be fuller and more elaborated with material developed in the body of the report.

If it is the exposition of a new idea, the reader is apt to require the writer's judgment, briefly stated, of the value of the new idea. Here, although the report is predominately factual and not critical, the concluding comment is critical.

It should be noted that, whenever such a final judgment is expressed in the concluding section, it should be soundly based on the discussion presented in the body of the report. It may be reinforced by quoting the supporting statements of recognized authorities.

2. Critical.

Criticism may take various forms; it may shade from an evaluation and appraisal to a definite damning of a thing with one's reasons for its condemnation. The terminal point of all critical discussion is, however, the final decision as to the status of the thing under consideration—a decision generally based on a summary of arguments developed in detail in the body of the report.

3. Advisory.

In reports the advisory function may range from mild suggestion to definite recommendations; it may take the form of argument, or sales talk, or advice. If argument is involved, the concluding section is apt to be a summary with conclusions; in a sales talk, the development and reemphasis of values, uses, applications of the thing for which the writer speaks; in definitely advisory reports, a formal setup of recommendations.

Whatever the purpose, the terminal section should mark the realization of that purpose.

Terminal sections are often camouflaged by the use of headings such as "Conclusion," "Recommendations," "Summary," "Results"; but whatever heading is used, it should always suggest the end of the report. "Limits of Application," "Some Common Uses," "Some Probable Developments," "Some Pertinent Suggestions," "Work in Prospect," "Merits of the Plan," "Some Important Correlations," "Important Precautions" often indicate more exactly the character of the terminal section than the stereotyped, and often inexact, heading "Conclusion." The term "terminal section" is never itself to be used as a heading.

Example 1. *Terminal Section.*

SUMMARY OF RECOMMENDATIONS

In the attempt to make recommendations for improvements in the printing department, an effort has been made to get at the source of the troubles and starting from there to arrive at the recommendations by a series of logical steps of reasoning. The several suggestions made constitute what are believed to be solutions for the various conditions which contribute to uneconomical operation. They show that by a process of standardization and the use of a stylebook the total amount of work required of the department may be considerably reduced. They show that by installing three new machines in the bindery and disposing of one linotype and by an easily executed rearrangement of the duties of half of the employees, two of the 12 employees may be completely eliminated and the loads on the remaining 10 be equalized so that none will have too much or too little to do to keep him fully occupied the full time employed. They show that, rather than causing the quality of work produced to suffer from this more economical operation of the plant, the new machinery will improve it. It is evident that partial use of these recommendations is not feasible, since most of them are inter-related in such a way that to put some into effect means using almost all of them. But, by doing so, the writer firmly believes that a beneficial effect cannot but show upon the balance sheet of the department.

Example 2. Terminal Section.

SUMMARY

Complete specifications for overhead lines more than justify their cost over the more simple type for several considerations, namely: the reduction in the number of stock items, better working conditions for the lineman, fewer service interruptions due to construction failures, lines which are better looking and less liable to complaints from the public, all at a lower cost. The success of overhead-lines specifications depends upon their being correctly applied, and to accomplish this the instructing of the users is very important.

Example 3. Terminal Section.

CRITICISM

The experience of the company with this method has led to three rather definite criticisms.

In the first place, the subjects presented for discussion should be carefully analyzed to make sure that the decisions required can not be obtained directly, rather than to take the time at the design conferences for obtaining such decisions. The tendency has sometimes been to insert items into the agenda for the conferences which could be answered by one individual, just because it was known that that individual would be present at the meeting and consequently readily available. If more care were taken in choosing the subject for discussion, this would not happen.

In the second place, the discussion of some subjects becomes sidetracked, and valuable time is wasted discussing unimportant details which may have nothing, or very little, to do with the questions under consideration. This could be prevented by the chairman if he would insist upon those present keeping to the questions in point.

Finally, the number of people attending the meetings should be more strictly limited to those who are directly interested in the subjects under discussion, and individuals should be encouraged to leave the meetings when the subjects affecting them have been considered.

Taken altogether, the present method of placing the responsibility for an individual job in the hands of one person as project engineer, and then helping him to expedite the design and construction by holding periodic design conferences, has proved very successful.

Example 4. Terminal Section.

ECONOMIES OF USE

The report has shown that the gross potential savings in cost of turbine operation effected by use of a turning engine will aggregate $15,640 per year.

The estimated cost of equipping a turbine with a turning engine complete with controls and auxiliaries, and including installation, is $7,400. The cost of purchasing and installing one set of diaphragm packing rings and high-pressure shaft packing is approximately $6,600, based on the assumption that the work is done while the turbine is opened up for routine inspection, making the total investment cost per unit $14,000.

Fixed charges, including depreciation, interest, and taxes, are estimated at 16 per cent, or $2,240.

The net saving is therefore estimated to be $13,400, and the annual return on the investment will amount to 95.6 per cent.

Example 5. Terminal Section.

REVIEW OF REPORT

In reviewing the process which has been followed to an ultimate conclusion in the form of a graphical estimate of available draft on Plate 6, there are two features which can well be recalled to mind. These are the method of investigation and the reliability of the ultimate result.

The adoption of the plan followed in this report shows that the present standard methods of draft estimation need some modification in order that their use produce results consistent with actual practice. The plan of this study is laid out so as to show very clearly the step-by-step calculations. By the use of this method, a comprehensive idea is obtained of the influence of each item upon the ultimate result together with a quick method of checking each computation. The actual calculations, because of their very voluminous nature, have not been included in this report, but are available for reference in the files of the Engineering Division.

In dealing with the data obtained from the various sources, certain assumptions have been made quite conservatively so that the results would not be in any way exaggerated. The preparation for an extreme condition adequately covers all other conditions which would affect the performance. Therefore, it is justifiable to conclude that a combination of accurate data, clear methods of development, and an adequate margin of safety has made possible the presentation of reliable data in a form suitable for the design of the induced draft fans for the proposed boilers at Connors Creek.

Example 6. Terminal Section.

SUMMARY OF CONCLUSIONS

This report terminates with a general summary of conclusions relative to the moisture content of boiler output steam. They are as follows:

1. The baffles and feed-water troughs in the stream drums have little or no effect on the moisture content of the stream, which is produced by Boiler 5.

2. By varying the water levels carried in the drums the water circulating tubes are covered or uncovered. This increases or decreases the velocity of steam through the circulator tubes resulting from a pressure difference between the center and outside steam drums. The velocity of this steam should be kept below 1,100 ft. per minute at all boiler steam loads. Inasmuch as the steam passing through the steam circulators was dry under all conditions and moisture was evidenced above the center of the outside steam drum, the source of the wet steam which was found in the output steam came from the high velocity of water and steam passing through the water circulators and the wet steam storage in the outside steam drum.

3. The velocity of the steam and water through the water circulators was lowered by increasing the number of steam circulating tubes. These tubes decreased the pressure difference between the center and outside steam drums and increased the steam-liberating space of the boiler. The output steam comes from the upper part of the steam drums where there is dry steam when the internal steam velocities between the drums is below 1,100 ft. per minute. Since Boiler 5 meets these conditions for all steam loads up to and including 500,000 lb. per hour, with normal water levels, the boiler produces dry steam.

NOTE: Analyze the functions of the terminal sections in the Annotated Reports (pages 162 to 230).

Chapter Fourteen

The Rough Draft

No inexperienced writer, unless he is a genius, can hope to produce a flawless report manuscript at the first writing, no matter how well he has done his preparatory work. The habit of carefully organizing one's ideas and concentrating on his main objective, if persisted in, should ultimately make it possible to dictate a report to a stenographer in almost perfect form. But it takes years to develop such facility of production. For a long time one must be satisfied to make first a rough draft which can be remodeled and revised and refurbished till it is free of its most glaring faults.

It must be a distressing experience for a student or young practitioner who has spent weeks or even months accumulating material or investigating some situation only to find that when he must write his report he is suffering a partial paralysis of his powers of expression or a severe case of writer's cramp. Even when one has prepared himself for his task by carefully organizing his material and making a plan for handling it, he may still have an overwhelming sense of insufficiency as he faces the actual writing of the report. The student whose major interest has been in some technological field is especially apt to develop this inferiority complex which he drags along after him, like a ball and chain, into his afteryears of practice, slowing down his writing or making it always a painful prospect for him. Engineers with years of experience, well known nationally as authorities in their field, even men on college faculties accustomed to lecturing on their special subjects, have admitted in confidence to the author their distress and discomfort when they had to do a piece of writing. It was perfectly evident in most cases that there was no basis for any such lack of confidence; the fear was a purely subjective condition. Often, unfortunately, it was so fixed by years of habitual use that it could be corrected only with great difficulty and with painful effort.

Every student or young practitioner who looks forward to a career in which his writing of reports must inevitably be an important part should free himself as early as possible from this subconscious drag since it is bound to make life miserable for him and greatly reduce his efficiency. It may be due to a variety of causes: an unfortunate language background in a home where English was spoken incorrectly; association with illiterate people in places of employment; high-school English classes in which too little composition was given or too great emphasis placed on the appalling hazards of English as a means of communication. But, whatever the cause, one must correct this unfortunate attitude toward his writing or he is doomed to a life of misery so far as any writing is concerned.

The first thing to do is to understand what actually happens in each case. The difficulty is evidently largely due to unfortunate mental and emotional attitudes. It is so subjective and individual that each person should understand what is wrong in his particular case and then set about correcting it. Young writers are apt to approach their writing surcharged with such thoughts as these: "I never could write," "I never shall be able to write," "I hate to write." Evidently, in some way, this negative attitude must be displaced by a positive attitude based on sound, reasonable considerations. The writer must somehow convince himself that he can write, that by persistent effort he can write better and better, and that he can learn to like it. He must subconsciously be carried forward by a new confidence in his own powers.

Not infrequently the trouble is due to the confusion of two quite distinct processes, the production of the idea and the criticism of the form it is taking. The moment the ideas begin to flow from one's mind down onto the paper and he has written a sentence or two, he begins to wonder how it sounds. Accordingly he demobilizes his production forces and interrupts the flow of ideas to examine his sentences critically. After such a critical session with himself, he starts up the machinery and produces another sentence or two. Thus he is always getting in his own way, interrupting any coherent, consecutive issue of ideas and slowing down the processes of production.

If the young writer who is overwhelmed with a feeling of his own insufficiency can recognize that this feeling is purely subjective and is due either to a timid, negative attitude toward his task or to a confusion of the two processes involved, he should read the rest of this chapter with great care; for the advice it contains, however simple and obvious it may seem, has freed several generations of students from their inhibitions with reference to their writing.

Whatever the cause, one can hope to acquire facility of expression only by ridding himself of his hampering self-consciousness—a holdover from one's adolescence when he suffered from physical as well as mental and emotional self-consciousness. One must displace it by a feeling of assurance that he has recognized and accepted as sound. This feeling of assurance should in the first place be solidly based on the knowledge that one has mastered his subject in every detail, that he has assembled all the necessary facts and data regarding it, has studied them until he understands them and knows what they mean. If he can say with confidence, "I know my stuff," then he is justified in feeling that he should be able somehow to get his ideas over to the other fellow. This assurance should be strengthened also by the knowledge that he has carefully determined the requirements which the report must satisfy, that he knows what is wanted, why it is wanted, and how it will be used. And finally nothing is more reassuring than the knowledge that one has a plan. The consciousness that one has given careful consideration to all the details of his material, and knows just how he wants to handle them in order to achieve a certain objective should give one an assurance that he can execute the design he has made.

To put it briefly and somewhat more incisively, the young writer should never allow himself to think: "I can't write," "I never could write very well," "I wonder if I ever shall be able to write." He must persistently and courageously say, instead: "Sure, I can do it; I know my stuff; I know what the other fellow wants; I have a perfect plan for giving him what he wants in a form he can use."

Approaching with a new assurance the task of actually writing the report he has planned, he should first prepare his rough draft. He will gain greatly if he will adopt a procedure that will concentrate his attention on the ideas to be delivered and on those to whom he is delivering them. Ridding himself of his subconscious fear of a poor performance and abandoning the habit of interrupting himself to examine critically how he is getting on, he should try to secure a continuous flow of ideas. To ensure an orderly result, he may rely on the plan he has made so carefully beforehand and that he must follow consistently; and then, to render the rough draft fit for public appearance, he must depend on long, careful criticism.

Temporary indifference to mechanics of spelling, punctuation, sentence form, and other really important details, will inevitably produce at first some rather bad looking copy. Its faults will, however, be largely superficial and mechanical, not to be minimized but quite easily eliminated in revision. It will be fundamentally good; it will have organic form and structural soundness, for it is based on a plan that resulted from an analytic study and classification of all the material. It will have unity; for being written with an intense determination to reach an objective, it must bear evidence of this effort to do a definite thing. It is much more apt to be developed with a due proportioning of component parts than if written piecemeal. Most important of all, it gives one something concrete to which he may devote his critical attention, not in any fragmentary way but with a comprehensive consideration of his whole subject. It thus eliminates the confusion which results from the effort to use those powers involved in projecting an idea while at the same time exercising those purely critical faculties by which the production is evaluated.

If a young writer is willing to use such a method of long preparation, rapid composition, and relentless criticism, he will in the end develop facility, ease, and speed, and at the same time he will produce reports that are structurally sound and practically adapted to the uses they must serve.

NOTE: Attention is called at this point to Part III of this book, which deals specifically with the criticism and revision of reports. It will be found helpful to those who feel the need of direction in making their rough drafts less rough.

Chapter Fifteen

Two Tests of Successful Performance

Engineers who are accustomed to test structures they have designed before submitting them to the strain of actual use will be quick to appreciate the need for having some systematic way of checking for themselves the soundness and integrity of the reports they have written before setting them up in final form for submission. Two such tests are suggested: (1) a synopsis, which will indicate how perfectly, after being immersed in the details of his subject matter, one has retained the grasp of his proposition in its larger aspects with which he began his study; (2) a table of contents, which will set up in final form the design that has actually been used in the report, incorporating such changes in the first working sketch as may have been found necessary.

It will be recalled that in Chapter III two tests were proposed to determine whether one has progressed far enough in his preliminary study of his material to begin writing his report. In the first stage in one's development of a report, when he was accumulating his material and getting acquainted with its limitations and possibilities, he worked toward a critical moment when he saw clearly what his material meant, what he could do with it, how he must limit it, what his objective must be in presenting it. When that moment arrived and the conception of his proposition for which he had been more or less groping became suddenly clear, it was suggested that he should seize that moment to write out in some simple, but definite, form this synthesis of his subject as a whole. The attempt to state the thesis, or proposition, or limits of his subject matter, in a single comprehensive sentence, forced him to a decision as to what precisely he proposed to do or disclosed to him how vague he still was regarding the task before him. The thesis sentence was a searching test of his fitness to handle the details of his subject matter without confusion to either himself or his reader because it gave evidence that he understood its meaning and the use to be made of it.

Since the writer met that test and set up his thesis in its simple, undeveloped form, he has torn it down by analysis into its logical components and has made a plan for handling the multitude of details necessary for developing those components. He has written the report, a task involving the actual handling of all those details. Now that it is done, and he has in the first rough draft an objective record of his performance, he needs to test himself again. He needs to determine whether, after the experience of presenting his subject matter, he has still the same clear, simple unifying conception of his proposition as a whole with which he began. Has he become confused by the details of his treatment as to what he was doing and why he was doing it, or does he still see it all simple and see it whole?

The preparation of a synopsis is an effective test to apply. One should attempt to condense the entire report into a single substantial paragraph which will represent the whole, divested of detail. As one tested his conception of his undeveloped subject by a thesis sentence, he now tests his conception of it as a more substantial developed unit by a synoptic paragraph. Thus the synopsis in a way is an expanded thesis sentence. For example, the thesis sentence for a report on a proposed installation of improved heating equipment reads:

It is found to be inadvisable to install an oil burner or an automatic stoker in place of hand-firing for the boilers at the X.Y.Z. Plant because it would result in no appreciable savings.

The synopsis of this report reads:

The advisability of installing an oil burner or automatic stoker in place of hand-firing for the heating boiler at the X.Y.Z. Plant is weighed in this report with respect to the additional investment required, fixed charges, operating expense, and intangible advantages. The proposition is not attractive since: (1) it is unprofitable where no reduction in janitor labor is contemplated; (2) much of the advantage in the automatic-control features used with an oil burner or stoker can be obtained with hand-firing, for an outlay of about fifty dollars ($50), through the installation of a thermostat and limit controls. With hand-firing the use of a water spray in the ashpit and a change to washed nut Pocahontas coal are recommended.

The drawing up of such a synopsis is a useful experience for the writer of a report since it forces him to lift the essential elements of his report out of the confusion of detail and simplify for himself what has become complex and confusing as he has elaborated it. It is a perfect test of the unity of the report. It indicates that the writer knows exactly what his report has done. It has, moreover, another and very practical value. If well executed it may be of great use to the reader who wants to get immediately, in the most condensed form possible, the substance of the report—the type of reader who may not care to read even the introductory pages. Displayed on a page by itself, following the title page and preceding the text, it offers for immediate attention a unified, coherent, but highly simplified, statement of what the report covers. Its use in a formal report of any length is well justified by the recognized value of similar devices in many technical publications, including circulars and reprints of technical papers, bulletins, and other documents from the experiment stations and research organizations—the familiar "Abstract," "Purpose," "Summary." The author recommends it in most cases for the long-form reports. As was noted in the treatment of the thesis sentence, some types of material will not readily submit to such condensation. But even if one's utmost efforts do not produce results, the habit of attempting a synopsis of all his long reports is a useful one for a young writer, since it accustoms him to seeing, in a comprehensive way, the salient features of all reports with which he has to deal. When one considers how large a part of a young engineer's writing has to do with the preparation of excerpts, abstracts, and digests of reports that others have written, the value of having developed a habit of analysis is evident.

One should not be disturbed if his synopsis seems at times to duplicate some of the functions of both the introduction and the conclusion. Often it is a combination of both; sometimes it is quite definitely the concluding summary of results or of recommendations thrust ahead of the introductory text, which is going to even a greater extreme than the display of such a summary following the introduction. It should always be kept in mind that the synopsis is to serve a class of readers who will probably get what they need from this condensed version of the report as a whole and will not read the report at all. An overlapping of functions or even a repetition of statement need not, therefore, be avoided.

Having demonstrated to his satisfaction that after completing his report he knows precisely what he has done, the writer should make a final check of the structural framework of his report. He began with a design based on an analytic study. That design, set up in schematic 'form, he has followed as he has written. But until one is thoroughly experienced, he is quite apt to let things slip out of alignment. He may mistake or misrepresent minor points for major points. He may easily become confused as to the relation of main and subordinate units in his plan. One will often find, too, that the plan which looked so logical and practical before he began his actual writing does not work perfectly. Concessions and changes have to be made in the original design as one progresses with his writing. Any such modifications of the original pattern are bound to get the inexperienced writer into more or less trouble. It is clear that all such evidences of confusion or loss of one's sense of direction or of relationships of parts must be eliminated not only because they are damaging to one's reputation as a writer but because they will be doubly confusing to the reader.

The preparation of a table of contents is the very best way to check all inconsistencies in the actual structural design of a report. As the outline plan represented the design pattern the writer proposed to use, the table of contents should present exactly and precisely the design pattern he did use. One should check it against all evidences of that design, the headings, both major and minor, if headings are used, or the paragraph topics if there are no headings. It is important to have the phrasing of the headings identical with that of the corresponding entries in the table of contents. And one should set up his table in a form that will make evident at a glance the relation of parts.

As was the case with the preparation of the synopsis, so with the table of contents the value of thus checking over the structure of one's report is greatest for the writer of the report. But in long or complex reports, the table of contents has also a very practical service to perform for the reader. Placed after the synopsis with the paging indicated, it not only gives him, at a glance, a correct impression of the pattern of the report but serves as a means of finding sections he may want to single out for special examination.

It seems hardly necessary to add that while the preparation of the table of contents should always be a final checkup by the writer of his performance and should never be neglected, the display of the table of contents as an integral part of the report is often uncalled for. When the design is standardized, as in test or progress reports, or where the pattern is too utterly simple, there is no point in using it.

The test of a good synopsis is to read it before reading the report and consider whether it gives one such a complete idea of the proposition to be treated that he need not read the report except for details and supporting facts. It will be a useful experience to subject the synopses at the end of this chapter to such a test. The final check on a table of contents is to make sure it corresponds perfectly with the headings displayed in the text. These two tests satisfactorily performed should give the writer confidence that his report will qualify on two important counts: it is a consistent unit of thought, and its component parts combine to produce a structural whole that is properly designed.

Examples of Synopses from Various Sources.

1. The relay protective methods used on the Electrical System of The Detroit Edison Company are designed to clear all faults in the minimum time consistent with satisfactory selectivity and reliability. Main generators, most transformers and important busses, and all parallel pairs of transmission lines have some form of instantaneous protection; such as over-all differential, bus-fault leakage, high-pickup overcurrent, or balanced differential. Highly inverse-time relays are used in most other applications and furnish a simple and dependable means of obtaining very rapid operation for severe faults near the source of power, together with the delayed action necessary in case of trouble which draws a lower current and may be cleared by a subordinate step of relaying.

2. The belief that ultraviolet could be substituted for cod-liver-oil feeding in poultry raising led to a comparative test on two flocks of poultry. One flock was given ultraviolet, the other cod-liver oil, to furnish the necessary vitamin D. Increased health, egg production, and ability of eggs to hatch in the flock that was given ultraviolet treatments showed this treatment to be superior to the feeding of cod-liver oil.

3. An analysis of standard screw-thread dimensions of nuts and bolts for piping work and the investigation of an experimental nut and bolt threaded to approach limiting dimensions shows that a neutral zone, or a difference in mating parts, should be provided to ensure interchangeability. On this basis, it is recommended that national standards for screw-thread dimensions be revised to include a neutral zone.

4. A steam-ejector cooler is one of the many systems now available for producing comfort cooling suitable for business establishments. The present method of installation makes the steam-ejector unit comparable with other systems with respect to installation costs, simplicity of operation, space required, and effectiveness of cooling. There are methods, however, which appear more favorable so far as cost of operation is concerned. It is the purpose of this report to discuss means of reducing the operating costs.

5. Load records are kept on all major equipment of the electrical system by the Planning Division of The Detroit Edison Company. The keeping of these records has developed through necessity of having this information available. The records pertain to loading on powerhouses, substations, transmission lines, distribution lines, and both the d.-c. and a.-c. networks. These load records are important because of their uses in planning work, in detecting undesirable conditions on an electrical system, and in the operation of the system. The records are practically of equal importance in times of below-normal load periods as they are in the higher load periods. The value and use of these records to the Planning Division alone more than justify the expense and time spent for their preparation.

6. It is the purpose of this report to demonstrate both the technical economic feasibility of cooling a residence by means of ice. The installation of an ice cooling system is described, and, from an examination of the operating characteristics and test data, conclusions are drawn to the effect that an unrestricted use of an ice cooling system will result in excessive operating costs but that it is possible, by simple and inexpensive means, to place an arbitrary limit on the use of the cooling system and accomplish a moderate degree of cooling at a reasonable cost. In a normal summer the minimum cooling requirements for a well-insulated and shaded house are found to be such that a central fan bringing in outdoor air will accomplish very satisfactory cooling on isolated hot days but in a succession of hot days artificial cooling will be required. The costs of cooling by means of ice, well water, and a refrigerating machine are compared, and methods are suggested for dealing with the commercial and engineering problems of estimating cooling requirements and choosing cooling equipment. The report concludes with recommendations on subjects proposed for investigation this coming summer.

7. This report gives a general review of a long series of attempts to determine why Boiler 5 at Beacon Street Heating Plant produced wet steam in excess of 4-per-cent moisture at boiler steam loads of 500,000 pounds per hour with high-water levels as indicated by the high-water alarms of the water columns. It deals with the difference in design of Boilers 1, 4, and 5; the effects of different water levels and internal steam velocities through the water- and steam-circulating tubes upon the moisture content of the output steam produced by Boilers 1, 4, and 5; the velocity moisture curve developed, limiting the internal steam velocities for dry output steam; recommendations made for Boilers 1, 4, and 5 to produce dry steam at all water levels and maximum steam loads; the number of additional steam-circulating tubes to be added to Boiler 5; the cost and method of installation; probable lower steam velocities by additional tubes; a summary of test results after tubes were installed; and concludes with a summary of factors which cause moisture in the output steam.

8. Requests for underground distribution in residential areas are nearly always occasioned primarily by a desire for improved appearance. Since the cost of underground distribution is at least ten times the cost of overhead, the latter is to be preferred if the use of underground can be properly avoided. Where underground installations are necessary, the cost may be minimized by the use of buried cables, buried transformers, and buried switches, designs for which are available. A new type of overhead construction offers promise of reducing the demands for underground by improving the appearance of overhead lines.

9. The determination of the available stack draft for the proposed 600-pound boilers at Connors Creek Powerhouse necessitates three operations:

1. The revamping of the present forms of the standard empirical equations.
2. The development of temperature corrections suitable for this particular installation, and
3. The application of the new equations and corrections in the ultimate determinations.

The available draft is between 0.78 and 0.56 inches of water for the range of increasing boiler loads.

NOTE: Additional examples of both synopses and tables of contents will be found in the Annotated Reports (page 162 and following).

Chapter Sixteen

The Short-form Report

A special comment on some aspects of the short-form report is evidently needed, for throughout the book thus far the treatment of the procedures involved in the design of a report has been based largely on the longer, more formal report. This is due partly to the fact that the short-form reports tend to become standardized or stylized so that their preparation does not so seriously involve the organization of detail, which, in the writing of longer reports, is often the supreme test of one's ingenuity. Then too, the consideration of the short-form report is fraught with difficulties so intimately related to practice that they can be met in each case only by those most familiar with the particular situation. It is even somewhat difficult to distinguish sharply between the two types as to length or to say when a report is to be regarded as a short-form report and when as a long-form report. It seems reasonable, however, to consider a report requiring six pages or more as a long-form report, since such a report is likely to be developed into a well-balanced, well-proportioned document; to such a report the principles worked out thus far in this book will apply with little modification. If a report falls below this norm of six pages, it is apt either to require less formal treatment or to be so highly stylized as to belong to a recognized class of standard type. Such reports are, in this book at least, somewhat arbitrarily called "short-form" reports. Some modifications of the report technique noted in the long-form report are often made to meet conditions of use of such short-form reports.

Sometimes, of course, a report that is usually of the short form because it is ordinarily a page or two in length, may, because of certain circumstances, go beyond the six-page limit without changing its form. For example, the daily reports on the interruption of service at The Detroit Edison Company, which are often only a page or two in length and which have a set form convenient for their use, on one occasion expanded suddenly to eight pages. A violent electric storm had enormously increased the number of interruptions of service in one outlying area. Of course, the report form was not changed, and the long report was still a "short-form" report. This merely illustrates how difficult it is to classify reports in these two categories.

Short-form reports are of two types, characterized either by a formal, impersonal treatment resembling on a small scale the style of the longer report, or by a more informal personal treatment cast in the form of a letter. In this exhibition of types, these short-form reports reflect the evolution of report forms. Originally most reports, no matter what their length, were conceived as letters and followed the conventions of letter writing. The submittal was accomplished by the first paragraph, often by the first sentence, which also served to set up the subject, or problem, and the purpose of the report.

Complying with your request of Oct. 6, for advice as to the best type of refrigeration system to install under the peculiar requirements of your plant, I have investigated the available types and submit herewith my report.

Gradually, the letter form with its rather stereotyped phrasing was limited to reports that were primarily advisory in character or to those in which the personal judgment of the writer and his expression of opinion gave the main value to the report. Reports that were concerned with presenting information that was largely factual came to be written with a complete elimination of the personal pronouns of the first and second person. The transmitting, authorizing function was performed by a separate letter. It was naturally difficult for the fiction of the letter to persist if a report were much beyond six or eight pages, so that the length of the report came to influence the use of these two forms. A long report tended to be presented more formally and impersonally, whether it was advisory or informational, and the shorter report to be conceived of as a letter if it were advisory or an expression of personal opinion, or as a formal exposition if it merely delivered facts.

At present the trend is strongly in favor of the formal, impersonal report in all cases where the treatment requires more than five or six pages. The longer reports rarely follow the form of the letter even when they are definitely advisory. Both forms persist, however, in the practice of shorter reports. If the report deals with routine procedure and is largely a record of facts, especially if it is to be distributed as a source of information to a number of people, if it contains few expressions of opinion and offers little occasion for personal initiative, it is apt to develop a more or less standard form in each category of practice. In these instances the impersonal form is used. If, on the other hand, it is a communication to a particular person, deals with a special situation, is the result of personal research, expresses one's personal opinion, it may be written as a letter, even though it employs the headings and other mechanisms of the report. Both the formal and the informal types of short-form report are apparently still needed in many ranges of practice.

Every fundamental consideration that applies to the longer report should apply to the short-form report, although with some modifications and limitations. The application of these considerations can be made only by those most familiar with the conditions of service in each particular case. Reports of the first type—routine, impersonal, formal—are prepared under rather difficult conditions; they must be written under pressure and without much time for revision; they are a part of routine practice; they are to be used for compilation of records; they must often be written by men with little or no training in the fundamentals of writing. Under such conditions, there is evident need for a very definite setup of instructions as to how to draw the reports, and there is need for uniformity. Standard forms seem almost a necessity, in spite of the fact that such practice discourages individual and personal initiative and produces inevitably a stereotyped report.

Reports of the second type are more personal and flexible in form. In all the reports not strictly on routine and necessarily standard procedure, initiative and originality of treatment should be encouraged. In this particular, the letter is rather stimulating, especially if the writer has imagination enough to write directly to the man addressed with a conscious effort to interest him and satisfy his needs.

It is difficult to set up any definite specifications for these two types of short-form report without knowing the exact requirements of use. The following suggestions may, however, be helpful in designing such reports.

1. For short-form reports of standardized type, which are formal and impersonal in treatment:

a. The display of title can do a great deal to economize the reader's time. It is particularly important that it give as complete an idea of the content as possible. The first page of such reports is apt to be crowded and confused by the display of too much detail. If the report is of a length to warrant it and is formal enough to demand the use of a folder, the use of a title page will relieve the first page of all such detail, leaving the title alone at the head of the text. If no folder is used, and therefore no title sheet, a letterhead is recommended.

b. There is often confusion about the function of the opening text. It is called, variously, "Statement," "Object," "Summary," "Materials Tested." These terms only partially represent its true function. As in the long-form reports it should be conceived as a unit giving the reader as complete an idea as possible of the whole project. There is often also the necessity of establishing the relation of the particular subject of the report to that of the general project. This is the case in progress reports, in reports in series, or in reports on supplementary tests. An intelligent integration of as much detail as possible in this first paragraph will often eliminate needless repetition. If, for example, one has in this first paragraph said all that is necessary about the thing tested, there is no need to set up a heading "Materials Tested," especially if no details regarding it need to be added.

One should appreciate the necessity of a complete performance of the indispensable functions of the introduction even in so brief a unit and especially the value of a good initial sentence that wastes no time in striking at the reader's interest or in focusing his attention sharply and immediately on the subject to be treated. Such an emphasis is sound since it results in the economical use of the reader's attention.

c. The arbitrary upsetting of the balance of the report by putting the conclusions first is less justified in the short-form report than in the longer report, where this illogical arrangement is intended to make it unnecessary for certain readers to read the body of the report at all. In the long-form report, one can make the first display of conclusions a mere tabulation of the utmost brevity from which the salient points of the conclusion can be gathered at a glance. In the short report, it would seem more likely that, if the coherence and proper sequence of the entire report can be maintained, the reader will read it in its entirety. This is highly desirable in the short-form report; it is hardly to be expected in the longer report. In both cases, however, there is an advantage in handling the conclusions at the end since the reader is in a better position both to grasp their significance, and to judge their soundness, if he has read their derivation. If the upset form seems desirable, it is essential that a semitabulation of points in the briefest possible form should be used. Such a section, following the introduction, should be headed not "Conclusions," "Findings," "Results," but "Summary of Conclusions," "Summary of Findings," "Summary of Results." The difference in phrasing is important for the preliminary character of the section should be stressed.

d. Since the design is being made for a report of five pages or less, the first-order headings used in the long-form report will be found too heavy. The side headings, displayed at the margin with the text below, will be found best for use as main headings. When a second order of headings is needed, the inset at the beginning of the paragraph should be used. In other words, only the second- and third-order headings used in the larger reports will be used in the short form. This keeps the system of headings in the long- and short-form reports as consistent as possible. Single spacing with double spacing between paragraphs is appropriate. These suggestions will be recognized as applying to typed reports only.

e. The organization of the body of such a report should represent a perfect and sharp classification of the material so that no duplication of statement will be necessary and so that the utmost economy of statement is achieved, and within that unit the sections should follow each other in a coherent order. There is unquestionably need for uniformity, especially in reports which serve as a means of compilation or record, but it is not necessary to follow slavishly, and without any flexibility, the test-report form or to use stereotyped, vague wording for the headings.

f. Whether concluding comment of some sort is needed will have to be determined for each type of report. It should seem likely to encourage some initiative if such a section were either required or preferred. To avoid a misnomer and too greatly to formalize this function, it might be called "Concluding Comment" or "Discussion of Findings" or "Results." Or, better yet, if the summary of conclusions can stand last, the balance of the little report is restored.

2. For informal, short-form reports, not of standardized type, that are cast in the form of letters:

a. The blocked title with "Re:" or "Subject:" is recommended.

b. The first sentence should include reference to the authorization.

As you requested in a recent interview. . . .
At the request of Mr. Blank. . . .
Following the directions you gave me on Oct. 6. . . .

c. It is not wise to assume that the reader will recall all the circumstances surrounding the problem. They should be recalled tactfully so far as one feels the reader will require; one should be sure to set up the problem or the proposition simply but clearly and adequately.

d. It is important to include in the first paragraph either the answer to the question with which the letter deals or a brief, concise statement of findings.

e. A letter gives one an opportunity to appeal to the reader's interest and to stress the importance of the subject of the letter.

f. Since the form is so simple, there is apt to be no statement of plan. If the treatment is unusual or highly individual, a very simple indication of plan may be helpful.

This may be an appropriate place to call attention to the fact that the question of whether one should write a long-form or short-form report and also whether the situation calls for a formal or an informal treatment is often one to be determined with great care. In practice, a preliminary estimate will often be made of the time that will be required and the time actually available for the preparation of a report on the project under consideration, and a careful estimate of the costs involved will be presented. Such estimates will then be weighed judicially against the value that such a report would appear to have for the organization concerned. The questions of whether it is to be presented in a formal or an informal report will depend on how it is to be used and by whom it is to be handled. These are clearly problems that concern one more after he gets into his engineering practice· than they do in a college course where the assignments are necessarily prescribed by the instructor.

NOTE: Examples of the short-form report are given on pages 90 and 218 to 225.

Chapter Seventeen

The English of the Report

In attempting to estimate fairly the importance of English in the report, one should admit at the outset that the success or failure of the report depends largely on the thoroughness and systematic care with which the preparatory processes have been performed. As has been repeatedly stated, the ideas to be communicated must be mastered, the objective of the report must be definitely determined, a plan must be made for getting the material over to the particular reader in such a way as to produce a certain effect. Curiously enough, none of these processes has anything whatever to do with English. To be sure, courses in English should develop a consciousness of the indispensable character of these preliminary stages, for they are in a way fundamental to all writing. Such courses may give excellent training in the planning or design of expository papers, but one would necessarily prepare himself to draw a report by exactly the same procedure whether it were to be written in French, German, or Russian or were to be set up in purely graphic or tabular form. This brings up squarely the consideration of what function English does or may have in the report.

English is evidently one medium of communication that may be used, but it is not the only one available. A report may conceivably have no running text at all; the material may be presented almost wholly by graphs or tables, displayed in a clear and orderly fashion. In so far as this method is possible, it is probably to be commended, but it can be practiced only when the writer is sure that in the use which will be made of the report there is no one to whom these graphical or tabular methods will be unintelligible or unduly difficult.

In most cases the reader will need to be given a preliminary statement of the problem or proposition or an idea of the boundary lines of the subject, some intimation of the writer's intent with reference to it, and a preconception of the plan of treatment. He will need to have definitions of unfamiliar or unusual phraseology, and explanations of details that he cannot be expected to get from either graphs or tables. He will need interpretive comment at points where his experience with this particular type of subject matter will not serve him adequately. Here are places where the graphical or tabular methods of demonstration must clearly be supplemented by verbal means.

The exact relation of these verbal means to the graphical means will be determined largely on the basis of the convenience to the reader and the conserving and economizing of his mental energies. Also, the degree of dependence on them will differ somewhat with the training and ideals of the writer. In England, for example, the report is primarily a written document. Recourse to diagrams, illustrations, and other supplementary means of demonstration are discouraged because it is felt they may serve as crutches which will ultimately lessen a man's ability to give a clear and adequate verbal account of his ideas. The ideal in England is a lucid text with a minimum of supplementary illustrative devices. In this country, on the contrary, engineers have been so ingenious in developing graphical methods and have been so conscious of their inadequate mastery of language as a means of demonstration, or at least of their lack of facility in its use, that they have tended to minimize the text and magnify the utility of graphical means. The text has been in danger of becoming supplementary to the graphs.

Professor Tilden's comment to the author years ago, when they first met at Michigan, seems to express the need for a proper balance of the two elements most cogently: "An engineer needs to be able to use his pen and his pencil with equal facility." He must be able to turn from one to the other at a moment's notice, and to use either when the case demands, with equal ease. In other words, there is need for a perfect correlation of all the means available for communicating the idea.

It will hardly be necessary to say that, if one is to use graphical methods, he must be thoroughly trained in the technique of drawing; he must be able to turn out drawings that are attractive in appearance, easy to read, and easy to understand. If one is to use French or German as his means of verbal demonstration, he must master these languages so that they become for him readily available mediums of communication. He must be able to use them correctly and fluently. If one is to use English for this purpose, he must likewise be able to express his ideas accurately and with almost unconscious ease. One must develop a diction that is fitted to his use, one that diverts none of the reader's attention to details of sentence structure, good or bad, at the expense of continuous, uninterrupted focus of attention on the development of subject matter. A style that is ornate, rhetorical, self-conscious, "literary" in a bad sense is distracting and does not serve the almost purely utilitarian purpose of the report as does a simpler style. It is, of course, equally true that the irritation and difficulty of a crude or illiterate style also absorb and waste attention. Simplicity, directness, brevity in one's way of putting things—these must be the ideals for which one works.

The problem of acquiring a good English style is greatly complicated in our country by a number of conditions that do not exist in most other countries. In the first place, we are an almost polyglot people with almost no standards of English usage. Our students, and even our instructors, come to us with variously bad language backgrounds and with mongrel language habits. We all of us hear English badly spoken most of the time and see it badly written so often that we are in danger of losing our sense of right and wrong so far as English usage is concerned.

As the author came out of the stadium one Commencement Day, after listening to a magnificent address from Dean Gaus of Princeton, he heard one girl, a member of the graduating class, say to another, "Ain't it hot? Maw set in the sun the hull time." Here were two young women who had just received, with all the pomp of a public ceremony, the stamp of approval of an old and respected educational institution but who still spoke the raw dialect of the farm. Four years of university training had been ineffectual in counteracting the fundamental and primary influence of "Maw" and her native speech. I fear this hideous example could be duplicated with all too little difficulty.

Our schools seem unable to combat the language influences of the home, the factory, and the playground. For one thing, the systematic training in the structure and reputable usage of the language such as was basic in the training of the older generation has been crowded out of the lower schools by the apparent necessity for "enriching the curriculum" with a host of "vocational units" and newly discovered educational fads and by the supposed necessity of allowing time for extracurricular activities. Then the efficiency of our instruction in English has been recently considerably lowered by the increasing pressure of financial stringency which has made it necessary to crowd the classes of our English teachers more and more till, as a measure of sheer self-preservation, they have had to reduce the practice work in writing to a point where it has little effect on the student's speech habits. Ideals in the teaching of English have been confused; at least, there has been a lack of a consistent emphasis from first grade to the last collegiate year on the indispensable need for every boy and girl, man and woman to be able to use English with correctness and facility, both as a practical equipment for life and as the one most evident proof of an education. All these conditions are far from favorable to the maintenance of high standards of English usage or the acquisition by the average young person of any sort of mastery of his native speech as a means of delivering his ideas, on the presumption, of course, that he will ultimately have ideas worth marketing.

From first grade to the last collegiate year, there is need for a consistent, unified policy of stressing the practical necessity of learning to speak and write correctly and fluently. There should be a new emphasis on the development of a feeling for the structure of the language and a basic familiarity with its syntax. The present occasional sporadic paper should be displaced by assignments of almost daily themes, which in the course of slow, painful years will develop habits of correct expression and ease and spontaneity in writing and speaking. Finally, a definitely critical attitude should be stimulated in every student toward his own performance and that of others.

To restate the author's main contention in this matter of English: The English of the report is just one of the means to be used in getting over to the reader the ideas to be presented. As is the case with all such other means, as graphs, tabulations, photomicrographs, diagrams of every sort, one needs to become expert in its use. One needs definite training in its technique and sufficient practice so that he may both write and speak with unconscious ease.

To repeat the quotation from Professor Tilden: "The engineer needs to be able to use his pen and his pencil with equal facility."

PART II

SOME SUGGESTIONS AS TO THE FORM AND STYLE OF THE REPORT

Part II is prepared for practical use in putting one's report in acceptable form. There are many details on which it does not presume to rule with any finality. Certainly it must not be expected to supersede the stylebooks prepared by the professional societies or, indeed, those of the industrial organizations in various fields of practice. Moreover, the thesis of the book, repeated so often, makes it logical to write in a style to which the prospective reader is accustomed. Every writer should have at hand the stylebook of his own professional group or of the company for which he works and a copy of Webster's "New Collegiate Dictionary." For anyone doing professional writing, "A Manual of Style," the University of Chicago Press, is indispensable. He should also secure all bulletins and other publications of the American Standards Association. One rarely gets beyond the need also of some convenient handbook. Smart's "Handbook of Effective Writing," "The Century Collegiate Handbook," and Woolley and Scott's "College Handbook of Composition," revised edition, are very satisfactory books for this purpose.

Some Suggestions as to the Form and Style of the Report

The first impression a reader gets of a report is quite definitely influenced by its appearance. Even such details as the color or texture of the cover, the quality of the paper, the neatness and evenness of the typing, the width and uniformity of the margins, affect one's first impression as he picks up the report and prepares to read. He is unconsciously, or at least subconsciously, attracted by the obvious evidences of careful, painstaking workmanship and meticulous attention to detail, or he is prejudiced from the first by the apparent indifference to conventions generally recognized as prerequisites for a satisfactory report. The author, in his early experience as editor of the Department of Engineering Research at the University of Michigan, once suffered the humiliation of having an entire set of 25 or more reports returned by an irate patron because a careless stenographer had failed to observe the specifications for the left-hand margins. Perhaps in self-defense he should recall that he himself was away on his vacation at the time. But the patron was quite right; it was irritating to have fairly to tear the reports apart in order to read them because the left-hand margin was entirely absorbed by the binding. A few such experiences will convince the most careless or the most stubborn that it pays to give attention to the minutest details of form. The directions that are presented should be studied with reference to the annotated reports displayed at the end of this Part II. Since comparatively few reports are printed, the directions apply in most details to the typewritten report, and most of the illustrative material has, for that reason, been given in typewriter form.

STENOGRAPHIC DETAILS

Materials and the way they are used have quite as much to do with the final results when one is dressing a report up for its public appearance as they do in the preparation of a drawing. In putting a report in final form, the student should recall the exact and specific directions he has been made to follow in his drawing classes and

135

accept, at least without resentment, the directions for his stenographic work.

Stationery.

For first copies, linen or bond paper of good quality, of medium weight, and 8½ by 11 inches in size should be used. Paper with a cloth weave is never to be chosen; it is appropriate for personal correspondence only. A lighter weight paper may be used for carbon copies. All paper stock should be fresh and should be handled with such care as to leave it unmarred after it is typed.

In the choice of covers, the student will be limited to what he can get at his local stationer's. Embossed covers of various color stock with a space indicated for the title display are available in most school centers. In choosing, the student is urged to secure a cover with as generous a display space as possible for his title; it will save him considerable distress later when he has to condense his title to a form that will fit this space. Also, it is suggested that in choosing his color stock he should exercise conservative taste.

In practice, the report writer may well devote some thought to the problem of getting just the type of cover that seems appropriate for his office. The Detroit Edison Company specifies, for reports concerning affairs of the company, an embossed gray cover with a title display space 2 by 4⅞ inches. For typing in the titles, labels are provided of stock that matches the cover stock. For reports that do not concern company affairs, a plain gray cover of flexible but substantial stock is used.

Typing.

Whether one does his own typing or has it done for him by a stenographer, he should be sure the type on the machine is clean and that a fresh ribbon is used. Black ink is certainly best. If one has his choice of type, he should use the small, so-called "elite" type; for a text that may be necessarily long when ideally it should be short, this type has the advantage of reducing considerably the apparent bulk of the document. Double spacing is recommended, with no increase in spacing between paragraphs, except to provide for topic headings, as will be specified later. Quotations of more than two lines should be single-spaced. Paragraphs should be indented from 3 to 6 spaces. It is best to avoid beginning a new paragraph on the last line or two of a page. It is well also to avoid displaying a heading within four or five spaces of the bottom of the page. One may better widen the lower margin in order to begin the new paragraph or the new section at the top of a page. Margins should be kept as uniformly as possible 1½ inches for the upper and left-hand margins and 1 inch for both lower and right-hand margins. If the report is to be put up in a folder, 2 inches should be allowed for the left-hand margin in order to provide for the binding. The pages should be numbered in the upper right-hand corner. Pages displaying full-page figures and tables should be numbered in series with the text.

STYLING THE REPORT

It will be found an ultimate economy to check carefully all details of spelling, punctuation, and capitalization before the final typing. In general one should follow the clear, simple exposition of such details given in Webster's "Collegiate Dictionary," fifth edition, or in any of the handbooks of recognized standing. It seems superfluous and confusing to repeat them here. There are three subjects, however, that fall in these categories, difficult in all forms of technical writing, which seem to warrant special mention; the use of the hyphen in compound words, the abbreviation of familiar terms, and the representation of numerical quantities.

Hyphenation of Compound Words.

In general, the use of the hyphen to indicate the relation of the elements in compound words has been increasingly recognized as a simple and effective means of saving the reader confusion and often misapprehension as to their meaning. There is still lack of agreement among reputable authorities as to how far the hyphenation process should go. One needs, however, only to observe any carefully edited text to realize how general the trend is toward a consistent usage. It is interesting, for example, to see to what extremes the hyphenation of compound adjectives has gone in such periodicals as the *Atlantic Monthly, Harper's* and the *Reader's Digest*. For example, one notes in recent issues:

> two infants with tonsilar-adenoidal expressions
> a chubby-faced, youthful-looking chap
> the end-of-the-day dull headache
> a civilization-destroying war

From "Honey in the Horn," a Harper book, a random glimpse gives one:

>   a high-sprung, glary-eyed two-year-old colt
>   hawk-struck, stiff-jointed old walrus
>   a grasshopper-eating Siwash Indian boy

Webster's Collegiate Dictionary succeeds in clarifying what has seemed a chaotic situation by a statement of the best present usages. The generalizations given in this dictionary may be summarized as follows:

1. Compound adjectives and compound verbs, with some few exceptions, are hyphenated.

Adjectives:
>   a well-to-do member
>   an eight-hour shift
>   a five-foot shelf of books

Verbs:
>   to double-asterisk
>   to cold-shoulder

2. Compound nouns are usually either solid or separate; there are, to be sure, six classes of nouns that are exceptions and are hyphenated. Fortunately, only one of these classes of nouns is of special interest to writers in the fields of technology, the class of nouns naming a technical unit of measurement, as "light-year," "foot-second."

Solid:
>   workman
>   blueprint
>   carload

Separate:
>   boiler room
>   slide rule
>   water power

These general rules are stated so simply that one would appear to need only to follow them to find the styling of a manuscript dealing with material of general literary character an exciting exercise in consistency. Unfortunately, in the field of technical writing, especially of reports, there are several conditions that make the problems involved much less simple. In the first place, the use of such compounds has been enormously increased by the necessity of finding names and descriptive attributes for new objects, new processes, and even new concepts. One has only to recall that in less than 50 years practically all the literature of aeronautical and automotive engineering has been written and that the airplane, the radio, the X-ray, the wireless, the submarine, the radio, radar, the rocket bomb, television, and dozens of other devices have come into existence and have become of such importance that almost a new language has had to be created for their demonstration. Teutonic instinct for making compound words, especially attributive adjectives, and the technologist's natural tendency to highly condensed statement have combined to create a style overloaded with such compounds.

When one considers that much of the writing on these subjects has been done by men technically trained in their respective fields but often quite inexperienced in writing, it is not strange that the value of the hyphen as a means of making the exact relationship of words evident has not always been appreciated. There has been, in consequence, a great lack of consistency and uniformity in practice and still is considerable disagreement among editors as well as writers of technical reports and papers.

In report writing, where every means must be used to safeguard the meaning and to economize the reader's time and attention, the consistent use of the hyphen has everything to commend it. Since the process of combining words of various sorts to form compounds is an almost continuous one for writers in any of the technical fields, it is well to have the general principles to follow stated very simply.

1. All compound adjectives are to be consistently hyphenated. This rule is in exact agreement with that stated in Webster for general application to all forms of writing.

> a water-free form
> two 75-ton storage bumpers
> a variable-speed direct-current motor
> a 110-volt alternating-current source
> a vanadium-chromium-molybdenum alloy
> a valve-in-head motor
> high-voltage lines
> a 50-per-cent increase

2. Almost no compound nouns are hyphenated; they are to be written either solid or separate. It should be recognized that compound nouns develop from the stage when the two elements are separate, as "horse power," through the stage when the relation of

the two elements is indicated by the hyphen, as "horse-power," to the final stage when the word is written solid, as "horsepower." The second stage is generally very brief; the word is, therefore, generally either "horse power," or "horsepower." Whether a noun is in present practice written as a separable compound or as an inseparable compound can be determined either by reference to Webster or, for combinations in common use in a specialized field but not to be found in Webster, by observation of the most authoritative texts in that field. Every report writer should build up for himself his own lists of separable and inseparable compound nouns. An excellent list is to be found in "Report Writing" Appendix E, by Gaum and Graves (Prentice-Hall, Inc.). It covers such compounds as the following:

SEPARABLE COMPOUNDS	INSEPARABLE COMPOUNDS
ball bearing	halftone
gate valve	setscrew
screw eye	spillway

There is one point on which the common practice in the technical field does not agree with Webster. Terms consisting of a capital letter and a noun are generally hyphenated. For example:

I-beam	T-square
X-ray	U-bolt
T-rail	U-gage

3. Compound verbs in general follow the generalization as to usage set forth in Webster; they are hyphenated, as in the following examples:

to heat-treat
to direct-connect
to single-space

To summarize in the form of a brief injunction: Hyphenate compound adjectives and verbs; do not hyphenate nouns. It is hardly necessary to add that one must be prepared to modify these simple directions by familiarizing himself with the exceptional cases and to be prepared to capitulate in the face of opposition in fields of practice where the hyphen is still a debatable point of issue. For example, logically chemical compounds should be hyphenated when used adjectively; actually in practice, there is a definite tendency to omit them. Example: "the carbon-dioxide content" would seem logical; in practice it is usually written "the carbon dioxide content."

Abbreviations.

The amount of abbreviation allowable in a report should be determined by considering the experience of the prospective readers and the use that they will make of the report. If there is any uncertainty as to their familiarity with the terminology, abbreviations of terms should not be used. One should certainly never risk employing abbreviations that will not be understood by all who will read the report. It is probably better, in general, to err by using too few rather than too many abbreviations. In all technical fields, recognized abbreviations are, however, used so generally as to have become almost standard. This is particularly true of units of measurement. To fail to use such abbreviations in reports within these fields is to appear pedantic. Everyone who expects to write reports should provide himself with lists of such standard abbreviations as have been agreed upon in his particular field. These lists are generally prepared by the various national societies or by the organizations in which one is working. Engineers, for example, should have the list prepared by the American Standards Association, sponsored by several of the most important engineering and scientific societies in this country. Each one should also build up for himself, by observation, a list of such abbreviations used in journals and proceedings of his own professional society.

One rule stated by the American Standards Association seems well worth observing. "Terms denoting units of measurement should be abbreviated only when preceded by the amounts indicated in numerals; thus 'several inches,' 'one inch,' but '12 in.' " This rule does not invalidate the general principle already stated that units of measurement are often in ordinary text to be written out, especially when the reader is not clearly understood to be one accustomed to the standard abbreviations.

There are a number of other details to be observed:

1. Although there is a definite tendency to drop the period following abbreviations of units of measurement, the author maintains the conservative position of retaining the period after all abbreviations.

2. In abbreviations of units of measurement the plurals are not indicated: "60 in." rather than "60 ins."

3. Conventional signs for inches ("), feet ('), pounds (#), per cent (%), and other similar devices are not to be used in a report text.

Numbers.

The question of whether to use figures or to write numbers has in general been determined by the rule that numbers below ten should be written out and that above ten they should be represented in figures. This rule still holds in technical reports, although the numbers from one to ten are also often to be represented in figures where they are employed to convey a concept of quantity or dimension involving several numerical quantities or when they are in some other relation closely associated with other figures. It should be appreciated that a reader gets a quantitative or dimensional concept much more quickly and easily from figures than from written numbers.

> There are three reasons for this reaction.
> The beam is 2 ft. 6 in. by 3 ft. 6 in. by 12 ft.
> At least 15 per cent of the product is wasted.

These specifications for stenographic detail should be followed meticulously by the student or laid down as absolutely mandatory in case he is having his copying done for him.

FORMAT

In deciding on the format of the report, it is well to keep in mind the steps by which it makes contact with the different classes of readers who are examining it for various purposes.

1. Title display.
2. Synopsis or abstract.
3. Table of contents.
4. A complete, coherent, self-contained introduction.
5. In some types, a summary of results following the introduction but preceding the first component unit in the analytic plan.
6. The body of the report so set up that it gives the impression of organization, order, system, which is apparent to the eye of one merely examining the report, but which will stand the most critical analysis.
7. A terminal section, summary, conclusion, or other organic final comment.
8. An appendix for the segregation of detailed data, computations, graphs, which may be checked by the reader concerned in determining the soundness of the report.

In addition to these usual elements, a letter of transmittal may also be required, especially in very formal reports, to detail circumstances of its authorization or execution, or to make the delivery of the document official and formal.

Each of these elements should function as perfectly as possible; they should be in absolute agreement among themselves. That is, no one should find his first conception of the subject matter or of the proposition of the report shifting or changing as he reads it in detail.

Cover Display of Title.

If a cover is used, the title display will give the reader his first contact with the report. It should be as significant and as indicative as possible of the subject and character of the report. In consideration of the limited display space, it should, of course, be reduced to the lowest possible number of words that will still convey its meaning.

Other information will also be required by the person handling the report; the name of the writer and the date appear to be the minimum and should be used by the student. In practice, the department, the report number in a series, and other details necessary for the proper filing and reference use of the report must often be added. These details should in all cases be reduced to a minimum.

The arrangement of these details often requires considerable ingenuity and feeling for design. The appearance of the display alone is not the primary consideration. The words of the title should be so grouped as to do no violence to their logical relationship. Disregard of this fundamental principle will result in a confused first impression of the title.

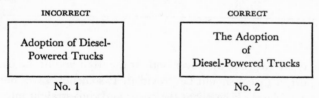

INCORRECT

Adoption of Diesel-Powered Trucks

No. 1

CORRECT

The Adoption
of
Diesel-Powered Trucks

No. 2

Arrangement 1 does violence to the sense; arrangement 2 groups the words according to the sense. Unless one has a title brief enough to permit a single-line display, it is well to spread the main lines by a short connecting line on which the connecting words "for," "by," "of," "for use of," etc., are placed.

The name of the author may be displayed in the lower left-hand corner and the date in the corresponding right-hand corner. If other details are required, the name may be centered below the title, the report number placed in the lower left and the date in the lower right corner. The title display should use capital letters underscored for the major lines and lower-case letters not underscored for the short connecting lines. The name, the date, the report number, and all other subsidiary details should be in capitals and lower-case letters, not underscored. If possible, there should be no abbreviations in this cover design.

It should be understood that not all reports will be so formalized. Obviously, routine reports and many short-form reports and interdepartmental memoranda would not justify the additional expense.

Examples of Title Displays on Cover.

```
              THE IMPROVEMENT

                    of

         SHEEPSKIN PROCESSING

W. G. Landwier                    January 7, 1938
```

```
                  MOLYBDENUM

                      in

                  GRAY IRON

P. N. Buckminster                January 12, 1938
```

Title Sheet.

Immediately inside the cover both at the front and at the back of the report, a flyleaf should be provided. It somehow saves one the jolt he experiences if he opens the cover and runs straight into text. The title page comes next unless a letter of transmittal is bound in with the report. In that case, this letter logically precedes the title page. This page is largely a replica of the title display on the cover with the elements spread out to suit the larger space. The title looks best if displayed in the upper third of the page. The name may be displayed either at the center of the page, if the author is of enough independent importance to warrant such prominence, or with the date and name of the department responsible for the report at the bottom of the page. A number of sample title sheets are shown on pages 146, 147, and 148.

Synopsis.

The student is urged to include this unit in all his formal reports till he determines for himself its utility and value. As a matter of self-discipline it is indispensable; for many reports it is most highly to be recommended. With growing experience in his practice, he will know where it is superfluous. In short reports, of course, it is quite unwarranted; in some forms of report, especially factual reports, it is difficult to use without its becoming too heavy. If a synopsis is indicated, it should follow the title sheet and should be on a page by itself; it represents the report as a whole in a highly condensed form. A sample display of a synopsis is given on page 149.

Table of Contents.

The table of contents lays before the reader the design of the report; it is the structural pattern in detail. Logically it follows the synopsis. If a report is of a standard type so that the average reader is familiar with the form, or if it is so simple in structure as to warrant no such layout, or if the report is less than six pages in length, evidently there is little justification for its use. For the longer or more complex reports, it is, however, indispensable. One very important thing is to set up the table of contents so as to make clear at a glance the relation of main and subordinate elements. Single-spacing the groups of minor topics helps to indicate their subordinate relation to the major topics. The letters and numerals used in the working outline are to be omitted from the table of contents. On page 150 is given a table without leaders; on page 151, one with leaders.

Example 1. *Title Sheet.*

THE SELECTION OF A HEATING SYSTEM

for

A MODERN HOME

Clifton M. Elliott

January 11, 19__

Example 2. Title Sheet.

THE CONTROL OF VOLTAGE SUPPLIED

to

INDUSTRIAL CUSTOMERS

R. E. Greene

The Detroit Edison Company
Electrical Section of Engineering Division

Report No. EE-11
February 14, 19__

147

Example 3. Title Sheet.

THE DETROIT EDISON COMPANY

DETROIT, MICHIGAN

THE IMPORTANCE OF LOAD RECORDS

January 9, 19___   Bronson Brant

Example of Synopsis.

SYNOPSIS

This report is the result of a study to determine the type of heating system which is best adapted for heating in a modern home, the specifications for which were submitted by the Ohio Realty Company. As the choice of an economical system was important, the field was limited to gravity warm-air, gravity hot-water, and steam-vapor systems. After calculating the heat losses from the home, the heating units, room heat-emitting units, piping systems, and initial and maintenance costs of the three systems were compared. Based upon the results of these comparisons, the system best suited for heating this modern home was selected. It was concluded that the hot-water system gave the most satisfactory performance, was the most economical, and was desirable from the standpoint of size. A hot-water system was therefore selected as the most desirable for the specified modern home.

Example of Table of Contents without Leaders.

TABLE OF CONTENTS

Example of Table of Contents with Leaders.

TABLE OF CONTENTS

The First Page.

The title of the report should be centered and displayed 15 spaces from the top of the page. It should be displayed in capital letters underscored. The same arrangement of the title may be used as was used on the title page. It is best if possible to avoid a single-line display since that is identical with the heading displays used through the text. Four to six spaces following the display of title will give it additional prominence. The use of the word "Introduction" as a heading is not recommended; it is evident that all text preceding the first topic heading is introductory. The first page is usually not numbered; it is reckoned as page 1, but the numeral is omitted from the upper right-hand corner. The title display marks it sufficiently at the first page of text.

The Body of the Report.

Perhaps the most important detail in setting up the body of the report is to be sure the headings are correctly aligned. In some types, especially in research reports, the details of footnotes need some comment. The following directions apply only to typewritten text.

Topic Headings: Main headings should be centered on the page, displayed in capital letters, underscored. In a double-spaced text four spaces should be allowed before and three following such headings. Secondary headings should be placed flush with the left-hand margin in a line above the text they mark. They are displayed in capital and lower-case letters, the main words having initial capitals; they are followed by a period and are underscored. The spacing should be increased before such headings but should be uniform with the spacing of the text following them; that is, there should be three spaces before and two after the headings. Third-order headings are set in 1 inch from the left-hand margin in capital and lower-case letters, the main words having initial capitals; they are underscored and followed by a colon. The text follows in the same line. It is customary to allow an extra space between the colon and the text. It should be kept in mind throughout reading these directions that they apply largely to the typewritten report. If one has occasion to use them in the setup of printed reports, he needs only to note that in the use of headings the underscoring in the typing is equivalent to the italics in printing. The relative usefulness of titles and headings can also be indicated by the use of different type sizes.

THE SELECTION OF A HEATING SYSTEM
for
A MODERN HOME

This report, prepared for Mr. D. R. Black of the Ohio
Realty Company, is the result of a study of three different types of heating systems to determine which is best
adapted to meet the heating requirements of the modern
home shown in Figure 1. As suggested by Mr. Black, representative systems of each of the leading types of residential heating plants were selected for comparison. As
the economy and simplicity of the systems were important,
those chosen were: (1) gravity warm-air, (2) steam-vapor,
and (3) gravity hot-water systems.

The investigation showed that the gravity hot-water
system is the most desirable for heating the specified
modern home. This conclusion was reached from the results
of a comparison of the three types of heating plants with
regard to heating units, room heat-emitting units, piping
systems, and initial and maintenance costs.

HEAT LOSSES FROM BUILDING

Before comparing the heating systems, it is necessary
to calculate the heating losses of the building, the
plans of which are shown in Figures 2, 3, and 4. The
principal sources of heat loss from this home are the
transmission losses through walls, ceilings, floors, and

153

Footnotes.

The use of footnotes should be avoided in reports. Generally, with a little ingenuity they can be integrated with the text. If they are used, they should be placed at the bottom of the page, separated from the body of the text by a line and a double space. They should be single-spaced. Reference to them is indicated by an asterisk or, in the case of more than one footnote on a page, by a small numeral. Sometimes when several footnotes are used throughout the report, they will be numbered in one series.

FIGURES

The placing of the figures and other illustrative devices in their proper relation to the text often troubles the young writer; even an experienced writer may find them quite a problem. One may get at a basis for deciding how to relate his figures to his text if he will consider why he uses figures at all. Should he not acquire such mastery of English that he can always make his ideas clear without resorting to pictures or graphs of some sort? Of course, the answer depends on the character of the ideas. In technical writing, where one is often dealing with highly complex mechanisms, it would seem at times impossible to convey adequately the conception of the thing demonstrated without some supplementary means. To realize the utility of objective means of demonstration, one has only to consider how much easier it is to explain a complicated mechanism, a dynamometer, for example, if one has a real dynamometer or at least a small working model or a diagrammatic sketch of one to base his demonstration on, than if he must depend wholly on oral exposition. Language as a medium of communication reaches its limit in such cases, and one must employ more objective and graphic means of demonstration. The figure must, therefore, always be thought of as a supplementary means of demonstration.

No figure should be included in a report unless it adds definitely to the understanding of the text. If it merely makes the report more attractive or more interesting, it may probably be better omitted. A report is primarily a document to serve a useful purpose; there is no place for mere decoration; there should certainly be little need for stimulating interest. This does not mean that a report should necessarily be unattractive or uninteresting. In fact, its appearance may do much to convey a first favorable impression. But an initial interest in the subject of the report on the part of the prospective reader may usually be assumed. That interest may, to be sure, be increased and made more intelligent; but, except in reports with a definite propaganda or sales purpose, the interest is inherent in the subject matter and not in the illustrative devices used in its demonstration.

Every figure should be thoroughly integrated with the text. The reader should be referred to the appropriate figure at every point at which he would be aided by such a reference. The reference should be related closely with the text rather than, as is so often done, insulated from it by the use of a parenthesis. If the reference is quite incidental and grammatically independent it should be set off by commas, but not by a parenthesis. Thus, one may say: "The crankshaft, Figure 4, is connected, ..." If the reference is of more importance than this incidental mention of it would indicate, one can say: "The crankshaft, which is shown in Figure 4, is connected . . . ." or "Figure 4 shows a diagrammatic sketch of the crankshaft which is connected . . . ." This conception of the figures as integral parts of one's text is the basis for the following directions for placing one's illustrative devices.

1. Place your figure as near as possible to the first point in the text where it is mentioned. This means that, if it is small enough or can be sufficiently reduced, it should be displayed on the page with the text. It is well to emphasize its integral relation to the text by so placing it as to allow some text to precede and some to follow it. If it is so large that such display would crowd out too much of the text, it should be on a page by itself following the page from which reference to it is first made.

2. If a figure is to be referred to from several consecutive pages, it should be put in on a folded insert following the last point in the text at which it is mentioned. This insert should be numbered uniformly with the other pages and reference made to it by page number at the first point in the text where it can be used. This makes it possible to unfold the insert and let it lie out before one as he reads till he reaches the last point of reference.

If a working model accompanies the report, as in the case of reports on new mechanical devices or on designs of equipment of various sorts, that fact should be made clear in the introduction to the report, and frequent reference to it should be made throughout the text. In this way, the reader should be stimulated to make use of the model at every point where it would help him to understand the verbal exposition. In some cases the importance of the model becomes so great that the relation of text and illustration is practically reversed; the text is written as an explanation or running comment on the model under consideration.

3. If there is such a large number of figures that they would overbalance the text if they were included in it, they should be segregated in the appendix. In such a case, reference should still be made to them at all points where the reader might profitably use them. It is also often well to keep sample figures, reduced to a scale fitting for display, in the text itself.

4. Figures should be numbered in arabic numerals placed above or below the figure. Although the integral relation of the figure to the text as a purely supplementary means of demonstration is the most important consideration to keep in mind, it is also true that, as reports are used, figures may sometimes have an independent value if they are clearly labeled. If every figure has a significant legend below it, a cursory reader may often get the whole drift of the exposition by merely looking at the figures with their explanatory legends. In a typed text, such legends must, of course, be kept very brief and very simple and must be so displayed as never to be confused with the text. They should be single-spaced if more than one line in length and should be separated from the text by at least three spaces.

The lettering of such legends on graphs and curves is an art in itself. It is so important a detail that the author has, with the permission of The Detroit Edison Company, quoted the detailed directions for such figures worked out for the reports of the Central Heating Plant of The Detroit Edison Company by A. S. Griswold, on the basis of the work of E. T. Heater of the University of Illinois.

Figures.

This classification includes illustrations of all kinds and all curve sheets, regardless of whether they occupy part of a page with the text or a separate page. They are to be numbered consecutively in arabic numerals placed below the illustration or curve. Provide a legend in single space beneath each figure that will indicate its character without making it necessary to refer to the text.

Expediency will require the use of several types of illustrations such as photographs, photostats, pen-and-ink drawings, etc. Directions for the use of these are given in the following paragraphs.

Photographs: It will be necessary to mount these either on the page with the text or on a separate page. When a separate page is used, the figure number, legend, and page number should be typed on a sheet of paper which can be duplicated by the black-and-white process with the text. The legend on the photograph is usually insufficient for the purpose and can be cropped off with other unnecessary parts. In mounting photographs use a generous amount of Nobuc or two or three small spots of glue. This prevents the wrinkling of the sheet. Paste or mucilage is unsatisfactory for mounting purposes since the pictures will eventually become loose and will then fall off.

Photostats: This type of reproduction can frequently be used where the reduction of large drawings, etc., is necessary. The positive copies should always be secured. If mounted on a sheet containing text or on a separate sheet, the same directions as for photographs are to be followed. Photostats large enough to insert as a sheet can be secured, but care must be used to see that the figure number and legend are properly arranged.

Pen-and-ink Illustrations: Care should be used to see that illustrations of this nature are legible and that they thoroughly fulfill their purpose. In making such drawings, first decide exactly what you wish to illustrate and then decide whether it should be placed on a page with the text, on a separate page, or on a folded insert. A pencil sketch can then be made and submitted with the text for the purpose of criticism and editing. Frequently much effort is needlessly wasted in making ink drawings before their purpose and their relation to the balance of the report are finally determined.

In making full-page drawings, be sure to retain sufficient margins and to use the standard line and letter sizes as outlined in following paragraphs. Most of the illustrations for reports can be made for full-size reproduction by the regular black-and-white printing process. In cases where this is not possible, follow the instructions regarding line and letter sizes for drawings which are to be reduced.

The inking of illustrations should not be done until the entire report has been approved by the editor. The neatest results will be obtained if the finished full-page drawings are made on tracing cloth. When the illustration is to be on a folded insert, leave sufficient blank cloth for the insert part of the sheet. This will eliminate the use of unnecessary mounting, etc. When the illustration is made on tracing cloth, the figure number, legend, and page number should be printed on the cloth, using standard letters.

Curve and Curve Sheets: It is frequently difficult to devise thoroughly acceptable curve sheets, and for this reason each sheet must be given special consideration. Small, simple curves may frequently be included in a page of text. In this case the exact size of the curve must be determined before the master copy is typed. The figure number and legend should be typed rather than printed.

When the curves are so large or complicated that it is impossible to include them in a page of text, the curves should be placed on a full page or on a folded insert. In these cases the legend, figure number, and page number should be printed in ink on the curve sheet.

In arranging curve sheets, considerable thought should be given to the matter of appearance and clearness. Do not include so many curves on one sheet that they appear crowded, and do not present curves which are not directly related to the subject of your report. Crowding can usually be prevented by the use of a larger sheet. Choose reasonable coordinates and print their value either outside or inside the cross-sectioned area. Do not draw the cross-section lines through notes on the curve sheet.

For purposes of criticism and editing, the curves may be drawn in pencil on ordinary cross-section paper or in any other suitable manner. For reproduction by the black-and-white process, they should be drawn on tracing cloth. The standard line and letter sizes, as given in the following directions, should be used. Cross-section lines should not be closer than ¼ inch. Sufficient margins for binding, legend, etc., must be preserved. Where the curve is to be on a folded insert, sufficient cloth for the insert should be a part of the curve sheet.

Lettering: It is preferred that all lettering for illustrations be made with the Wrico lettering guides. In some cases, however, freehand lettering may be used. The lettering should conform to the following standards:

1. When the illustration is to be reproduced full-size:

    a. For title or caption, use lettering guide VCN-140 with No. 6 pen.
    b. For coordinate values on curve sheets, use lettering guide VCN-120 with No. 7 pen.
    c. For notes on drawings or curve sheets, use lettering guide VCN-90 with No. 7 pen.

2. When the illustration is to be reduced in size by photographing or photostating, the lettering must be made correspondingly larger.

3. The letter sizes and line weights recommended are those developed by E. F. Heater of the University of Illinois.

Experience has demonstrated that these specifications will nearly always provide an acceptable appearance. The exception to this is the case of very complicated drawings when sufficient detail and contrast cannot always be secured with lines of a given weight.

TABLES

Tables are, of course, not means of supplementing the text; they are devices for substituting highly condensed massing of material for text. They economize space and verbal statement by presenting factual material in a form easy to read and easy to refer to. Their relation to the text is, therefore, quite as integral as that of the figures. All that was said regarding the placing of figures applies to the placing of tables. One should be warned, however, never to allow his tabulations to outbalance the text, unless, as is sometimes the case, he is presenting a report which is best reduced to "tables and labels." There are such reports where the text is purposely suppressed or totally eliminated in the interest of a purely graphical or purely tabular presentation. When there are more tables than can be well displayed in the text, they should be assembled in the appendix and only such sample tables used in the text as will be required.

Tables should be numbered either in Roman or in Arabic numerals placed above the table and, as with figures, should be given titles that make them understood at a glance. These titles and the column headings should be complete, accurate, and significant. In a typed text, it is best to rule the tables so as to set them off distinctly from the text and to precede and follow them with three spaces. Sample tables are shown on pages 160 and 161.

Example 1. *Table Displayed on Page with Text.*

The average mass velocities of the hot gases during the tests with the scaled tube were, for three of the four groups, somewhat lower than the average mass velocities during the clean-tube tests. The present writer is inclined to interpret the positions of the points as indicating that the effect of the 0.083-inch scale upon the over-all heat-transfer coefficient, and hence upon heat utilization, was rather less than the experimental error in the investigations.

TABLE 4.—SUMMARY OF ESTIMATES OF HEAT LOSS DUE TO BOILER SCALE
(Only values based upon experiment are included)

Thickness of scale, in.	Heat conductivity coefficient of scale, $\dfrac{\text{B.t.u.-ft.}}{\text{ft.}^2\text{-hr.-}°\text{F.}}$	Rate of heat transfer, $\dfrac{\text{B.t.u.}}{\text{ft.}^2\text{-hr.}}$	Decrease in over-all conductivity of scaled tube,* %	Estimated decrease in heat utilization, %	Observer	Year
0.06	....	......	....	14.7	Graham	1860
0.02	....	5,250	2.9	....	Schmidt	
0.03	....	5,250	4.1	....	and Snod-	
0.04	....	5,250	6.8	....	grass	
0.05	....	5,250	4.6			
0.06	....	5,250	6.2			
0.07	....	5,250	4.7			
0.08	....	5,250	8.6			
0.09	....	5,250	8.1			
0.11	....	5,250	15.8			
0.13		5,250	6.6			
0.07	0.67	3,900	....	1.7	Eberle and	1909–
0.19	0.67	3,900	....	6.0	Reutlinger	1910
0.10	1.75	3,015	....	1.67	Croft	1927
0.10	1.75	7,540	....	3.83		
0.20	1.75	3,015	....	2.99		
0.20	1.75	7,540	....	5.98		

* The values given in this column have been recalculated by the writer from the original data of Schmidt and Snodgrass with the use of logarithmic mean temperature drops, all values for different scales of a given thickness being averaged together.

This discussion of heat losses due to scale thus leads to the conclusion that these losses are relatively small, since theoretical calculations are well supported by the data of competent contemporary investigations in placing them at a figure of not greater than 2 per cent for scales of ordinary thickness and heat conductivity.

Example 2. Table Displayed on Page with No Text.

TABLE 8.

SOLUBILITY PRODUCTS OF SCALE CONSTITUENTS AT BOILER TEMPERATURES

Anhydrite

Temp.	Solubility		Ionic Strength	Tentative Ion Activity Coefficients		Solubility Product-K_A equivalents/million grams		Degree of Ionization, %
°C.	p.p.m.	mols./1000 gr.		Ca^{++}	SO$_4^-$	Activities	Concentrations	
100	650	0.00477	0.01908	0.535	0.477	23.2	25.6	53
110	535	0.00393	0.01572	0.555	0.503	17.3	16.7	52
120	435	0.00320	0.01280	0.577	0.532	12.6	10.7	51
130	350	0.00257	0.01028	0.598	0.558	8.82	6.88	51
140	280	0.00206	0.00824	0.620	0.580	6.10	4.25	50
150	222	0.00163	0.00652	0.637	0.605	4.10	2.66	50
160	176	0.00129	0.00516	0.658	0.627	2.75	1.73	51
170	140	0.00103	0.00412	0.678	0.645	1.86	1.15	52
180	112	0.000823	0.00329	0.708	0.666	1.28	0.760	53
190	92	0.000675	0.00270	0.722	0.684	0.899	0.551	55
200	76	0.000558	0.00223	0.736	0.700	0.641	0.390	56
210	64	0.000470	0.00188	0.752	0.720	0.479	0.297	58
220	55	0.000404	0.00162	0.767	0.737	0.369	0.235	60

Calcium Hydroxide

Temp.	Solubility		Ionic Strength	Tentative Ion Activity Coefficients		Solubility Product-K_H equivalents/million grams		Degree of Ionization, %
°C	p.p.m.	mols./1000 gr.		Ca^{++}	OH$^-$	Activities	Concentrations	
100	658	0.00890	0.0222	0.522	0.885	2310	3000	81
110	544	0.00735	0.0184	0.540	0.893	1370	1752	82
120	433	0.00585	0.0146	0.564	0.904	738	916	83
130	344	0.00465	0.0116	0.588	0.914	395	495	85
140	277	0.00374	0.00936	0.606	0.923	216	266	86
150	225	0.00304	0.00760	0.625	0.933	122	148	87
160	185	0.00250	0.00625	0.641	0.942	71.1	88.1	89
170	154	0.00208	0.00520	0.658	0.949	42.7	52.5	90
180	129	0.00174	0.00435	0.680	0.953	26.0	31.7	91
190	111	0.00150	0.00375	0.699	0.957	17.3	21.0	92
200	99	0.00134	0.00335	0.719	0.961	12.8	16.0	94

Brucite

Temp.	Solubility		Ionic Strength	Tentative Ion Activity Coefficients		Solubility Product-K_B equivalents/million grams		Degree of Ionization, %
°C.	p.p.m.	mols./1000 gr.		Mg^{++}	OH$^-$	Activities	Concentrations	
100	4.5	0.0000772	0.000141	0.969	0.997	0.00354	0.00325	96
110	4.0	0.0000686	0.000125	0.972	0.997	0.00250	0.00229	96
120	3.5	0.0000600	0.000109	0.976	0.998	0.00168	0.00153	96
130	3.0	0.0000515	0.0000935	0.979	0.998	0.00107	0.000997	97
140	2.6	0.0000446	0.0000810	0.982	0.998	0.000694	0.000648	97
150	2.2	0.0000378	0.0000688	0.985	0.999	0.000425	0.000394	97
160	1.8	0.0000309	0.0000563	0.988	0.999	0.000233	0.000223	98
170	1.5	0.0000257	0.0000467	0.990	0.999	0.000134	0.000128	98
180	1.2	0.0000206	0.0000375	0.992	0.999	0.0000693	0.0000658	98
190	1.0	0.0000172	0.0000313	0.993	0.999	0.0000403	0.0000395	99
200	0.8	0.0000137	0.0000250	0.994	0.999	0.0000204	0.0000200	99

ANNOTATED REPORTS

The reports and memoranda that follow are not presented because of their technical excellence; the author assumes no responsibility for the soundness of their statements. The Detroit Edison Company has permitted the use of some of the reports and memoranda written as assignments in the author's lecture course; this permission was made with a similar understanding that the reports were presented simply as a basis for comment on report technique. It has been thought that a study of these reports with the author's comments would make clearer the details of form presented in this part of the book.

In order to reproduce the appearance of the typed report as exactly as possible, the paging of the book has been placed, throughout this section, at the bottom of the page and that of the illustration reports in the upper right-hand corner as is specified on page 137 for typed reports.

Example 1.

In a professional long-form report the title page must often contain information that would not be required in a student report. Here the name of the company and of the division are of sufficient importance to require a prominent place on the page.

This information is given for use in filing the report for reference uses.

THE DETROIT EDISON COMPANY

ENGINEERING DIVISION

TWO SUGGESTIONS FOR IMPROVING THE DESIGN

of

WELDED PIPING SYSTEMS

or

HIGH—TEMPERATURE SERVICE

Arthur McCutchan

Report ME77

January 9, 193_

This paragraph gives in a highly simplified form the substance of the entire report. It is like the statement of a thesis to be developed in detail in the document to follow. It would be invaluable to one who wished to know what this report does with the subject proposed, but who has no time to read the report to find out. Its display on a page by itself gives it the prominence it deserves.

Reference should be made to pages 115 to 117, and 145, 149.

SYNOPSIS

The method proposed for the design of welded piping
systems for high-temperature service provides for dividing the piping system into units so that connections between pipe and valves may be welded in the shop. It also
includes a simple loose-sleeve guard for field-welded
joints. These two suggestions are based on studies of
flanged joints and welded piping made in connection with
the rebuilding of Commons Creek Powerhouse.

The spacing and use of type have much to do with the appearance of a table of contents. This table of contents seems well placed on the page; it makes clear the relation of groups of minor topics to their major headings. It also stands the ultimate test for such a table: the plan, set up schematically here, corresponds perfectly with that used in the report and represented by the topic headings of the text.

Reference should be made to pages 118, 145, 150, and 151.

By using the title sheet for such information as is needed only for purposes of filing and identifying the report, this first page is cleared of confusing detail. The reader's attention is concentrated at once on the title display. The spacing and spread of the title give it the prominence it deserves.

See page 152.

The purpose of the report and the pattern are both suggested in this first sentence. $X = a + b$.

The two suggestions a and b are stated in their simplest form.

This paragraph elaborates the first suggestion and makes clear its relation to a similar plan suggested by the Chief Engineer.

TWO SUGGESTIONS FOR IMPROVING THE DESIGN

of

WELDED—PIPING SYSTEMS FOR HIGH—TEMPERATURE SERVICE

The purpose of this report is to present two suggestions for improving the design of welded piping for high-
temperature service. It is suggested that a new method of
dividing piping into welding units would improve the
design of welded piping by securing more satisfactory
connections between pipe and valves. It is further suggested that a ''loose-sleeve'' guard for field-welded
joints could be used to advantage. These suggestions are
the natural outgrowth of studies of flanged joints and
welded piping made in connection with the rebuilding of
Connors Creek Powerhouse.

In examining the main—steam piping system proposed for
Connors Creek as well as those systems used in former
plants, it soon becomes apparent that the majority of the
joints are between valves and pipe and between fittings
and pipe, rather than in the line itself. Consequently
before it is possible to secure a satisfactory welded
main—steam system, it appears essential to develop a
practicable means of welding pipe to valves and fittings.
In a conference on Connors Creek piping, Feb. 23, 1932,
Mr. Parker suggested that short lengths of pipe might be
welded to the valves in the shop under Class I welding
requirements of the ASME Boiler Code. This procedure
would make possible a completely welded system without
involving unusual welding problems in the field. A plan
which is somewhat similar to that proposed and is in

171

This paragraph elaborates the second suggestion. It should be noted that in both cases the suggestions are not given in sufficient detail to overtax the reader or overload the introduction.

The pattern of the report, suggested in the first sentence $X = a + b$, reinforced by the full statement of a and b, is now set up in a form explicitly indicating the plan to be followed in the report. Such a statement is usually needed just before one takes off in his flight over the area thus mapped.

Refer to Chapter V, pages 35 to 41.

fact, a simple extension of that plan, is developed in this report. In place of welding short lengths of pipe to the valves, as suggested by Mr. Parker, it is proposed to weld pipe fillers of approximately half the length between adjacent valves to the valves in the shop. The reduction in number of field—welded joints required to erect the resulting welded assemblages constitutes the improvement which may be obtained by the substitution of fillers for short lengths of pipe. The elimination of bolted connections at valves and fittings is an advantage which these plans have in common over present welded design.

The second suggestion is concerned with protecting the field joints used in assembling these welded units. A number of methods of reinforcing and guarding field—welded joints for high—pressure work have been used, such as straps, sleeves, and so—called ''backing—up'' flanges. All such methods are expensive and some of doubtful utility, as usually applied. The loose—sleeve guard described in this report is intended to be used as a ''limit stop'' rather than as a reinforcement. In this respect the proposed guard is designed to serve the same purpose in the case of field—welded pipe joints as cotter pins serve in mechanical assemblages.

In presenting the development of the welding units, the division of the piping system into suitable units for shop welding of pipe to valves and fittings and the method of procedure suggested for making and installing such welded units will be first described, after which the design and application of the loose—sleeve guard will be explained.

Writing the Technical Report

This page illustrates the design of a section in which two orders of heading are used. The main heading, which is displayed at the center of the page in all capital letters underscored, is followed by such introductory text as was needed to set up the topic for consideration.

Reference should be made to pages 86 to 94.

The secondary headings are displayed at the margin in a line above the text in capital and lower-case letters, the main words having initial capitals. It is thus made easy for the cursory reader to find the list of methods at a glance. It should be especially noted that these headings have not in any way lessened the functions of the text.

3

DEVELOPMENT OF WELDING UNIT

The development of a satisfactory welding unit for the main-steam piping of a 600-pound 825-850 F power plant requires a departure from the practices and principles followed in flanged piping design. The usual elements of a piping system, pipe fillers, bends, fittings, and valves, cannot be readily and economically assembled on the job by welding while the retention of bolted joints at valves and fittings represents an undesirable compromise. A satisfactory welding unit should, therefore, reduce the number of field-welded joints to a minimum and eliminate bolted connections at fittings and valves. A unit consisting of a valve or fitting with a part of a pipe filler or bend shop-welded to each end would seem to meet these requirements for a satisfactory welding unit.

Division of Piping into Suitable Units.

In order to demonstrate the practicability of dividing a piping system into suitable welding units, a study has been made of one of the main-steam header systems proposed for Connors Creek Powerhouse. The sketch on Figure 1 shows the header as at present laid out with its combination of welded and bolted joints. Possible locations of field-welded joints to secure suitable welding units are indicated on the sketch. Actual division of the system would have to take into account erection interferences, transportation limitations, and a number of other features requiring careful study. The division indicated is intended to serve only as an illustration of the ease with which a piping system may be divided into units for shop fabrication.

The writer of this report has understood correctly the relation of the topic headings to the topic sentences. The heading is, for all practical purposes, the topic sentence reduced to its lowest possible terms in order that it may be used as a topic label. It provides a ready point of reference to the eye of the reader as he skims the page either to get his perspective or to find a part of special interest. The topic sentence performs the same service for the person actually reading the text; it is therefore not objectionable to find a similarity in the wording of the two.

It is interesting to study this technique throughout the report.

The footnote is correctly single-spaced.

4

Shop Welding of Pipe to Valves and Fittings.

Shop welding a part of a pipe filler to each end of a
valve involves welding a rolled-steel part to a relatively heavy steel casting. While cast-steel fittings in
some instances can be replaced to advantage by welded-
steel assemblages fabricated from steel plate and forgings, it is probable that cast-steel valve bodies, owing
to their rather intricate shape, will continue to be used
in place of forgings in the larger sizes. Welding rolled-
steel pipe and cast-steel valve bodies together in the
shop does not involve difficulties which have not been
successfully overcome in other lines of construction. As
confirmation of this statement, reference may be made to
a discussion of welding cast-steel and rolled-steel parts
together by Mr. T. S. Quinn of the Lebanon Steel
Foundry.*

---

*Paper on 'Fusion Welding as Related to Steel Cast-
ings,' by T. S. Quinn, presented at the ASTM annual meeting at Atlantic City, N. J., June 20-24, 1932.

This is a third-order heading. Such headings are to be used sparingly. They are displayed 3 to 6 spaces in from the margin in capital and lower-case letters, the main words having initial capitals, followed by a colon and an extra space. The text follows in the same line.

Note the single spacing of this quotation, as well as the way it is inset from the margin.

5

Preparation of Valves for Welding: Valves intended to be welded solid into the line should be designed so that valve seats may be replaced through the bonnet opening. Present practice is to insert a tool from either end of the valve, but this change need not occasion difficulty. The saving in weight of metal due to elimination of flanges should more than offset the cost of pattern changes or the cost of dry-sand cores to secure a valve body casting without flanges. Whether valve seats should be finally screwed in position before welding the valve ends to the pipe will depend upon the amount of distortion which results from the welding operation. In any case, the bonnet and moving parts of the valve should be assembled after the welding and annealing operations are completed.

Welding: Welding is to be done in accordance with the requirements for Class I pressure vessels of the ASME Boiler Construction Code. These requirements involve:

1. ''Test Plates for Circumferential Joints: . . . where a vessel has only circumferential joints, two sets of test plates of the same material as the shell shall be welded in the same way as the joints in question.'' This requirement would necessitate additional test bars being cast attached to the valve casting over the number called for by ASTM Spec. A95-29 for Carbon-steel Castings for Valves, Flanges, and Fittings for High-temperature Service. Two test plates consisting of these cast bars and sections from the pipe welded under the same conditions as the valve and pipe joint would apparently meet the demands of the code. Tensile tests of both joint and weld metal, bend tests, and specific-gravity determinations shall be made from coupons cut from one of these test plates.

6

2. ''Nondestructive Tests of Vessel: . . . At least 25 per cent of the length of each welded circumferential joint equally divided between not less than four uniformly spaced intervals around the circumference shall be radiographed. Where any one radiograph fails to comply with these requirements, all parts of that circumferential seam represented by that radiograph shall be radiographed.'' Sample radiographs are included in the code with which comparisons may be made in determining acceptability.

In order to provide a reliable guard for field-welded joints, rings having the general proportions indicated in Figure 2 are to be welded a few inches from the beveled outer ends of the pipe fillers or bends which are welded to the valve. These rings, in conjunction with a loose sleeve, which will be described in a later section of this report, are designed to prevent actual separation of the joint in case of a faulty field weld.

Testing: In addition to the special tests for Class I pressure vessels, a hydrostatic test of the complete welded unit which consists of a valve, two lengths of pipe, and guard rings welded together is required to assure that all parts and welds are suitable for the intended service.

Annealing of Complete Unit: In order to relieve stresses induced by welding, the entire assemblage shall be annealed as specified for Class I vessels. After the annealing operation, the valve is ready to be assembled and tested for tightness and ease of operation.

This page shows the design for a section employing both second- and third-order headings.

7

Installation of Welded Unit.

The completed assemblage of valve and pipe fillers or bends with guard rings attached at each end is now ready for connection to a like assemblage in the field.

Welding: Adequate clearances are provided to facilitate lining up the pipe ends of the different welding units by means of the loose-sleeve guards. Whether an inner ring should be used to prevent weld metal falling inside the pipe is a debatable point. No ring is shown in Figure 2, as it would tend to complicate the sketch, but it would seem desirable to provide some form of inner sleeve or ring for this purpose.

Electric-arc welds using heavily coated electrodes would seem most suitable for a field-welded joint which is not intended to be annealed. In the electric-arc process a number of beads are used to build up the joint. Each bead tends to anneal the previous bead, while peening of each succeeding layer further tends to refine the structure and reduce residual stresses. Considerable evidence of both laboratory and field experience indicates that an electric-arc weld made under these conditions does not require a final annealing operation.

Testing: Upon completion of the butt welds connecting the various units of the pipe line and before placing the guard sleeves in position, a hydrostatic test should be made. While it will be desirable to check the practicability of certain of the nondestructive tests which have been developed for field-welding control, chief reliance will have to be placed on destructive tests of specimens

welded at the same time and under the same conditions as
the field-welded joints.

PROTECTION OF FIELD-WELDED JOINTS

Since plain butt-welded joints, as made in the field,
are not as yet generally considered sufficiently reliable
for high-pressure work, different methods of reinforcement have been proposed and used. Heavy strap reinforce-
ments, as used on the field-welded joints in the main-
steam lines at the station,* while doubtless safe enough,
are expensive and require annealing of the completed
joint to minimize welding stresses set up while welding
the straps in position. Sleeves welded to the pipe on
either side of the butt weld have been used, but they
also set up undesirable stresses which should be relieved
by annealing. Backing-up flanges, as used in the turbine,
lead to the 10,000-kilowatt high-temperature unit at
Delray Powerhouse 3, are expensive, and defeat some of
the advantages of welded construction, such as a saving
in insulation cost, and an improvement in appearance.

The consensus of opinion seems to be that a reasonably
sound weld does not need reinforcement. Where adequate
means of testing exist, a plain butt weld is recognized
as a satisfactory connection. But, in the case of field-
welded joints in high-pressure lines, some form of guard
or ''limit stop'' appears desirable to prevent actual separation of the joint and limit the steam leak which might
develop as a result of a faulty weld. The simplest guard

*See Report ME 66 for description of piping at station.

which will effectively give this security would seem to be a logical basis for design.

Design of Loose—sleeve Guard.

The loose—sleeve guard illustrated in Figure 2 consists of two rings shop—welded to the pipe ends over which the two halves of the sleeve are placed. The two parts of the sleeve are then welded together along the beveled edges parallel and perpendicular to the pipe axis, respectively. Since these sleeves are not to be welded to the pipe, no stresses are induced in the main butt weld by the addition of the guard.

Fabrication of Guard.

While other methods of making the loose—sleeve guards may be used, the following procedure would secure sleeves suitable for the purpose. Short lengths of heavy walled pipe of the length required for the sleeves could be placed in a lathe and the inner section removed as indicated on Figure 2. The sleeve after being hollowed out could be cut in halves with a torch or a saw and beveled for welding.

Application of Guard to Joint.

Sufficient clearances should be provided to facilitate assembly; but it is expected that in welding the sleeves together; they will be tightly clamped around the pipe and that shrinkage after welding will provide something of a shrink fit between the pipe and sleeve. In the event of the main butt weld parting, the rings will tend to be forced against the ends of the sleeve by the steam pressure and the escape of steam further restricted. If a

This summary reduces the detailed discussion contained in the body of the report to a greatly simplified form.

Reference should be made to pages 104 to 110.

This final sentence, while it ventures a critical comment on the value of the suggestions, is commendably modest and restrained. It is interesting to observe how well it agrees and balances with the introduction.

steam leak should develop the loose sleeves could be removed with a torch without danger of damaging the pipe
and probably could be replaced after repairing the main
weld.

SUMMARY

Two suggestions have been presented in this report
which are designed to secure a more satisfactory welded
piping system for high-pressure high-temperature service.
The practicability of the new method of dividing piping
into welding units, which has been described, has been
demonstrated by application to the main-steam header system proposed for the Connors Creek Powerhouse. A loose-
sleeve guard also has been described which is a simple
means of preventing separation of the joint in case of a
faulty field weld. These suggestions, if found workable,
would seem to make possible a completely welded main-
steam system which would be more satisfactory than either
present flanged or welded construction.

Example 2. Student Long-form Report.

This form of title sheet is recommended for student reports on which no information is required except the title, name, and date.

The title is set up in capital letters for the major lines and lower-case letters for the connecting lines. It looks best if begun, at least, in the upper third of the page. The liberal spacing gives it prominence on the page it would not otherwise have.

The name should come about on the center of the page.

The date is displayed about 1½ inches from the bottom of the page.

THE PREQUALIFICATION OF BIDDERS

on

PUBLIC WORKS

Ralph S. Lewis

January 15, 19__

This synopsis gives the substance of the report in the form of a compact paragraph. One who reads this gets in advance the thesis of the writer and a complete idea of what he intends to present in the report.

Refer to Chapter XV, Part I, pages 115 to 121.

SYNOPSIS

Prequalification of bidders on public works, which requires each bidder to submit in advance on standard forms
a sworn statement as to his experience, equipment, finances, and contracts on hand, results in benefits to the
contractor and to the contracting party. It protects the
unqualified contractor against undertaking work he cannot
do satisfactorily; it thus saves him embarrassment and
the useless expense of bidding on jobs he should not
attempt; it relieves the awarding official of the elimination of unqualified bidders and enables him to proceed
at once to the determination of the lowest bidder. So
obvious are these benefits of prequalification that it is
increasingly recognized as decreasing defaults, increasing the percentage of work completed on time, and encouraging competition of the right kind.

TABLE OF CONTENTS

The introduction is most concerned with a careful definition of the terms used in the statement of the subject as given by the title. The first sentence defines prequalification in its broadest sense, the second in its application to construction.

The second paragraph goes specifically into its relation to public contracts.

The third paragraph attempts to establish that prequalification is not confused with qualification simultaneously with the opening of the bid.

THE PREQUALIFICATION OF BIDDERS

on

PUBLIC WORKS

Prequalification in its broadest sense is the determination of an applicant's qualifications for a given responsibility before entrusting him with that responsibility. Applied to construction, it is the determination of a contractor's competency and responsibility to complete satisfactorily a given construction project before he submits a bid.

There is nothing new or mysterious in prequalification except in connection with public contracts. Private corporations, architects, railroads, public utilities, and others have always required it. They limit bidders for their work to contractors whom they believe to be financially responsible, to have experience for the particular work, and to have a suitable plant or means with which to secure such a plant. It is only within recent years, however, that prequalification has come into use on public works.

For a long time it has been admitted that in awarding public contracts the successful contractor shall be the responsible contractor with the lowest bid. But determination of responsibility after bidding has often been troublesome. The solution of a difficult problem is by

195

This last paragraph indicates the purpose of the report in contributing to the struggle to secure prequalification and states in a simple form the plan of treatment—the analytic pattern of the report. If such a statement of plan is used, it should come at the end of the introductory text and should be so simply stated as to make it possible for the reader to retain the scheme of points as a guide to his reading of the report.

Refer to Chapter VII, Part I, pages 50 to 63.

This paragraph, following a main heading, is a typical example of introductory text to a section large and complex enough to warrant such treatment. The first sentence is a good, crisp topic sentence.

prequalification reduced to the solution of two much simpler problems. With actual prequalification, a group of qualified bidders is established in advance of the opening of bids and as a separate act. Determination of the qualifications of the bidder simultaneously with the opening of his bid, or subsequent to the opening of his bid, is not real prequalification.

So far it has been the contractors' associations that have had to wage the battle for predetermined competency of bidders and to carry conviction of its importance into engineers' associations. The task has been a tedious one, but it very definitely needs to be continued. It is the purpose of this report to outline the procedure, note the legal aspects, and explain the advantages and objections relative to prequalification.

PROCEDURE

The procedure itself is simple. The advertisement states that prequalification of bidders will be required, and those who cannot qualify are denied the bidder's sheet on which bids must be made. In a great many cases, however, the right to bid on public construction is re- garded as a right parallel to the right to vote, and hence it is necessary to have a thorough and scientific method of investigating prospective bidders.

A second-order heading.

The initial emphasis in this topic sentence is on the subject of the paragraph.

Here the first clause is transitional; the second gives the topic of the paragraph.

This is an example of a paragraph in which the topic is not, as in the two previous paragraphs, thrust forward to the point of first attention. The topic sentence really is the last in this paragraph.

3

Determination of Qualifications.

The method employed in qualifying a contractor consists
in requiring each bidder in advance to submit on standard
forms a sworn statement as to his experience, equipment,
finances, and contracts on hand. The awarding agency
checks the truth of the information submitted. Discretion
is then exercised as to the ability of the bidder to perform the contract in question. The bidder is notified
whether or not bids will be accepted from him on a particular job or what sort and volume of work he will be
permitted to bid on in the future.

Obviously there is no mathematical formula for comput-
ing a bidder's skill, but a reasonably accurate idea can
be obtained from his record of previous construction
projects successfully completed. The bidder's reputation
for honesty is especially important in reference to the
quality of work performed. No amount of supervision and
inspection can force a first-class job from a contractor
who is unwilling to produce such a job or who is incompetent to do such work. A prospective bidder who is known
to be a habitual tardy finisher or a poor manager is
discouraged.

The Bureau of Contract Information, Inc.

In any attempt to verify the statements of bidders as
to their qualifications, there is one particular difficulty. For, in spite of the fact that where the standard
questionnaires are used statements are submitted under
oath, there are those who will not only falsify but fail
to give complete information and thus try to hide or
cover up some part of their record. When the awarding

This is really the topic idea.

This paragraph is both transitional and introductory; all of it except the last sentence is largely transitional in its effect.

authority attempts to check up, he often finds there is no reliable source of information that will enable him to make a check. To remedy this condition there was inaugurated in August, 1929, the Bureau of Contract Information, Incorporated, with offices in Washington, D. C.

The Bureau is now well started on the huge task of building up its files on the thousands of contracting concerns throughout the country. It is a non-profit, fact-finding, and reporting institution within the construction industry for the service of that industry, and its service is without charge to those responsible for the award of construction contracts. It asks payment for its service only from those who sell to and give credit to contractors for profit. Already the bureau has made its influence felt in promoting better bonding practices, in curbing overextension by contractors, and in upholding the responsible elements in construction.

LEGAL ASPECTS

Prequalification procedure, as has been shown, is based on an interpretation of the administrative authority of the contracting party, and has in most cases been productive of good results. Authority to withhold the bidder's sheet from a contractor to whom award would not be recommended has never been questioned, and likewise authority to require a qualification statement in the form of a standard questionnaire has also never been questioned; these are the two essential elements of prequalification of bidders. Nevertheless, the legal status

The emphasis on the words "until recently" prepares one for the initial emphasis on the date in the next sentence.

The transition from one paragraph to another is well made.

of prequalification has until recently been very
uncertain.

The Philadelphia Case.

Previous to 1929, no case had ever come up in court
involving the principle of prequalification, and its
advocates looked forward with some anxiety when a contest
was started in the lower courts of Philadelphia County,
Penna., against a Philadelphia city ordinance providing
for prequalification. Shortly after the ordinance was
effective, three bidders were refused qualification by
the awarding officer, the director of city transit, in
connection with the project on which he was receiving
bids. All three appealed. A board was appointed and a
hearing held as provided in the ordinance. The decision
of the director was sustained.

After being appealed through several other courts, the
case was finally taken to the Supreme Court of Pennsylvania, the contentions being that no plan could be
devised under the method specified in the ordinance regarding prequalification which would not violate the
provisions of a former ordinance and that in any event
the method specified in the ordinance under which the
contract was awarded violated that act. The Supreme Court
disagreed with the first contention but upheld the second
contention on the possibility of committing fraud upon
the public where the qualifications were passed upon by
one individual.

This case is extremely important from the fact that the
Supreme Court sanctioned the right to enact an ordinance
providing for prequalification in spite of the fact that

The transition is effected by the words "A similar case," indicating the relation of this case to the one before.

Note the single spacing of this quotation. Such single spacing is recommended for quotations of more than two lines.

This sentence is both a topic and a transitional sentence. The words "these and similar cases" refer to the preceding text; the rest of the sentence sets up the topic for the paragraph.

it declared the particular ordinance in question invalid
due to the faulty method of applying the principle.

The Oregon Case.

A similar case has to do with the failure of proposed
prequalification legislation in Oregon in 1929. Perhaps
the most unworkable feature of this proposed Oregon bill
was the following:

> The letting of any contract for a public improve-
> ment concerning which a prospective bidder has
> taken an appear shall be postponed, and no bids
> shall be opened or made public until such appear
> has been determined.

Under such language a dissatisfied bidder could, under
unfavorable conditions, hold up the award of important
contracts about three weeks. While this Oregon act was
pending, however, overzealous partisans sponsored the
submission of a bogus bid to the Highway Commission, and
this hoax undoubtedly helped defeat the bill. Probably
also the mandatory character of prequalification of
bidders for all county and municipal contracts caused
opposition.

Lessons Derived from Adverse Experience.

A review of these and similar cases shows that they do
not contain much argument against the prequalification
principle. The Supreme Court of Pennsylvania explicitly
sanctioned the principle and questioned only the method.
The failure in Oregon was evidently due to clumsy provisions.

Where new legislation is required, the evidence indicates that it is preferable: (1) to have sufficient time
for contractors to present their qualifications in ad-

Note the transitional and topic functions of this sentence.

This paragraph, which is an introductory paragraph to this section, is concerned with limiting the discussion of advantages to those accruing to the contractor and the contracting party.

vance; (2) to have those qualifications passed upon by a
board or committee, rather than by an individual; (3) to
avoid any variation whatever in the treatment of prospective bidders; and (4) to avoid any method of appeal that
would delay the letting. In other words, it would seem
unwise to try to write into any proposed prequalification
law or any set of rules and regulations governing its
application anything that is calculated to take the place
of wise discretion.

ADVANTAGES

In spite of the several cases of adverse legislation
just discussed, prequalification has in most cases worked
out to the satisfaction of the contractor and general
public alike. The owner of a highway, for instance, is
interested only in the prompt completion of a sound product at a fair price, and the advantages accruing to him
may be summarized by saying that prequalification, if
properly administered, will result in the public's securing a uniformly high quality of service without increased
cost. It is necessary then to discuss only those advantages accruing to the contractor and to the contracting
party.

Protection of the Unqualified Contractor.

There is almost unanimous conviction that what benefits
the contractor most in the matter of prequalification is
the better understanding and the increased good will resulting from the practice. Safeguarding of the contractor
by confronting him with the questionnaire is of the

Note how the words "Another advantage" aligns this paragraph as one in a series.

Note the effect of the word "Finally." It does several things: it reminds the reader that he is engaged in reading a series of points; it also announces that this is the last in that series and that he is approaching the end.

utmost value. Too many times he has only a vague notion
of the job in hand—of its remoteness, the short season,
the difficult transportation, and other unfavorable conditions. The number of prospective bidders who have
quietly withdrawn from bidding after a thorough discussion of the situation is evidence not of a stifling of
competition, but rather of a protection of the unqualified contractor against his own poor judgment.

Saving of Useless Expense.

Another advantage of prequalification is that the incompetent or irresponsible contractor is advised of that
fact before he has gone to any expense in estimating a
project. With the other method of qualifying bidders,
that is, postqualification, the contractor may proceed
to incur the expense of figuring the job not knowing that
when he does submit his bid it will be rejected on the
ground that he is not qualified to handle that particular
project. He is therefore saved money by prequalification
and is also relieved from the embarrassment of having his
bid thrown out after bids are opened.

Criticism of Awarding Official.

Finally, since the bidders have all been investigated
and their qualifications reviewed with reference to the
project on which they are bidding, all bids received are
from contractors who have been judged competent and responsible to handle the particular job. All that remains
is to determine the lowest bidder. The temptation of the
awarding official to follow the line of least resistance
and award to the low bidder, whether he is competent or

This is a good example of a paragraph commenting on a section and marking an important point of arrival in the discussion.

Here, because of the decisive marking of the end of the discussion of advantages, no transition is needed. The word "objections" is in obvious and emphatic contrast to the idea of "advantages" with which the previous section had to do.

The words "One objection" set up the beginning of a series of objections. One previsions an alignment of such points of discussion.

not, is removed because competency was determined before
the bids were submitted. Likewise, the awarding authority
is relieved of the criticism entailed under postqualification when he rejects the low bid of an irresponsible or
incompetent contractor.

Prequalification, then, is a step forward. It is a
measure, as the court said in the Philadelphia Ordinance
Case, ''whose design and effect will be to substitute the
scientific for a haphazard method of determining the lowest responsible bidder.'' It is not claimed here that prequalification is a panacea for all the ills which beset
the construction industry, but it does for the first time
eliminate the troublesome irresponsible low bidder.

OBJECTIONS

It would seem that any objections to the practice of
prequalification would be directed along lines other than
those having to do with the elimination of the irresponsible low bidder, but such is not the case.

Complexity of the Questionnaire.

One objection to the prequalification of bidders is
that the questionnaires are too complicated. For large
concerns the objection would have no weight; they must
keep complete records. But it is said that a surprising
number of the smaller contractors have incomplete and
perfunctory records. To such, an accurate response to a
definite set of questions would doubtless loom large and
discouraging. However, it would seem that a man with
sufficient responsibility to enter any commercial field

This objection is met and shown not to be a serious one.

Here is the second in the series. It is shown to be based on a misconception.

Evidently this objection is not valid.

This is the last in the series of objections.

should keep books—for his clients' safety, if not for his own. If questionnaires did no more than promote the general use of proper accounting methods by contractors, they might be worth while.

Expenditure of Time and Labor.

Another objection would involve undue expenditure of time and labor. This idea may be due to a misconception. It is not necessary for a full set of questionnaires to accompany each bid. Ordinarily one experience questionnaire a year, submitted when the lists of qualified bidders are being compiled, should be sufficient. Financial questionnaires should be needed only twice, or at most four times, a year, from those on the eligible lists, with a current statement from the contractor to whom an award is about to be made. And an equipment schedule for the job in question should be filed with each bid. At the most, then, there should be needed one experience statement and four financial statements a year, an equipment statement with each bid, plus a current financial statement from the contractor to whom an award is about to be made.

Reduction of Competition.

The last objection to prequalification is that it restricts competition. It is important to remember, though, that there is undesirable as well as desirable competition. Engineers and contractors alike agree that, whatever the bid price, it is less expensive to have work done on time in a workmanlike manner than to have it drag or be done carelessly. Experience indicates that the

This is a final summary for the section on objections. The conclusion is that, in view of the major purpose of prequalification, the objections are outweighed by the benefits of this practice.

This first paragraph in the conclusion summarizes the points developed in the body of the report. The conclusion stated is based on that summary.

This quotation greatly strengthens the conclusion based on the writer's arguments.

removal of the competition of the irresponsible encourages bids from contractors of the better class who have previously refused to compete. If inferior men had been bidding previously, prequalification should at the outset reduce the number of bidders, but the reduction would probably be only temporary.

Glancing over these objections, it is difficult to escape the feeling that the few arguments against prequalification of bidders ignore the disaster that irresponsible bidding may bring the individual. Hence it must be evident that the objections are not especially discouraging, because the elimination of the irresponsible bidder is the ultimate aim of prequalification.

CONCLUSION

It has been shown in this report that the procedure necessary for prequalifying bidders is a simple one, that the principle itself is open to no legal objection, and that the advantages of the practice are sufficient to far outweigh the several objections. The result is that those organizations which have adopted the policy of prequalification are strongly in favor of it.

In a signed communication on Feb. 15, 1929, Thomas H. MacDonald, Chief, U.S. Bureau of Public Roads, writes:

> The experience of this Bureau in the prequalification of bidders for forest and park road contracts under our supervision has been eminently satisfactory.

In March, 1930, the American Association of State Highway Officials submitted a ''yes'' and ''no'' ballot on the principle of prequalification to the various state-high-

The results of the questionnaire still further strengthen his case.

The writer precludes the criticism that, in spite of his arguments, only two states have statutes requiring prequalification. In spite of this fact, it is gaining in popular usage.

This final summary leaves little to be desired. The reader knows he has reached the end, and he knows what the conclusion of the whole matter is. Note how well this whole conclusion balances and agrees with the introduction to the report.

way departments. This referendum resulted in an overwhelming number of votes in favor of the principle. Only
two states voted ''no.''

As a matter of fact, there are only two states using
prequalification as provided in specific statutes;
namely, California and South Carolina. Legislative
action, however, represents only a fraction of the advance. If the adoption of prequalification did not extend
well beyond its specific requirement by statute, the
situation would indeed be discouraging. Most of the
state-highway departments prequalifying bidders base
their authority not on the enactment of a specific statue
on this subject, but on the broad powers granted them
under the law to select ''the lowest responsible bidder.''
The following states at present operate on this basis:
Arizona, Colorado, Georgia, Iowa, Kansas, Minnesota,
Missouri, North Dakota, South Dakota, Montana, Tennessee,
and Wisconsin. In all 14 states there are now prequalifying bidders on state-highway projects.

In conclusion, then, it may be stated that prequalification is ceasing to be a matter of academic debate and
is becoming a prevalent method of letting contracts. Its
use has been endorsed by public officials, engineers,
architects, contractors, manufacturers and producers of
equipment and materials, surety companies, and prominent
national associations representing the construction industry. Their unanimous opinion is that prequalification
has decreased defaults and increased the percentage of
work completed on time and has encouraged competition of
the right kind.

Example 3. Short-form Report.

Mr. W. A. Carter
Technical Engineer of Power Plants
622 Service Building

Subject: Comparison of Operation
of the Four Power Plants

Dear Sir:

In accordance with your request, I have compared the operation of the four powerhouses during April, 1932, with that during April, 1933, to determine why the coal rates were higher for the latter period. As there are several contributing factors, I shall discuss those for each powerhouse separately.

Delray.

There are two reasons for a higher coal rate at Delray, namely: a less efficient turbine combination during the second period, and lower output in that period.

Turbine Combinations: Unit 21 was running about three-fourths of the latter period, while it was idle in April, 1932. Although the coal rate on the portion of load carried by this unit was substantially that on the other units, the oil used in additional superheating added about 2 per cent to the over-all rate of the powerhouse.

Output: The output of this powerhouse was reduced 20 per cent during the latter period, partly because of allocating a lesser portion of load to Delray.

Connors Creek.

The coal rate increased at Connors Creek because of a coal supply with lower heating value and because of reduced output.

Heating Value of Coal: The heating value of the coal was 210 B.t.u. per pound less in April, 1933, which accounts for most of the increase in coal rate.

Output: The output was 30 per cent lower in April, 1933, principally because of the allocation of less load to Connors Creek.

Marysville.
The reduction of 15F in steam temperature at the turbine throttles was the principal factor contributing to a higher coal rate at Marysville. The output, boiler-room efficiency, and heating value of the coal were unchanged. Although the steam temperature reduction does not account for all the coal rate increase, it was chiefly responsible.

Trenton Channel.
The Trenton Channel coal rate increased because of lower-heating-value coal and because of lower boiler-room efficiency.

Heating Value of Coal: The coal burned during April, 1933, had 500 B.t.u. per pound less heating value, accounting for most of the increased coal rate.

Boiler Room Efficiency: The efficiency was two points lower, but this was partially offset by better steam temperature and turbine exhaust pressure.

Summary.
To summarize briefly, the coal rate was higher in April, 1933, than in April, 1932: at Delray, because of operating No. 21 unit and because of lower output; at Connors Creek, because of lower-heating-value coal and of lower output; at Marysville, because of lower steam temperature; and at Trenton Channel, because of lower-heating-value coal and of lower boiler efficiency.

Very truly yours,

Signature
Name typed.

AWT:HS

This short-form report is of the letter type. Although highly skeletonized, it is a perfect example of all the fundamentals of report writing as they apply to longer reports. It follows the conventions of letter usage as to heading, introduction so-called, salutation, and complimentary close. It retains the use of the headings, in spite of its miniature proportions. The side headings are used as main headings and the third-order headings of the long-form report for the secondary headings.

The blocking of the "Subject" is especially advised not only in these reports but in all interdepartmental correspondence. Note that this block balances with the so-called introduction in which the name and address of the person addressed are given.

The brief introductory paragraph may well be studied analytically for its essential functions. In small space it gives authorization, the purpose, the general method or plan of treatment.

The third sentence sets up the pattern of this little section.

Refer to Chapter XVI, Part I, pages 122 to 127.

Example 4. Short-form Report.

<u>THE DETROIT EDISON COMPANY</u>

<u>Detroit, Michigan</u>

<u>COPES FEED–WATER REGULATOR STUDY</u>

at

<u>BEACON STREET HEATING PLANT</u>

Arthur S. Griswold

June 10, 193_

    This short-form report is less personal in character than that shown in Example 3. It is on a study made as part of company routine, not as in Example 3, in response to a personal request of the one to whom the report is submitted. It appropriately takes an impersonal form. As it approaches the formal report in tone and is of the maximum size usual for the short-form report, it is formalized by being put up in a folder. In such a case the title sheet is used, as in the long-form report. The synopsis and table of contents, are, however, not required.

The purpose of the investigation, and therefore of the report, is given.

The second and third paragraphs state briefly what was found out by the investigation.

The limitation of the study to the Beacon Street Plant. When any limitation is placed on an investigation which was not anticipated in advance, it should be made clear why this was done.

Emphasis is given the value of the findings to be presented because of the bearing on subsequent studies of other plants.

The relation of this report to the longer report to follow is indicated. There seems no need of a further statement of plan than has been already suggested by the wording in the previous paragraphs—"many points concerning these regulators which will facilitate the studies at the other plants," etc. The plan is merely to list in series the points noted. No complex structure is needed.

FEED—WATER REGULATOR STUDY

at

BEACON STREET HEATING PLANT

In December, 193_, a study of the feed—water regulators, used in the heating plants, was begun in order to
secure information concerning the operation of these instruments and to determine whether the modernization of
some of these regulators might be advisable.

The operators at Congress Street and Willis Avenue
stated that practically no difficulty was encountered
with their regulators and a log kept at Congress Street
showed that it was necessary to adjust the thermostat nut
of only one tube but once during a four—week period.

At Beacon Street, however, considerable difficulty was
being experienced with two regulators. Because of this,
the work was started at Beacon Street; and because of
time limitations, no work has been done at other plants.
The investigation at Beacon Street, however, has brought
out many points concerning these regulators which will
facilitate the studies at the other plants when they are
undertaken during the coming winter.

This report is a brief review of the results obtained
during the investigation at Beacon Street. A complete detailed report is being prepared.

Writing the Technical Report

Note on this page the use of the side headings, which, in the long-form report, mark the secondary topics but which here become the main headings.

Mechanical Difficulties of Boilers 4 and 5.

The regulators of Boilers 4 and 5 were giving considerable trouble at the start of the investigation. It was necessary to adjust the thermostat with boiler load changes of not more than 75,000 lb. per hour. A careful checkup disclosed that the thermostats were not properly located and that there was severe binding in the levers of Boiler 4. These conditions were corrected and the action of the regulators improved until it was equal to that of Boilers 1 and 2. These were mechanical difficulties which could have been detected at the time of the installation.

Tests to Determine Performance of the Regulators.

The next step was to determine whether the regulators were performing in the desired manner. The regulators are expected to maintain the water within working limits without adjustment from the minimum to maximum boiler steaming rates. The boiler gauge glasses are 14 in. long and there is only 8 in. between high- and low-water alarms. During the investigation, it was found that the water level swells appreciably with small load changes when operating at steaming rates below 100,000 lb. per hour. To prevent high-water whistles, the water must be kept $2\frac{1}{2}$ in. below the high-water alarm point. With high steaming rates, the swell or shrinkage is not large and it is possible to operate with the water down to 1 in. above the low-water alarm. The permissable variation in water level, therefore, is only $4\frac{1}{2}$ in. from minimum to maximum boiler loads.

Friction in Stuffing Boxes of Bonnet.

One other mechanical difficulty was encountered. The valve bonnets have double stuffing boxes in which a very soft packing is used. It is possible to tighten the stuffing-box nut with the fingers so that the valve becomes inoperative. In attempting to stop small leaks these nuts may be turned too tightly, and this will certainly cause poor action. The bonnets can be refitted for single stuffing boxes. This would halfway eliminate this source of trouble.

1. Summary of Investigation to Date.

In summing up the work to date, it appears that the valve travel with the present arrangement at Beacon Street is insufficient, the valve cages are unbalanced with high excess pressures, and the thermostats are not sufficiently rigid. The feed-water excess pressure can be controlled, but numerous adjustments to the feed-pump governors are required.

2. One suggestion concerning the purchase specifications should be made. The practice has been to specify a valve which will have a definite flow at a definite valve opening and excess pressure. It would seem to the writer that the specification should be changed. The valve called for should be able to control the flow over the entire boiler-load range and keep the water level within prescribed limits.

NOTE 1: The summary is exactly what is needed. The reader at the end of this report wants to know what has been found out up to the present time. This first paragraph satisfies that requirement.

NOTE 2: If those who prepare short-form reports can be stimulated to give their own reactions to and their concrete suggestions on the findings of a study in which they are engaged, they will be given a sense of responsibility which will increase their usefulness manifold.

Example 5. *Memorandum.*

The memorandum is a modified form of short-form report that is quite useful in some practice. It resembles the letter type, except that it omits the salutation and complimentary close and does not use the personal pronouns of the first and second person as does the letter. It usually should retain the introductory paragraph, although this never stresses the plan, for the organization is generally very simple, often a mere listing of points. The careful setup of the "Subject" is especially to be noted. This particular memorandum was bound in a folder and was provided with a title page.

Memorandum To: June 26, 19____

Mr. J. H. Walker
Superintendent of Central Heating
522 Service Building

                    SUBJECT: Operating and Testing Program
                             for the Cooling Installation
                             in the C. M. Drake Home and
                             the Attic Fans in the A. D.
                             McLay and R. E. Greene Homes

    The cooling and ventilating equipment installed last
summer in the homes of Messrs. C. M. Drake, A. D. McLay,
and R. E. Greene will be tested in accordance with the
following program as agreed upon in our conference of
June 10.

Test on C. M. Drake Cooling Installation.
    The occupants of the home will be requested to operate
the cooling system with a view to maintaining reasonably
comfortable conditions with ice quantities arbitrarily
restricted in the interest of economy. Cooling by night
air will be used to the maximum extent in order to reduce
the consumption of ice. During the three weeks absence
of the occupants, tests will be made to determine accurately certain quantities affecting the cooling capacity
of the system for which time was not available last
summer.

    Methods of Operation: The system should be operated
according to the following directions:

    1. Using ice for cooling, start the system when the
temperature downstairs reaches 77° to 78° F., which will
normally occur at around 2:00 to 3:00 P.M. Do not start
the system before noontime except in case of extreme
heat. Limit the charge of ice to from 500 to 700 lb., depending upon the heat of the day. Block off one-half of
the upper coil surface, close the by-pass dampers, and
throttle the pump discharge to about 5 g.p.m.; continue
the operation of the water pump until there seems to be
no cooling power left in the water. On this basis the
pump will usually be operated for from 3 to 4 hr. Fan
should be operated continuously from the time the system
is started until about 6:00 A.M. the following morning.
The dampers should be changed to night-air cooling as
early in the evening as outdoor temperatures are favorable. Experiments can be made to determine the effect on
cooling of closing the downstairs registers. The effect
of exhausting the air from the downstairs rooms plus the
effect of the cool air coming down the stairway may result in sufficient cooling.

    2. For a period of about one week prior to July 15 the
charge of ice should be limited to about 300 lb. and the
system started not earlier than 3:00 P.M.; otherwise, the
operation is to be the same as in paragraph 1. The object
is to determine whether comfortable conditions can be

produced by only artificially cooling the house for a brief period and then allowing the temperature to rise gradually until night air is available.

3. On one or two days prior to July 15, experiment with the cooling effect which may be produced by simply operating the fan throughout the day, recirculating the air in the house.

Tests: The following tests will be run during the absence of the house occupants:

1. Measure quantity of air delivered at supply registers and at fan discharge, using an anemometer.
2. Measure air movement in rooms by use of Kata thermometer.
3. Check floor temperatures, and check for stratification of air.
4. Measure basement losses.
5. Measure duct and coil friction losses; also pumping head.
6. Check water temperatures in ice tank.
7. Operate cooling system for one day, using both well water and ice water. Estimate possible saving in operating cost.

Test of Attic Ventilating Fans.

The attic ventilating fans installed in the homes of Messrs. A. D. McLay and R. E. Greene will be tested during the week of June 12 to 18. During these tests, comparative temperature data will be gathered to determine the cooling effect accomplished by these fans. These data will be presented to the Association of Fan Manufacturers when they meet in convention at Detroit during the last week of June. If necessary, the tests will be continued into the week of June 18 to obtain sufficient data.

Centrifugal Fan Tests: The performance of the centrifugal fan installed in the A. D. McLay home should be tested as follows:

1. Compare the temperatures in the two bedrooms with and without the use of the fan, making the comparison under similar outdoor conditions, if possible. Start the fan at about 7:00 P.M. or when outdoor temperatures are favorable. Have bedroom windows wide open and doors closed, and run the fan until about 6:00 A.M. For the temperature test without the fan running, bedroom doors will, of course, be opened. Measure power input to the motor, fan speed, and air flow through the grilles.

2. With bedroom doors open and windows only partially open, determine whether it is possible to draw air into the house through open windows downstairs and accomplish any appreciable cooling. If results are promising, an all-night test should be run.

Propeller Fan Tests: The propeller fan installed in the R. E. Greene home will be tested for performance in the following manner:

3

1. By means of recording thermometers placed in two bedrooms, a comparison should be made of inside temperatures with and without the use of the fan. To be truly indicative of the effect of the fan, outdoor temperature conditions during these tests should be similar. The fan should be started as early in the evening as outdoor temperatures are favorable and should be run until about 6:00 A.M. the following morning. The bedroom windows should be closed. Measure the power input to the motor and the flow of air up the attic stairway. Determine whether any air is drawn up the front stairway under these conditions.

2. With bedroom windows only partially open and downstairs windows partially open, determine whether it is possible to accomplish cooling for the upstairs and downstairs simultaneously. If results are promising, comparative all-night tests should be run. A recording thermometer should be placed in a downstairs room.

3. With bedroom doors closed, during the early evening, tests should be made to determine whether the fan will draw air through open downstairs windows and accomplish any effective downstairs cooling.

Very truly yours,

Signature
Name typed.

PART III

THE CRITICISM OF THE REPORT

The final test of a report is, of course, whether it meets satisfactorily all the conditions under which it is used; that is the most important thing to determine. The report should be judged from the point of view of the man who will first read it and then from the point of view of all subsequent readers. If it can qualify on these two counts, it will probably be acceptable, even if it does not accord with all the other requirements for a perfect report. The critical studies in this part of the book should be useful to both student and practitioner who wish to carry the quality of their reports above this standard, and who realize how much the refinements of writing technique are appreciated in their ultimate effect by those who handle reports. Part III takes the form of a few clinical studies such as were a feature of the course on which the book is based.

Finding the Point of Attack

The development of a consciously critical attitude toward one's own work and the work of similar sort of others is an important means of self-education. One can learn more by observing how others succeed or fail in their efforts to get their ideas over than by listening to any number of lectures on the art of writing. One needs to cultivate a conscious habit of noting the source of effects in the things he reads; he needs to be alert for new methods of demonstration and intelligent in his judgment of their value.

As a class, men trained or experienced in any field of technology are already critical of facts. They appraise the accuracy of statement in a report or paper, the intelligence exhibited in the presentation of a proposition, the soundness of the conclusions drawn, the reasonableness of the judgment shown in the recommendation of measures based on the discussion of the facts. They are apt, however, to be so concerned with these considerations that they are only vaguely aware of the writing technique. If without undue effort they can get what they want from a report, they are satisfied. They are apt to judge it purely on its service aspects. This is quite correct. This critical attitude is neither to be deprecated nor to be belittled. As has been repeatedly stated, a report is a communication. If it functions to make that communication in such a way as to meet fully all the requirements of the person to whom it is directed and specifically all the conditions of use he may require, it should be regarded as a satisfactory communication.

But there is involved in this communication of ideas a writing technique that itself may be viewed critically, since it has much to do with the effectiveness of the composition. One may learn much and improve greatly his own methods of communication by consciously observing this, and noting where it is or is not effective. The case is somewhat analogous to studying conveyor systems till one has developed a system perfectly adapted to his own use.

The purpose of this part of the book is to make the student and the practitioner more interested in observing critically the technique of others who write reports, in order to make them more sensitive to effects and thus to improve their own methods of presentation.

One difficulty presents itself at once. An engineer, forester, or architect, young or old, student or professional, will find it difficult to keep interest focused on a report as a problem in communication. His interest in the material presented will constantly lure him from any critical attitude he may assume toward the report as a piece of writing. This is a natural and, under ordinary circumstances, a perfectly correct state of mind. If, however, one is to strive consciously to profit by the mistakes of others or to improve his own writing by observing the sources of their success, he must try to keep himself detached, to inhibit or postpone the full exercise of his real interest in the subject matter until he has got some first impressions of the form or general method of the report he is reading. It is suggested that as the first part of his critical procedure one adopt definitely the rule of making, first, a general examination of the report. This is an attempt to see it as a whole, before he becomes confused by the massing of details—to see it in perspective, to check the balance and proportion of parts, the soundness of the structural pattern, and to discover in advance any obvious occasion for possible confusion. If one will refrain from reading a report through in detail until he has thus first got his bearings with reference to its functional features, he will be surprised to find how much more easily he will get through it when he does settle down to a careful, considered reading of the detailed text. Most important, however, in this critical approach will be the discovery of the fundamental points of attack.

In his first general survey of the report, one should attempt, not to settle issues, but merely to raise them; he should not even try to diagnose the difficulties he seems to see. He may more profitably make a few notes to be used later in his detailed examination of the queries he has noted. "Why should an eight-page report have an introduction of four pages?" "If the report is supposed merely to assemble in an orderly way the information the chief engineer requires, why does the writer presume to recommend the action to be taken?" "Why should the first section be four pages long, the second only a half page, the third six and a half?" These questions raised by the reader handling the report for the first time can evidently be answered only after a more careful reading.

The procedure outlined for such a general survey of a report will often in five minutes disclose the weak points or the apparent confusion in a report or will satisfy one that it will qualify as an orderly presentation of a well-motivated proposition. The following directions will make this procedure more concrete:

1. Consider, separately and in relation to each other, the title, the synopsis, if one is used, the table of contents, and the introduction. Are they in agreement? The introduction, in particular, should be read carefully. It represents the writer's mental attitudes as he began his task. Analyze it, first as an evidence of what he thought he was going to do, what he hoped to accomplish by doing it, and how he planned to do it. Was he clear in his own mind about these three aspects of his task? Then, consider how clearly the introduction sets up in your mind a conception of the proposition, of the writer's purpose, and his plan or organization. These are really two distinct analytical examinations, first of the writer's evident intent, and second of your own reactions.

2. Next, read the terminal section of the report; it may be a conclusion, a summary, a recommendation, or some other appropriate final comment. This terminal section presumably is significant of what, at the end of his performance, the writer thought he had done. He looks back and sums up the substantial aspects of his material, reinforces certain points of emphasis, draws his conclusions, or makes his recommendations. Has he come out as he expected, or at least as he said in his introduction he hoped he would? Here is where one can often catch the writer unawares. Here will be evidence of his wandering or of his becoming muddled as to the objective or limits of his proposition. One can discover whether the report is out of alignment, or whether its purpose is confused, or whether it has spread out beyond its legitimate limits.

If there are any apparent inconsistencies or if there is any lack of agreement between the introduction and the conclusion of the report, these can be definitely diagnosed only after a critical, detailed reading. One should, however, make, for future use, some such notes as these: "The concluding section seems to exceed the purpose as stated in the introduction"; "The summary contains a point not even suggested in the statement of proposed points for discussion in the introduction." Somewhere in the detailed treatment of the subject matter, the writer forgot what he was doing and why he was doing it; it will be your task to discover where the point of confusion was. If for any reason you are responsible for the editing of the report, you will have to understand why he stumbled or blundered as he did and be able to suggest a correction.

3. Then, examine in a general way the system of headings. The headings are presumably the mapping devices. They mark, or

should mark, the route to be followed from start to finish. Before trusting them, it may be well to check them through. Take an airplane view of the entire area thus mapped. Are the markers consistently used? Does the plan they indicate agree exactly with the plan set up in the introduction and in the table of contents? Is the perspective clear? Is the relation of major and minor parts correctly indicated? Are there any evident cases of bad proportioning or a lack of balance of parts? Is there any order of points that strikes you as open to question?

It is surprising how much more easily one can discover defects or weaknesses or inconsistencies in the structure of a report by studying the pattern as set up in the table of contents or represented by the heading system than by the most careful analysis of the text. Any lack of alignment, any twisting of the structure, any slip of the writer in relating parts properly can be seen almost at a glance.

4. Finally, examine the transitional text—the text that introduces and, in some cases, concludes the sections of the report. This text should serve to keep clear the relation of part to part, to orient the reader at the critical moments when he passes from one topic to another and may easily be confused. Since the coherence of the report is so largely dependent on these transitional functions, it is well to examine them as representing the articulation of parts.

In all these general examinations of a report, one is trying to make sure that from first to last the writer of the report has kept clearly in mind what he has set out to do, and that he never forgets what his original plan for doing it was, and to discover any points at which he became confused or lost his sense of direction, or of perspective, or of proportion. One is studying his psychology at three stages: before he began, when he was through, and as he was actually delivering his ideas. Such an examination is intended to put one in a critical mood toward the report before his interest in the subject matter is too sharply enlisted by a reading of the text. It should serve to suggest points of attack, to provide leads to be followed by careful study later. The clinical studies that follow will illustrate more in detail how such critical analyses may be made.

NOTE: It is suggested that the student try out this method of approach to the criticism of reports by applying it to the Annotated Reports (pages 162 to 230).

A Study of Introductions

In any critical examination of the introduction to a report, one should be sure that he takes the point of view of those for whom the report is written, not only those to whom it will be directly submitted, but those whom they in turn will want to have read it for various purposes. Will it serve to get them a complete picture in miniature of what the report presents on a larger scale and in multiplied detail? One should recall the ideal of the introduction as a complete, self-contained unit given in Chapters V, VI, and VII. He should then appraise the particular introduction under examination on the basis of that ideal. It should not depend for its meaning on the title, the accompanying letter of transmittal, the synopsis, or even collateral knowledge assumed to be in the mind of the reader. An extreme test, and one that will appear to some fantastic, would be to consider whether the introduction would be self-explanatory fifty years hence to someone who happened to come upon the report in an old file after all those familiar with the situation it was prepared to meet were dead and gone.

Having assumed the point of view of the reader and having recalled the fundamental relation of the introduction to the report, one might follow systematically the following procedure:

1. Check on the three fundamental and indispensable functions of an introduction: the statement of the subject, including an adequate setup of the problem, or of the proposition to be considered; the indication of the purpose of the report; and the plan to be followed in the presentation.

2. Consider whether there is included a sufficient summary of findings or conclusions or recommendations to mark for the reader the terminal point of the report.

3. Study in particular the initial focus of attention produced by the first sentence, or at least by the first paragraph.

4. If a preliminary section is used as a means of relieving the burden of the introduction, consider whether it is justified and has been properly handled or has robbed the report of an effective ending.

5. Read the whole introductory text aloud to test whether it reads smoothly and coherently. In launching the reader, the ways should be so smooth and so well greased that he will slide down without a jar or conscious effort into the body of the report on the reading of which he is embarking.

The examples of ineffective introductions that follow are taken from student papers. A study of the original text, the editor's notes, and the revision may prove suggestive.

Example 1. *Subject Not Fully Enough Stated.*

ORIGINAL

The Class II thermometer has recently become of importance in the use of precision instruments by industry, not only because of its low first cost, but because of the simplicity of design and operation. Since the design of the instrument is so very simple, practically the only difficulty of manufacture arises in the filling of these thermometers with the actuating fluid. The difficulty is caused by the variation of the amount of volume filled in each different thermometer.[1](x) The new method of filling has almost entirely eradicated this problem and has thus produced thermometers which are more nearly uniform in action.(xx)

It will be the object of this report, therefore, to discuss the investigation of this new method and to determine whether the new method is a satisfactory solution for the problem of filling Class II thermometers. Since the new method is to be recommended for use, the emphasis will be placed on the discussion of the new method and only a perfunctory review of the limitations of the old method will be given.

The presentation of this investigation includes first, a few preliminary considerations; next, a detailed discussion of the new method of filling; then the factors influenced by the new method are considered;[2] and at the end of the report is given a summary of the more important points and a discussion of the conclusion reached regarding this new method.[3] [A number of instruments were tested for the purpose of determining the results of using the new method of filling the thermometers, and the data were found to be not easily expressible. The information obtained by testing is, therefore, discussed in the report only in a general way.]

NOTE: [1] At (x) there is need of indicating more definitely what "the" means. The exact character of the subject is not clear. The insertion of the following sentence should remedy this defect:

Quite recently a new method has been suggested by technicians in this field which has almost entirely eradicated this problem by controlling the filling operation as a function of the percentage volume of the system. The system, under the new method, is completely filled with liquid while the bulb and capillary temperatures are at a maximum.

[2] The concluding summary is not ordinarily to be regarded as a section to be announced as part of the analytic scheme. It is a purely functional unit.

[3] Obviously the bracketed text at the end of the introduction is misplaced; it belongs at (xx).

It is best never to add any text after one sets up the pattern of this report. Such text blurs the sharpness of the outline, which one needs as he begins to read the body of the report.

REVISION

The Class II thermometer has recently become of importance in the use of precision instruments by industry, not only because of its low first cost, but because of its simplicity of design and operation. Since the design of the instrument is so very simple, practically the only difficulty of manufacture arises in the filling of these thermometers with the actuating fluid. The difficulty is caused by the variation of the amount of volume filled in each different thermometer.

Quite recently a new method has been suggested by technicians in this field which has almost entirely eradicated this problem by controlling the filling operation as a function of the percentage volume of the system. The system, under the new method, is completely filled with liquid while the bulb and capillary temperatures are at a maximum. The new method of filling has almost entirely eradicated the variation of the volume filled in the different thermometers and has thus produced thermometers which are more nearly uniform in operation.

A number of instruments were tested for the purpose of determining the results of using the new method of filling the thermometers, and the data were found to be not easily expressible. The information obtained by testing is, therefore, discussed in the report only in a general way.

It will be the object of this report to discuss the investigation of this new method and to determine whether the new method is a satisfactory solution for the problem of filling Class II thermometers. Since the new method is to be recommended for use, the emphasis will be placed on the discussion of the new method and only a perfunctory review of the limitations of the old method will be given.

The presentation of this investigation includes, first, a few preliminary considerations; next, a detailed discussion of the new method of filling; and, finally, an analysis of the factors that have influenced its success.

Example 2. Initial Focus Misleading.

ORIGINAL

The[1] Stant Manufacturing Company's Connersville plant is essentially engaged in job shop production but also manufactures large lots of one or two popular gas caps. Mr. C. B. Hyde, General Manager of the firm, requested an investigation of production delays on the large-lot jobs. The investigation showed the materials-handling system the cause of the delays in large-lot production.

The[2] report presents a study of the present system, showing the delays, and then proposes a materials-handling system for the large-lot jobs which will minimize the delays discovered in the present system.

The findings of the investigation may be briefly summarized as follows: the present system wastes the operator's time, allowed him to loiter, and interrupts his rhythm of motion, besides wasting floor space and machine time. The solution is the use of conveyors to eliminate the operator as a trucker or anything but a machine operator. Incident savings in overhead and floor space will be realized. (x)

[1] Would not anyone likely to read this report know this? The initial focus of attention is on a fact perfectly familiar to the reader. In the revision the focus is on the report, its content and its purpose.

[2] This statement of plan should come last in the introduction. It belongs at (x).

Example 3. Initial Emphasis Misleading.

ORIGINAL

[Aviation[1] is essentially a means of transportation, and as such it can be stated that it is based on flights from one point to another. If these points are so close together that they can both be seen from the air at once, then no problem in aerial navigation exists; but there is usually a period of time in which the flyer cannot see the spot from which he started or the destination at which he expects to arrive.] Consequently it is imperative that he have some means whereby the ship can be directed quickly and safely to its goal. There are three general methods for aircraft navigation, and naturally there is no best one, since the use of any method depends to a large extent upon the type of course flown and the conditions surrounding it.

[1] The approach to the subject is such as one would use if the reader had no conception of the problems of aerial navigation. The bracketed portion should be cut altogether. The three methods should be given by name, as they are in the revision; and since the purpose of the report is to recommend the method best suited to the Los Manaos Airline, this recommendation should be added.

REVISION

This report presents the findings of an investigation requested by Mr. C. B. Hyde, General Manager of the Stant Manufacturing Company, to determine the causes and to provide a solution for the serious delays in the production of large-lot jobs. The investigation showed that the materials-handling system was the cause of the delays in large-lot production. The present materials-handling system wastes the operator's time by allowing him to loiter and, by interrupting his rhythm of motion, wastes floor space, and wastes machine time.

The findings of the investigation may be briefly summarized as follows: the present system wastes the operator's time, allows him to loiter, and interrupts his rhythm of motion, besides wasting floor space and machine time. The solution is the use of conveyors to eliminate the operator as a trucker or anything but a machine operator. Incident savings in overhead and floor space will be realized.

The report presents a study of the present system, showing the delays, and then proposes a materials-handling system for the large-lot jobs that will minimize the delays discovered in the present system.

REVISION

This report, prepared at the request of Mr. Castillos, recommends the method of aerial navigation best suited to the conditions under which the new Los Manaos Airline will be operated. The problem is to determine not what is inherently or technically the best method, but rather what is the method that is best fitted for the course flown and the conditions likely to be encountered.

The methods to be discussed are the piloting method, the method employing celestial observations, and the dead-reckoning method. The consideration of these three methods with reference to the requirements of the Los Manaos Airline indicates that the dead-reckoning method is the most advantageous.

Example 4. Initial Emphasis Misleading.

ORIGINAL

The[1] corn-products industry, which is related in many ways to the cane-sugar industry, developed after cane-sugar technology had been firmly established. For lack of a better alternative, much of the sugar technology was adopted by the younger industry. With the development of new industrial equipment, there have appeared many instances where a break from sugar practice would prove beneficial to the corn-products industry. This is especially true in the field of evaporation. This report is an attempt to present some of the new evaporating equipment which is available and to point out how it might be introduced into the corn-syrup process.

The present writer has been authorized to prepare this report by Mr. (x) Jackson so that he may have a basis upon which to judge the relative merits of the several kinds of evaporating equipment now available.

After[2] considering, in some detail, (xx) the process and equipment now in use by the Corn Syrup Company, the report will continue with a discussion of the physical details of the two new types of evaporator, the vertical-tube basket type and the long-tube vertical type, which are now available. The application of these new evaporators to the corn-syrup process will be considered, not only from the standpoint of ability to accomplish the necessary concentration, but from the standpoint of the benefits to be derived from their use by the Corn Syrup Company.

---

[1] The title and the first paragraph give the reader who has no previous contact with this report project the impression that he is about to read a perfectly general paper on this subject. To be sure, when he reaches (x) in the second paragraph, he will see that he is mistaken, but that means a loss of motion because he must correct his first impression. The revision strikes immediately at the purpose of the report.

[2] It would hardly seem necessary to go into such detail as suggested at (xx) regarding the installation, with which the reader must already be quite familiar. This discussion of the present installation is needed, but it might be better to minimize its place in the report. For example, "After reviewing briefly the. . . . "

Example 5. Initial Sentence Dependent for Its Meaning on a Reference to the Title.

ORIGINAL

Before taking up the specific aspect of the question indicated by the title, a few remarks concerning the subject in general may well be made. The use of electric-arc welding as a substitute for riveting in ship construction has increased greatly in recent years. Since 1927, when the American Bureau of Shipping Rules first provided for the classification of all-welded ships without reference to such classification being experimental, the percentage of welded ships has grown until about half the vessels now being classed are of welded construction.

REVISION

This report has been prepared at the request of Mr. A. S. Jackson of the Corn Syrup Company to provide a basis upon which he may judge the relative merits of the several kinds of evaporating equipment now available for use in the company's plant.

The corn-products industry, which is related in many ways to the cane-sugar industry, developed after cane-sugar technology had been firmly established. For lack of a better alternative, much of the sugar technology was adopted by the younger industry. With the development of new industrial equipment, there have appeared many instances where a break from sugar practice would prove beneficial to the corn-products industry. This is especially true in the field of evaporation. This report is an attempt to present some of the new evaporating equipment that is available and to point out how it might be introduced into the corn-syrup process of the Corn Syrup Company with worth-while results.

After reviewing briefly the evident limitations and disadvantages of the process and equipment now in use by the Corn Syrup Company, the report will discuss the physical details of the two new types of evaporator, the vertical-tube basket type and the long-tube vertical type, which are now available. The application of these new evaporators to the corn-syrup process will be considered, from the standpoint not only of their ability to accomplish the necessary concentration, but of the benefits to be derived from their use by the Corn Syrup Company.

REVISION

Before taking up the specific question of whether welding or riveting would be the better method to use in the construction of the tugboats to be built by the XYZ Company, a few remarks concerning the subject in general may well be made. The use of electric-arc welding as a substitute for riveting in ship construction has increased greatly in recent years. Since 1927, when the American Bureau of Shipping Rules first provided for the classification of all-welded ships without reference to such classification being experimental, the percentage of welded ships has grown until about half the vessels now being classed are of welded construction.

NOTE: The text should never be made to depend for its meaning on a reference to the title or even to a heading. The text should be so complete in itself that it may be read orally to one who does not have the text before him and still be self-explanatory.

Example 6. Initial Focus Misleading.

ORIGINAL

A[1] dial flowmeter is a fluid-metering instrument for which certain industries have voiced a demand; and the Meriam Company, engaged in the manufacture of fluid-metering instruments, should produce such an instrument to meet these existing demands.

In[2] this report it will be demonstrated how the dial meter evolved from earlier and simpler instruments through the needs and demands of certain types of industries—in short, what the dial flowmeter is. Next will be discussed the nature of, and arising of, these demands for the instrument; and finally will be discussed the feasibility of manufacturing it by the Meriam Company.

---

[1] This definition is too obvious to be essential. All members of the Meriam Company would surely know what a dial flowmeter is. Such a definition should be subordinated so that it is quite incidental, as it is in the revision.

[2] In this case it might be a good thing to state the authorization of the report.

Example 7. Lack of Coherence between Sentences.

ORIGINAL

This report has been prepared for the information and guidance of members and examiners of the American Red Cross Lifesaving Service.

Swimmers are urged to learn the methods by which those in peril of drowning may be rescued with the least possible risk to the rescuer.

By study and practice of the methods described herein, swimmers of ordinary ability should be prepared, in case of necessity, to bring a person to safety.

The method of inducing artificial respiration merits serious study and practice, as it is a most effective means of saving life if applied in time.

Examiners in lifesaving assume a great responsibility in passing upon candidates for the test. Everyone passing the test is thereby encouraged to believe himself capable, in time of necessity, of rescuing persons in peril of drowning.

NOTE: There is a great lack of coherence between sentences in the original text. This is unfortunate, for an introduction especially should read smoothly. Paragraphing each sentence makes it especially disjunctive.

In the revision the italicized words indicate an effort to avoid shifting the logical subject except where it is necessary.

REVISION

The demand on the part of certain industries for a dial flowmeter that will meet their requirements for a fluid-metering instrument is so great that the Meriam Company, engaged in the manufacture of fluid-metering instruments, should produce such an instrument to meet these existing demands.

This report has been prepared at the suggestion of several members of the Board of Directors who are keenly aware of the opportunity for the Meriam Company to take advantage of a promising new field for their products. In view of the rapid development in this field, the report will trace the evolution of the newest type of dial flowmeter from the earlier and simpler instruments. It will then analyze the demand for its use and finally consider the feasibility of its being produced by the Meriam Company.

REVISION

This report has been prepared for the information and guidance of members and examiners of the American Red Cross Lifesaving Service. *It* proposes to present a simple account of the method by which those in peril of drowning may be rescued with the least possible risk to the rescuer. *By study and practice of the methods it describes,* swimmers of ordinary ability should be prepared, in case of necessity, to bring a person to safety. Emphasis is placed on the methods of inducing artificial respiration since it is a most effective means of saving life if applied in time.

Examiners in lifesaving assume a great responsibility in passing upon candidates for the test, for *they* encourage those who are passed to believe themselves capable in emergency of rescuing persons in peril of drowning. Remembering this, *they* should not encourage too much confidence on the part of the swimmer.

The report treats in considerable detail both the work to be done in the water and the artificial respiration that is so imperative when the rescued person has been brought to land.

Example 8. *No Indication of Use, and Therefore No Suggestion of Purpose.*

ORIGINAL

In modern high schools, (x) locker systems have come to be used universally, as a place where students may safely store their personal property while they are attending classes. The success of such locker systems depends entirely on the security of the lockers, so that, since a locker is only as secure as its locking mechanism, the method of fastening them is extremely important. Thus, it is essential that the best lock available be used on high-school lockers.

Locker locks are of two sorts, the key lock and the combination lock. Key locks may be further classified as worded, disk tumbler, lever tumbler, and pin tumbler; but, since the pin tumbler type is far superior as a locking mechanism to the other three types, it alone will be compared with the combination lock. In this comparison, it will be shown that the combination lock is superior to the key lock for locker-lock use and, therefore, should be used exclusively. (xx) Also, to assure complete understanding of this comparison, a detailed description of each lock will be presented before their merits are considered.

In pointing out the superiority of the combination lock over the key lock, (xxx) the following characteristics will be discussed: (1) costs; (2) security; and (3) adaptability to use in locker systems.

REVISION

In modern high schools like the Foxboro High School, locker systems have come to be used universally, as a place where students may safely store their personal property while they are attending classes. The success of such locker systems depends entirely on the security of the lockers, so that, since a locker is only as secure as its locking mechanism, the method of fastening them is extremely important. Thus, it is essential that the best lock available be used on high-school lockers.

Locker locks are of two sorts, the key lock and the combination lock. Key locks may be further classified as worded, disk tumbler, lever tumbler, and pin tumbler; but, since the pin tumbler type is far superior as a locking mechanism to the other three types, it alone will be compared with the combination lock. In this comparison, it will be shown that the combination lock is superior to the key lock for locker-lock use and, therefore, should be used exclusively in the proposed installation at the Foxboro High School. Also, to assure complete understanding of this comparison, a detailed description of each lock will be presented before their merits are considered.

In pointing out the superiority of the combination lock over the key lock for the Foxboro High School, the following characteristics will be discussed: (1) costs, (2) security; and (3) adaptability to use in locker systems.

NOTE: The phrases which have been inserted at x, xx, and xxx in the revision indicate how definitely the report purposes to recommend the best locker system for installation in the Foxboro High School.

Example 9. *Purpose Not Clear.*

ORIGINAL

This report contains the results of a library investigation in regard to the visual qualities of the light from mercury-vapor and incandescent tungsten-filament lamps, especially considering the lighting of a machine shop on a 24-hour-day basis. (x)

No attempt has been made to investigate the relative qualities of other types of industrial lighting as they have already been eliminated by a committee (xx) in charge of the reorganization of the production facilities as unsatisfactory for the purpose. Also the investigation has not covered such considerations as cost, maintenance, dependability, or durability.

The quality of light may be considered, first, as to its physical characters, such as color spectrum and results of use, and, secondly, as to its clarity, and visual acuity.

REVISION

This report contains the results of a library investigation of the visual qualities of the light from mercury-vapor and incandescent tungsten-filament lamps, with special reference to the lighting of a machine shop on a 24-hour-day basis.

The information given in the report is to be used by Mr. W. K. Mulligan, an industrial engineer now engaged in a study of the production methods which are now being used by the A.B. Stores, Inc., manufacturers of gas and electric cooking ranges. Mr. Mulligan intends to use this report as a basis for deciding the type of lighting to be used in the machine shop of this factory to replace the present unsatisfactory system.

No attempt has been made in the report to consider the relative qualities of other types of lighting, since they have already been eliminated by a committee in charge of the reorganization of the production facilities of the A.B. Stores, Inc., as unsatisfactory for the purpose of lighting their machine shops on a 24-hour-day basis. Also the report contains no such considerations as cost, maintenance, dependability or durability. The report covers only a comparison of the visual qualities of the two lamps in question.

The quality of light has been considered, first, as to its physical characteristics, such as color spectrum and results of use, and, secondly, as to its clarity, and visual acuity.

NOTE: In the original text there is nothing to suggest the purpose of the report or the use to be made of it. At (xx) there is a vague reference to a committee in charge of some reorganization program, but "the" purpose remains undefined. At (x) and at (xx) this should be cleared up.

Example 10. *Statement of Plan Too Detailed.*

ORIGINAL

The first part of this report deals with the circuit design of the transmitter. [It is purely theoretical to the extent that it has not been actually tried in practice. However, such a method of design is good practice, since all the component parts of the circuit have been proved practical, and the general circuit itself is similar to some of the standard ones in present-day use.

Three divisions make up this part. The first describes the radio-frequency circuit. A crystal controlled "tri-tet" exciter with type-59 tubes is used to drive a pair of type-46 tubes in push-pull, which in turn drive the output stage of type-800 tubes also in push-pull.

In the second, the audio-frequency system, consisting of two type-56 tubes in a speech amplifier, driving two 2A3 types, driving two 800 types as class B modulators, is described. The third tells about the power supplies used.]

Part II deals with the actual construction of the transmitter. [The first division concerns the frame, which is of all-aluminum welded construction. It is composed of three sections, which, when placed together, have dimensions of 27 by 18 by 12 inches. The second division shows how the apparatus is arranged to the best advantage of circuit design and ease of operation.]

Part III covers operation of the transmitter. [It tells how the transmitter may be set up in different locations such as on shipboard, in lighthouses, and in amateur radio stations. It explains how to use the main-line power, gasoline engine, and other sources of power. Different ways of arranging the units are also discussed. The adaptability to different antenna systems is mentioned. Finally, tuning operations are covered, and why they are easy— as demanded by the market.]

Costs are dealt with in Part IV. [Individual parts are itemized, and the extra expenses such as labor, advertising, and shipping are considered.] It is shown that the transmitter can be built to sell within the limit of $200.

NOTE: Unless the report is very long, this statement of plan is evidently too detailed. It actually occupies more than one-half the space devoted to the introduction. Since the object of any such setup of plan is to give the reader an impression of the pattern of the report that will guide him in his subsequent reading, the statement should be reduced to a simplified outline of major parts. The bracketed detail may well be omitted.

The report is presented in three parts: Part I deals with the circuit design of the transmitter; Part II with the actual construction of the transmitter; Part III with its operation; Part IV, estimating the various costs involved, shows that the transmitter can be built to sell within the limit of $200.

Example 11. *Statement of Plan Out of Its Normal Place.*

ORIGINAL

The design problem considered in this report was taken up at the request of the L.C.L. Container Co. of New York. Its purpose is to determine the preliminary physical design characteristics of a vessel to be built especially for the transportation of this company's product, which is now nationally standardized. The investigation has been strictly limited to the mechanical design only; the particular advantages which would be derived from its use are stated only in general terms, with no attempt to estimate their exact economic value. This report is, therefore, intended to furnish the basis for such a detailed study of costs, which may be made in the future.(x)

The results of the investigation will be presented in the following order: first, the general disadvantages of the conventional type of cargo vessel will be stated for the purpose of indicating desirable features to be employed in the new design; second, the special features to be incorporated in the design of the hull will be considered; and third, the system and devices to be used in handling the cargo will be explained in detail.

A detailed section on the container equipment to be handled is unnecessary, as these data were specified by the company for whom the report is intended. The two standard types of outer container which were developed for rail transportation were accepted as a basis for the ship design. Briefly, their characteristics are as follows:

Designation	Dimensions, ft.	Capacity, lb. lading	Type of lading
A	8 by 8 by 10	25,000	Dry, packaged, dense goods
B	8 by 8 by 24	30,000	Dry, packaged, low density

The standard refrigerated container is of the same dimensions and lading capacity as type *A*, so that it may be considered as identical for the purposes of carrier design. It is to be noted that two *A* containers occupy approximately the same floor space as one *B* container.

NOTE: The statement of plan—in this case the second paragraph, should come last in the introduction. Any comment following it blurs the impression of plan which is to aid one in making his way through the details of the text following. The third paragraph with the table, and the paragraph following it should go to (x), at the end of the first paragraph.

Example 12. *Introduction That Fails on All Counts.*

ORIGINAL

The reduction of the funds which are allowed to the maintenance departments of the railroads today has been about 50 per cent as compared with the amount allowed those departments between the years of 1920 to 1930. The reduction in available funds has required that some means be taken to reduce the amount of maintenance required per mile of track.

The items which affect the maintenance of track are numerous, and various solutions have been found to remedy the maintenance costs of these items. I shall list only a few of the items and show the relation of the cost of maintaining the rail joint to the other items of maintenance.

First, the treating of ties has generally increased their life.

Second, the rail joint, the weakest point in the track structure, should be eliminated in some manner or made as strong and elastic as the rest of the track.

Third, it has been found that mare rails are renewed yearly because of the battering and splitting of the rails at the joints than for any other reason. This can be remedied only by eliminating the joints.

From the above discussion it is seen that the maintaining of rail joints is the major expense in the maintenance of the track structure. Therefore it is highly desirable to eliminate the joint by some means. Welding of the joints is an entirely feasible method of eliminating these joints, as shown in this report.

NOTE: The introduction in the original text seems to fail on all counts; it does not perform satisfactorily any of the three functions of an introduction.

REVISION

Track maintenance on the Delaware and Hudson Railroad has been greatly decreased by eliminating the joints between the rails. This company made its first installation of welded rail in 1933 at Albany, N. Y. It consisted of 2,700 feet of continuous rail. Since that time the company has made several other installations until at the present time it has 45 miles of welded rail in service. Its experience has shown that welding the rail ends together is an entirely feasible method for eliminating joints. It has apparently encountered no difficulties due to creeping of rails or to stresses set up in the rails.

In order to understand why such long sections of continuous rail do not cause difficulties due either to creep or to stress, this report will review the results of the study made by Mr. Clarke, Chief Engineer of the D & H. It will then discuss the methods that this railroad has found to be practicable for laying and transporting the rails and particularly the new type of rail fastening it has developed. The results that it has achieved in its use of welded rail seems well to justify the advantages it claims for it.

Example 13. *Abortive Attempt to Use a Preliminary Section.*

ORIGINAL

This report of an investigation of the hydraulic conditions of the Millpond is submitted at the request of Mr. E. F. Green, defense counsel for Mr. Fred Siegle, in an attempt to settle a dispute between the latter, a gristmill operator, and the Père Marquette Railway, a corporation interested in harvesting ice from his pond. The interpretations and results are set forth in a simple straightforward manner easily understandable by the nontechnical layman. (x)

From this report, it is concluded that the removal of ice slightly affects the efficiency of this pond as a source of power while the use of water for power seriously limits the ice harvest.

This report is presented in the following order: first, a description of the natural resources and property concerned as well as the data taken on investigation; second, the effects of the removal of ice and the use of power; third, the interpretation of results; fourth, conclusions and recommendations.

Analysis of the Problem.

The past four years with their exceedingly dry seasons have given rise to a definite problem at Farwell, Mich. This little Central Michigan town has a small millpond which has two reasons for being very useful. The body of water is fed by the Little Tobacco River and one other small stream. The water of these streams is a pure nonmineral spring water, so that, consequently, in the winter as the pond freezes over a very pure ice is formed. The Père Marquette Railway, recognizing this fact, built an extremely large icehouse and yearly takes comparatively enormous quantities of ice from this small body of water for railroad icing purposes. On the other hand, Mr. Siegle is operating a gristmill using the pond as a source of power. Thus, in the winter season, when the grinding business is at a peak, the operation of this mill apparently affects water levels. Changing water levels ruins the ice formations, seriously handicapping the railroad company. Also, taking ice from this pond seems to lower the water level and affect the mill efficiency. As the result, the Père Marquette Railway has charged Mr. Siegle with maliciously operating the sluice gates of his dam so as to destroy ice by changing the water levels. In return, Mr. Siegle is suing the railroad for time and profit loss ensued while his mill was idle.

NOTE: The section headed "Analysis of the Problem" is an evident attempt to lighten the introduction by the use of a preliminary section. It should be noted that, although such a section will usually be somewhat shorter than the other major sections, it should not be insignificant in size. In this case the attempted preliminary section is only one page in length as compared with other major sections four to six pages in length. It would be better to throw this analysis of the problem back where it belongs at (x) in the introduction. The heading is wrongly displayed. A preliminary section, in a long-form report, is marked by a main heading.

Studies in Reorganization

In any examination of a report that has as its purpose a critical appraisal of the writer's method of treatment, one should give primary consideration to checking the soundness and consistency of its structure. If it is well designed, that is, if the design is simple, logical, strategic, and easy to discover, if the structure is so coherent that it defeats one's efforts to tear it down, if the relationship of part to part is evident and is evidently right, if the report is well proportioned and well balanced, it may perform its task satisfactorily and qualify as evidence of sound reasoning and sound engineering sense, even though the style may leave much to be desired.

There are two methods of attack in seeking evidence regarding these qualifications of a report. In the first place, the heading system and the table of contents are the most obvious and the most explicit evidence of the structural features of a document. Any fault in the structural pattern is quickly seen by examining these in detail. If the report is so brief or simple as to require neither headings nor a table of contents, one can check the topic sentences in order to discover any inconsistencies of structure. In the second place, analyzing a proportioning of unit parts that does not appear to be in accord with the relative importance of those parts or their evident complexity and need for detailed development will often lead to the discovery of defects in organization. When one understands what the difficulty is, he may often easily suggest the reorganization that will correct it.

In examining the heading system with reference to the table of contents, there are a number of things to observe, some of them of minor importance, but others that may serve as a check on the consistency of the structural plan.

1. If a heading system is used, it should be simple, obvious, and consistent. Any inconsistencies in its use will confuse the reader. Headings of the same order should be similar in form in details of

type used, underscoring, spacing, position of the page. Important headings should not be displayed too near the bottom of the page, which is not an effective point of display. These things can easily be checked. One should see that the main headings are all in alignment throughout the paper and, similarly, that second- and third-order headings line up with the others of their respective ranks. No section should show only a single heading of a subordinate order, since in that case no division takes place. One should also consider whether the headings have been used to excess so that the text is split up in a fragmentary way.

2. The wording of these headings is quite as critical as that of the title. The heading must, if possible, be displayed in a single line; it must therefore be brief, but it must be significant. It must indicate exactly the content of the section it heads. The wording of a heading should be as nearly identical as possible with the wording of the reference to this unit of the report in the table of contents and in the introduction. It is well to check this point specifically, for such an agreement makes it easier for the reader to recognize and identify the parts of the report as he reads. Where sections are related in parallel, the wording of the headings can help keep that similarity of function clear in the reader's mind. For example: The Original Installation, The Present Installation, The Proposed Installation.

3. The most important check is, of course, the determination of whether the plan as set up in the table of contents or in the introduction is perfectly represented by the heading system. Is there perfect agreement through the document as to the scheme of organization of the material?

4. Often, when a plan that looked logical and sound in outline is worked out, it shows defects that one did not anticipate. It is well to consider whether the plan as indicated by the headings would be improved by revision.

It is surprising how many suggestions for constructive criticism one can get from a thoroughly searching analysis of the structure of a paper as marked by the heading system.

If one discovers a section of a report that appears not to be developed in proportion to what one would expect, it is well to study such a section to determine whether one can justify its being developed more briefly and in less detail than other similar sections. Often, as in the case of a discussion of costs, the weight of the material compensates for the lack of detailed treatment. This is especially true if there are extensive tabulations. Such material occupies relatively little space but is highly condensed and therefore relatively important. If, however, one cannot account for the lack of balance, he may often find a complete reorganization of plan advisable. This is one symptom of trouble that is most useful in diagnosing defects in the plan of a report.

There are three alternatives available in case revision is necessary:

1. One may eliminate the diminutive section altogether.

2. One may develop it on a scale comparable with that used in similar conditions.

3. One may absorb it or combine it with some other section to which it evidently belongs.

There are two specific points at which such sections are apt to occur. If a section, clearly too brief to rank as a major unit, occurs immediately after the introduction, it may often be thrown back into the introduction and integrated with it. It is often an abortive attempt to employ a preliminary section. If such an ill-proportioned section appears immediately preceding the final summary or conclusion, it can sometimes be combined with this terminal section; for generally, in such a case, it contains material which evidently belongs to the terminal comment of the report.

The studies of reports that have defects of design, which follow, will be found helpful to the student when he is trying to decide on the best plan of organization for his own subject matter. He should review Chapter III, pages 12 to 22, in which procedures are given for making an analysis and classification of one's material in preparation of a plan. Fair warning has been given, however, that, no matter how scrupulously one follows the method of analysis suggested, he is apt to find his first plan of treatment needing modification and reshaping as he continues to work with the details of his report. The studies in reorganization of report plans will be suggestive of how to mold one's material to his purpose.

Example 1. *Confusion of Title with First Main Heading.*

DESIGN AND OPERATION

of

THE CERINI DIALYZER IN THE RAYON INDUSTRY

CONTENTS

(Original)

Introduction	1½ pages
Development of Dialyzer[1]	16 pages
Early Equipment	
Modern Dialyzer[2]	
Design	
Operation	
Plant Layout	
Raw-material Storage	
Production	
Conclusions	¼ page

---

[1] The writer has here developed as his first main heading something that is approximately the same as his title. Consequently he throws his entire report, except "Conclusions," under this one heading. He has therefore no unit sections to correspond with this one. That throws the whole system of headings out of alignment. There is evident need of a reorganization that will give the component parts of the report their proper prominence; not $x = x$, but

$$x = a + b + c + d.$$

[2] Everything to this point needs to be reorganized. Part of the text thus far is introduction, part is a preliminary section, but much of it can be condensed. The main headings would then be "Design," "Operation," "Plant Layout," "Production." Note that the proportion of parts is greatly improved in the revision.

(Revision)

Introduction	1½ pages
Early Equipment	2 pages
Design	1½ pages with a full-page diagram
Operation	1¼ pages
Plant Layout	1¼ pages
Production	3 pages with two full-page diagrams
Conclusions	¼ page

Example 2. Superfluous Heading.

CAMPUS SITUATION[1]

(Original)

Before an intelligent understanding of the problems involved in this report can be begun, the manner in which the *Michigan Daily*[2] controls the campus situation should be explained and the probable need for some improvement established.

The Michigan Daily.[2]

The present situation on the campus at the University of Michigan in regard to the circulation and distribution of the *Michigan Daily*, the campus newspaper, is a result of its business policy.

Policy: This paper has been in continuous service since 1890, serving its function of conveying the latest news of the campus to its readers.

---

[1] Awkward and not clear. What is meant by "campus situation"? What is meant by the *Daily's* controlling the campus situation? There are so many points of view, and so many situations. Probably "Present Method of Circulation" is a more accurate title.

[2] The heading "*The Michigan Daily*" seems superfluous and breaks the text up unnecessarily.

Example 3. An Unaccountable Proportioning of Parts.

RADIOSTAT CONTROL

(Original)

Introduction	¾ page
Description and Function of the Radiostat Units	
(Introductory text ½ page)	
Outside Unit	2 pages
Return Unit	1¼ pages
Boiler Unit	1 page
Master Control Unit	1 page
Operating Performance	2½ pages
Advantages	¾ page
Conclusions	1 page

NOTE: The proportion of major parts is 5¾, 2½, ¾, 1 pages. By breaking up the unit that is out of proportion, one gets a 2-, 1¼-, 1-, 2½-, ¾-, 1-page proportion. The ¾ page on "Advantages" should then be combined with the 1 page of the "Conclusions" to provide the terminal comment. In rewriting this combined section, it can be reduced to a page or less.

PRESENT METHOD OF CIRCULATION

of

THE MICHIGAN DAILY

(Revision)

Before it is possible to give an intelligent presentation of the problems involved in this report, the present method of distribution and circulation of the *Michigan Daily* should be explained. The present method of circulation and distribution of the *Daily* at the University of Michigan is the result of its business policy, which has a long and established tradition; but it is certainly open to question whether there might not be need for improvement.

Policy.

This paper has been in continuous service since 1890, serving its function of conveying the latest news of the campus to its readers.

Present Method of Circulation.
Need for Improvement.
Summary.

RADIOSTAT CONTROL

(Revision)

Introduction	¾ page
Outside Unit	2 pages
Return Unit	1¼ pages
Boiler Unit	1 page
Master Control Unit	1 page
Operating Performance	2½ pages
Conclusions	1 page

Example 4. Proportioning Incorrect; Analysis Faulty.

AIR CONDITIONING IN THEATERS

TABLE OF CONTENTS

(Original)

---

[1] It should be evident that three pages of introduction are too many for a report in which the unit sections average two pages or less. Moreover, most of the three pages develop in detail the topic "Limits of Application of Air Conditioning in Theaters." This would seem to suggest a brief introduction with a preliminary section concerning this topic.

[2] A one-half page section set up with a major heading, as in the original, seems out of proportion to the other sections of the same order. Study of the text of the report suggests that it should be absorbed and integrated with the section on "Methods of Air Distribution."

(Revision)

Example 5. Proportioning Incorrect.

THE USE OF CONTINUOUS RAILS

for

THE NEW YORK CENTRAL SYSTEM

CONTENTS

(Original)

Introduction	½ page
Welding Processes[1]	10½ pages
Electric Flash Welds	5¼ pages
Oxyacetylene Welding	4¼ pages
Stress Relieving[2]	½ page
Transportation of Rails	5 pages
Rail Fastening[3]	1 page
Advantages[4]	¾ page
Conclusions	¾ page

---

[1] The section on the welding processes, 10½ pages, is evidently out of proportion to the other coordinate units. In the revision, each of the two processes is given a main section.

[2] This section of less than one page is so evidently a fragment that it must be integrated with the account of the processes, as a minor detail.

[3] Some combination of this one-page section possibly with the one on "Transportation of Rails" would seem a reasonable disposition of what appears too brief a section to rank with the other major sections.

[4] The brief critical comment must be either developed at a length somewhat commensurate with its importance in the report or thrown forward and combined with the conclusion.

(Revision)

Introduction	1 page
Electric Flash Welding	5½ pages
Oxyacetylene Welding	5 pages
("Stress Relieving" is integrated with the account of the welding processes)	
Transportation and Fastening of Rails	6 pages
("Advantages" to be combined with concluding section)	
Conclusion	1 page

Example 6. Proportioning Not Satisfactory.

CONCRETE-HOUSE CONSTRUCTION

TABLE OF CONTENTS

(Original)

CONCRETE-HOUSE CONSTRUCTION

TABLE OF CONTENTS

(Revision)

NOTE: The proportion of parts in the original plan is 7½, 2, 2, ½, ½ pages Some better plan or organization would seem desirable. The one suggested in the revision simply breaks up the overlong unit into its components. This results in the following proportion of parts: 1, 1½, 2, 2, 1½, 2, 1, 1 pages. The further suggestion is made that the diminutive section on "Comparison of Concrete and Wood-frame Construction" should be combined with the equally diminutive "Conclusion" to form the terminal comment.

Example 7. Lack of Agreement as to Plan.

SYNOPSIS

In the design of an earth dam, certain requirements must be met to ensure safety. The designers must have an accurate understanding of the foundation. The height must be great enough to provide ample freeboard protection against overtopping. The side slopes must be stable. (x)

TABLE OF CONTENTS

STATEMENT OF PLAN
IN THE INTRODUCTION

A half century of success and failure in earth-dam construction reveals four fundamental principles that must be followed in the design of a safe and successful dam. The designers must have an accurate understanding of the nature of the foundation and its behavior under different loadings. The height must be sufficient to prevent any probable overtopping. The side slopes must be stable under all conditions. (xx)

NOTE: The heading system in the completed text, which agrees with the table of contents, shows four fundamental requirements of design; the synopsis evidently intended to list four but lists only three; the introduction omits the fourth. Evidently the plan as represented by the headings and the table of contents is correct; the text of the synopsis and the introduction would need to be made consistent. This may be done by adding at (x) in the synopsis and at (xx) in the introduction this sentence: "Finally, provision must be made for the control of all percolating water."

Studies in Coherence

It is a great convenience in reading a report to be able to find things where one has reason to expect them. Marking the component units in a report distinctly by some system of headings is important since it makes it easy for the reader to discover at a glance the structural pattern of the report. Here is *a*; here is *b*; they are labeled conspicuously and significantly. There are reports where such a well-indicated setup is all that is needed; little or no text is required. In many memoranda, tabulations, compilations, listings of equipment, and other routine records of this sort, it is only necessary to be sure of a reasonable and fundamentally sound classification of details and to set the classes of material up in their proper order with little or no textual comment. In such reports the use of a consistent heading system is quite indispensable, since it is the sole means of assuring a coherent structure.

There are reports that consist of parts having no very close relation to each other, because each part is prepared for the use of a different class of reader. No one person is going to depend for his understanding of the report on reading the entire document through as a coherent, continuous development of a unified subject. The important requirement is that each part should be made so distinct from the others that each reader will be able to find his pew easily. In large reports of this type a separate title sheet—the so-called "bastard" title sheet—is provided for each part.

Such reports are the exceptional types; the special conditions of use make it most important to emphasize the component parts rather than their mutual interrelationships and to produce a disjunctive rather than a coherent effect. In most reports, and of course in all papers where a coherent text is required, the relation of part to part and to the development of the whole must be sufficiently marked to make it easy to apprehend these essential relationships. The headings alone cannot be depended on to accomplish this; the text itself must be so coherently written as to indicate these relationships without any dependence on the headings, which in such documents must be regarded as purely supplementary means. The reader must be safeguarded against confusion, his time and energies must be economized, he must be assured that at the critical points, where he passes from one part to another, he will not mistake the relations involved or that he will not have to spend valuable time figuring out what the writer is doing or what point he has reached in his discussion.

It is important, and interesting, in viewing a report critically to make a study of the articulation of parts. One should take the structure apart by analysis and examine each component unit, first by itself, and then in its relation to the other units of the structure. One should study, in particular, the introductory, transitional, and concluding texts in all such component parts.

One should study first the initial emphasis in each section, considering whether it is sufficient to focus and fix attention accurately on the subject of the section. He should then examine critically all the topic sentences to determine whether they are incisive enough to mark the subordinate units effectively. The purpose of this first examination is to see whether, without the aid of the supplementary means provided by the headings, the reader would in all cases be aware of the points at which new units are introduced.

Having assured himself that the unit sections are well marked as distinct components of the whole, one should next study all the means used to indicate the relation of these sections to each other and to the subject as a whole. One should consider whether the writer is depending too much on his headings to perform this function, and is thus impoverishing the text, and whether, deprived of the headings, the text would be coherent and the relations of part to part clear.

There are a number of defects one may discover by such an examination.

1. Lack of introductory text at the beginning of a section. This will result in a heading of a secondary order following one of a next higher order with no text between. This is allowable, of course, in certain types of report that are intentionally highly skeletonized— "tables and labels"—but it is for most reports a defect that indicates too great a dependence on the headings as a means of achieving coherence.

2. Misplacing of introductory text of a section. Usually this defect occurs where the introductory text to a section is mistaken for part of a subordinate unit of that section or for a part of the concluding paragraph of the preceding section. The use of the forward reference as a means of transition from one section to another often robs the second of the two sections of its topic sentence.

3. Labeling of the introductory text of a section as if it were one of the component units of the section.

4. Omission of a needed and logical subordinate heading. This can usually be discovered by noting an introductory text to a section which is, in length, out of all proportion to the units it introduces.

5. Unnecessary elaboration of the transitional text. It is easy to make the conveying machinery too conspicuous; it should function smoothly and unobtrusively. If it attracts attention to itself, it is too obviously a mechanism.

6. Repetition of any one transitional device till it becomes noticeable. One will discover this most easily by reading the transitional texts consecutively, without reading the intervening text.

One of the very best final tests of the coherence of a text is to read it aloud, preferably to an alert, keen listener, omitting in one's reading all headings. Most reports should read smoothly and be intelligible without dependence on sectional headings to indicate relation of part to part.

Note: It will be helpful to review Chapters VIII, IX, and X, Part I, since these deal with the paragraph as a means of coherence. The examples that follow, illustrating some of the defects listed, are taken from students' reports.

Example 1. *Lack of Introductory Text.*

(Original)

CORRECTION OF ACOUSTICAL DEFECTS

Soundproofing.

Walls: Traffic noises can easily be heard inside the theater.

NOTE: The writer of the original seems not to have appreciated the value of introductory text. Where such text is lacking, the writer is apparently depending on the headings to keep the parts of the report coherently related. Except in reports in which little text is required and a highly labeled, highly skeletonized treatment is desired, one should avoid having headings of different orders follow each other, as here, with no connecting text. The third-order heading seems superfluous.

Example 2. *Lack of Introductory Text.*

(Original)

ACOUSTICAL DEFECTS

External Noises.

Traffic: The Millbrook Theater is situated in a very noisy district. It was built 40 years ago without any provision for keeping out outside noises.

NOTE: In the original, introductory text is lacking between the main heading and the secondary heading and also between the second- and the third-order heading. There seems an excess of headings for such limited text; the third-order heading might well be omitted. One must be careful not to overdo the use of headings.

Example 3. *Apparent Lack of Introductory Text.*

(Original)

PRESENT SYSTEM

Description: The organization of most fraternal groups is along two separate, distinct lines: the Alumni Association, and the active undergraduate chapter. Michigan Alpha of Phi Kappa Psi has followed this practice.

Alumni Association. The Michigan Alpha Alumni Association is a nonprofit corporation, membership in which is comprised solely of initiated members of this chapter.

NOTE: In the original, the use of the superfluous heading "Description" leaves the section on "Present System" without introductory text.

The secondary headings are not according to the specifications for such headings, as given in Chapter XI, Part I, pages 86 to 94.

(Revision)

CORRECTION OF ACOUSTICAL DEFECTS

It is evident that measures must be taken to correct these acoustical defects. Just what these measures should be can be determined only after a thorough investigation of the sound conditions in the theater.

Soundproofing.

Soundproofing, if done properly, will eliminate practically all external noises. Traffic noises can at present be easily heard inside the theater.

(Revision)

ACOUSTICAL DEFECTS

The disturbing defects are due to external noises, to excessive reverberation, and to the uneven distribution of sound.

External Noises.

Naturally the roar of traffic is the most obvious source of annoyance, but those who have sat through a performance in the theater will hardly fail to recall the additional distraction of the ventilating fan. The Millbrook Theater is situated in a very noisy district. It was built 40 years ago without any provision for keeping out outside noises.

(Revision)

PRESENT SYSTEM

The organization of most fraternal groups is along two separate, distinct lines: the Alumni Association, and the active undergraduate chapter. Michigan Alpha of Phi Kappa Psi has followed this practice.

Alumni Association.

The Michigan Alpha Alumni Association is a nonprofit corporation, membership in which is comprised solely of initiated members of the chapter.

Example 4. *Lack of Introductory Text.*

(Original)

INJECTION INTO INLET PIPE

The Test.

Tests were made first with the conventional carburetor to afford a basis of comparison. The carburetor was then removed and replaced by a section of plain tubing. Then the injection valve was placed in position in the inlet pipe to inject spray in the same direction as the incoming air for the first set of runs. For the next set of runs, injection was down the pipe against the air flow.

Results.

The performance curves for these tests are shown on curve sheet 1, in which the curves obtained with the carburetor functioning are plotted for comparison.

NOTE: In the original, introductory and connecting text is lacking between the main and secondary headings. Even a single sentence will often be sufficient to provide a text that will read coherently without undue dependence on the heading.

Example 5. *Apparent Lack of Introductory Text.*

(Original)

THE ABILITY OF PYREX BRAND GLASS EQUIPMENT TO WITHSTAND STRAINS

Thermal Strain.

[As has been pointed out in the preceding paragraphs, one of the first requisites of a material for this installation is that of holding up under the enormous thermal strains imposed upon it by] the drastic cooling of the gases from a temperature of approximately 1000°F. to a temperature well below the condensation point, which is in the neighborhood of 200°F.

NOTE: It is well to keep all headings brief enough to permit a single-line display; if they run to more than a line, they are too much like title displays.

 In the original, apparently, the writer is depending on the headings to indicate the relation of parts. Introductory text is lacking. This apparent defect, however, is largely due to misplaced introductory text, for the bracketed portion of the first sentence, with its backward reference, is both transitional and introductory. It needs only to be made a little more general and inclusive to serve very well as topic text.

(Revision)

INJECTION INTO INLET PIPE

Tests were made first with the conventional carburetor to afford a basis of comparison. The engine was then prepared for solid injection of the fuel into the inlet pipe.

The Test.

An injection valve was placed in a piece of plain tubing which replaced the carburetor. The injection valve was first placed in a position in the inlet pipe to inject the spray in the same direction as the incoming air. A complete engine-performance test was run on the engine with the injection valve placed in this manner. For the next engine-performance test, the injection valve was placed so that the fuel spray was down the inlet pipe against the air flow.

Results.

The performance curves for these tests are shown on curve sheet 1, in which the curves obtained with the carburetor functioning are plotted for comparison.

(Revision)

ABILITY TO WITHSTAND STRAINS

As has been pointed out in the preceding paragraphs, one of the first requisites of a material for the installation is that it must hold up under the enormous thermal and physical strains imposed upon it in the cooling of the product.

Thermal Strain.

The first strain is that due to the drastic cooling of the gases from a temperature of approximately 1000°F. to a temperature well below the condensation point, which is in the neighborhood of 200°F.

Example 6. Apparent Lack of Introductory Text.

(Original)

A REVIEW OF FUNDAMENTALS

DEFINITIONS.

In order to eliminate, as far as possible, confusion as to terms, the following definitions are given. They will be found to agree with those used in the literature on the subjects but are so scattered as to make it very much of a chore to discover for oneself the meaning of each term.

THE ELECTROSTATIC FIELD: The subject of electrostatics is becoming of more and more importance with the ever-growing application of the vacuum tube, and, while a few years ago an electrical engineer considered this something to be skipped over lightly in some physics course, he must now consider it very intently.

NOTE: The original constitutes apparently a case of no introductory and no connecting text; actually it is a case of badly displayed headings. The main heading is not especially significant; it is too general. The section presents certain basic definitions. Why not use "Definitions," then, as the main heading? The introductory text needed is then evidently at hand. It should be noted that the second- and third-order headings in the original do not follow the specifications for such headings. See Chapter XI, Part I, pages 93 to 101.

Example 7. Forward Reference as a Means of Transition.

(Original)

The foregoing sections have given a picture of what results can be expected on the performance of a propeller at high tip speeds; so let us now see how these results can be applied to actual problems and how the proper corrections can be made. To do this, we shall proceed with a practical demonstration of the material.

CORRECTION DATA FOR DESIGN PROBLEMS

In the full-scale tests, it was necessary to use propellers of low pitch in order to obtain the high tip speeds which were desirable, and consequently any effects due to tip speed would be greater than for a common-pitch propeller.

NOTE: The forward reference, which in the concluding paragraph of the first section of the original is used as a means of transition, would be more effectively combined with the introductory text of the new section. It is better to combine the transitional functions with those of the introductory text rather than to use the forward reference from the concluding text of the preceding section.

(Revision)

DEFINITIONS

In order to eliminate confusion as to terms as far as possible, the following definitions are given. They will be found to agree with those used in the literature on the subjects but are so scattered through the literature as to make it very tedious to discover for oneself the meaning of each term.

The Electrostatic Field.

The subject of electrostatics is becoming of more and more importance with the increasingly common application of the vacuum tube, and, though a few years ago an electrical engineer regarded this something to be considered as a purely theoretical detail in a physics course, he must now consider it as an exceedingly important practical subject.

(Revision)

CORRECTION DATA FOR DESIGN PROBLEMS

All the tests have given a clear idea of what can be expected from the performance of a propeller at high tip speeds. The application of these results can now be made to actual problems in order to make the proper corrections. In the full-scale tests it was necessary to use propellers of low pitch in order to obtain the high tip speeds which were desirable, and consequently any effects due to tip speed would be greater than for a common-pitch propeller.

Example 8. Forward Reference as a Means of Transition.

(Original)

The last and most conclusive test is a test of the fatigue of the metal under service conditions, for even if the elastic limit were not exceeded the element still might fail by fatigue of the metal.

Fatigue of the Element: For these fatigue tests a number of the spirals and helices were fastened to a specially designed machine which applied full-scale pressure alternately and then allowed the element to return to zero pressure. The number of applications per minute was about 5, and the test was carried on continuously until each element had failed. Failure was indicated by a cracking of the element and a consequent failure to expand. The results of the tests are indicated in Table III as the average number of expansions before rupture.

NOTE: The first sentence of the original is wholly concerned with introducing the test of the fatigue of the metal. Placed, as it is, at the end of a section, it is evidently conceived of as a forward reference used as a means of transition. This robs the following paragraph of its topic sentence. It belongs at the beginning of the paragraph on "Fatigue of the Element."

Example 9. Forward Reference as a Means of Transition.

(Original)

With this general description in mind, the next step would be to consider the requirements for the use of these elements in precision instruments. Then, too, these requirements might give reason for the elimination of some types of elements.

Requirements of the Elements.

Since these instruments using pressure elements are nearly always self-actuated, a most important requirement would be for the element to produce sufficient torque and deflection to operate the mechanism of the instrument without the use of outside power.

NOTE: The forward reference as shown in the first sentence of the original should be used sparingly as a means of transition. This first paragraph, reduced somewhat and rewritten, should be used at the beginning of the next section. If it seems necessary to mark the end of the description before proceeding to a consideration of requirements, this can be done without using any forward reference.

(Revision)

Fatigue of the Element.

The last and most conclusive test is a test of the fatigue of the metal under service conditions, for even if the elastic limit were not exceeded the element might still fall under the fatigue of the metal. For these fatigue tests a number of the spirals and helices were fastened to a specially designed machine which applied full-scale pressure alternately and then allowed the element to return to zero pressure. The number of applications per minute was about 5, and the test was carried on continuously until each element had failed. Failure was indicated by a cracking of the element and a consequent failure to expand. The results of the tests are indicated in Table III as the average number of expansions before rupture.

(Revision)

This description of the general construction and action of the element in performing its service will provide a better understanding of the application of the element to use in the industrial instrument.

Requirements of the Elements.

In proceeding to a consideration of the requirements that the particular use of these elements makes necessary, certain types of elements may be eliminated. These elements are to be used in precision instruments, and their exactness of use and application sets up immediately very rigid requirements which must be met. Since these instruments using pressure elements are nearly always self-actuated, a more important requirement would be for the element to produce sufficient torque and deflection to operate the mechanism of the instrument without the use of outside power.

Example 10. *Forward Reference as a Means of Transition*

(Original)

Now that the importance of current magnitude and timing control are evident, the means by which the ignitron controls these factors will be considered. This will necessitate first an understanding of what the ignitron is and how it works.

WHAT THE IGNITRON IS

Essential Form.

A schematic drawing of an ignitron is shown in Figure 2.

NOTE: Here the use of a very common stock form of forward reference as a means of transition leaves the following text wholly dependent on the headings to suggest the relation of component parts. The text of the paragraph, which is largely introductory rather than conclusive, belongs between the main heading and the secondary heading, where introductory text is evidently needed. A slight change in the headings is suggested in the revision.

(Revision)

THE IGNITRON

Now that the importance of current magnitude and timing control is evident, the means by which the ignitron controls these factors will be considered. This will necessitate first an understanding of what the ignitron is and how it works.

What the Ignitron Is.

The ignitron is a new form of electronic device. Although the commercial ignitron assumes a variety of forms, depending upon its size and service, all these forms are essentially the same from a functional viewpoint.

Essential Form: A schematic drawing of an ignitron is shown in Figure 2.

PART IV

SUMMARY OF BASIC PRINCIPLES OF REPORT WRITING

The basic principles involved in the writing of technical and scientific reports have been discussed in this book at length and illustrated in considerable detail. A brief summary of this detailed material may be found useful for ready reference and occasional review. Used faithfully whenever the student has occasion to write a report, this summary should serve to make the principles and procedures the book has presented so familiar that their use will come to be followed habitually.

Summary of Basic Principles

A report is an important document for those who must use it. It is fundamentally the communication of information or counsel which is desired and which will be used by a specified person for a particular end. Its success will depend on how intelligently it is planned to meet all the conditions it is to serve. It must economize the reader's attention and must make it possible for him to get the essential ideas easily and without confusion.

A report should satisfy the following requirements:

1. It should present all such material, but only such material as is pertinent to the subject.

2. It should present the subject matter according to a preconceived plan, based on a logical analysis and classification of the pertinent material.

3. It should make this plan so evident that it can be easily understood and save the reader confusion.

4. It should be written in a simple, concise style that permits no possibility of misinterpretation.

5. It should be intelligible to all who are likely to read it, even though they may not be specially versed in its technical detail.

FUNCTIONS OF THE PARTS OF A REPORT

The functions of the various parts of a report have become quite generally standardized.

The Title Page.

The title page gives the reader his first contact with the report. It indicates the subject matter and, as far as possible, the character of the report. It consists of an effective display of the title, the name of the writer, the name of the person, or persons, the organization, or department, for which the report is made, the date, and any other information as may be required for reference or for filing (pages 142–145).

In reports of more than a half-dozen pages, such a title page is almost indispensable. It is not usual in short-form reports unless they are of sufficient length and importance to be enclosed in a formal folder. In that case the title page can be used to relieve the first page of text of certain details (pages 218 to 223).

Synopsis or Abstract.

The synopsis gives a statement of the substance of the entire report in a highly condensed form (page 145). It makes clear the purpose of the report and the general character of the conclusions or recommendations made (page 149). It is limited, if possible, to a single paragraph, usually displayed on a page preceding the first page of text (pages 166, 167).

In formal reports of any considerable length, a synopsis is indispensable. In short-form reports, however, it is generally not required. In certain types of factual or statistical reports, it is difficult to use because it tends to become too heavy and too detailed.

Table of Contents.

The table of contents gives the reader, at a glance, the design of the report and its structural pattern in detail (page 145). It is so set up as to make clear the relation of the main and subordinate units. These units should be phrased exactly as the corresponding headings in the text are.

The table of contents is usually omitted in reports of standard form, such as text reports or progress reports, and in reports so simple as to require no such detailed layout. Short-form reports seldom need such a table.

Introduction.

The introduction gives the reader his first contact with the subject and prepares him to receive what the writer has to tell (pages 35 to 36). It does three things: (*a*) it states the subject of the report; (*b*) it indicates the purpose for which the report is written; and (*c*) it announces the plan of treatment (page 36). Because the character of the subject matter and the capacity and experience of readers vary, all three of these simple functions take many varied forms (pages 36 to 41).

Preliminary Section.

A preliminary section is a special device for relieving the introduction of preliminary material in case such material requires a fuller statement in order to be treated adequately in the introduction itself, where it logically belongs.

A statement of results would seem to be an integral part of any introduction that purports to be complete. The person most interested in the report will want to know as soon as possible the results of the investigation (page 52). If, however, this information cannot be stated briefly, it is best presented in a preliminary section, which will appear as the first main section of the report (pages 53 to 55).

The preliminary section in such a report gives the required fuller development of (*a*) the results or findings, (*b*) the conclusions reached, and (*c*) the recommendations. It does not, however, necessarily rob the terminal section of its important function (page 55).

Body.

The body of the report should fulfill all promises made in the introduction. It contains, in as condensed a form as possible, a statement of the character of the investigation, the equipment used, the procedure followed, the detailed results obtained, an analysis of these results leading to such conclusions as seem warranted, and such recommendations as logically follow from these conclusions.

Such charts, tables, diagrams, and drawings as are required to make the subject matter clear may supplement the text as desired.

When the amount of statistical data is so great that it tends to make the body of the report cumbersome, supporting information is frequently placed in the appendix, where it can be referred to in the main text.

Throughout the body of the report, the reader should be kept aware of the structural pattern on which he can rely to direct him through the discussion. The two most obvious means by which this pattern is made apparent are the use of sectional headings and a consistent paragraph system.

a. Sectional headings indicate the relation of main and subordinate units of the plan. They should agree perfectly with the table of contents (pages 86 to 94).
b. The paragraphs, both those representing the units of the plan and those purely functional—topic, concluding, and transitional—serve to provide a coherent text (pages 64 to 103).

Terminal Section.

The terminal section may take various forms and be denominated by a variety of terms (pages 104 to 110). It lifts the essential points out of the mass of detail and displays them as the things to be remembered. It indicates that the task has been completed according to the preconceived plan.

Although this section develops no new material, it is an organic part without which the report would be incomplete. It reinforces the conclusions drawn and the recommendations made, and it indicates that the goal announced in the introduction has been reached.

The terminal section is the final checkup which makes sure that the essential ideas and the purpose in presenting them are understood by the reader.

Appendix.

An appendix relieves the body of the report from congestion. It presents pertinent data that are too detailed to be given in the text and displays supporting data, computations, tables, graphs, and other material which the reader may wish to use in confirming the soundness of the report (pages 51, 142). A system of numbering makes this additional material easily accessible when reference is made to it in the main text.

The appendix is usually unnecessary in a short report, but it is an indispensable part of one that is bulky or involves the use of considerable statistical information.

Bibliography.

A bibliography is added when the report is based on material from the literature on the subject treated or when it is assumed that the reader will wish to supplement the report by further reading.

Letter of Transmittal.

For formal reports, a letter of transmittal is often required to detail circumstances of authorization or execution or to make the delivery of the report official. This letter precedes the title page.

PROCEDURE TO BE FOLLOWED
IN WRITING A REPORT

In the preparation of a report, a writer must, in one way or another proceed through four distinct stages.

Stage I. A period of preliminary study (page 8).
Stage II. A period of careful planning (page 9).
Stage III. A period of rapid composition (pages 9 to 10).
Stage IV. A period of criticism and revision (page 10).

To any writer, experienced or inexperienced, such a procedure is indispensable. If he follows it, not slighting any one of the periods nor confusing any two of them, his reports will give evidence of intelligent planning and will do what is expected of them. The following directions may be found helpful.

Stage I. A Period of Study.

Master the material for your report; determine its possibilities and limitations; decide what can be done with it (page 8).

1. Collect all pertinent material.
2. Check details.

   a. Determine the relative value of details.
   b. Eliminate those obviously irrelevant.
   c. Add details that are lacking.

3. Consider the purpose of your report (page 9).

   a. Who will read it?
   b. Why does he want it?
   c. What does he require of it?
   d. How will he use it?

4. Draft a thesis sentence (pages 12 to 14). This sentence should state your main objectives, the most important point of emphasis of your report. It is your working sketch, your lead sentence. It tests your grasp of your subject as a whole, keeps you at all times aware of the structural plan you purport to follow, and prevents your including extraneous material or exceeding the limits of your subject.

The thesis sentence will rarely appear in your text. It is merely a working device.

Stage II. A Period for Planning.

Arrange the assembled material in a structural plan that will support your thesis sentence (pages 14 to 18).

1. List, preferably on cards, the topics you propose to cover.
2. Test these topics by means of your thesis sentence, with special reference to the purpose and limits of the report.

3. Arrange the topics under their main groupings. These groupings will provide the subject matter for the major sections of your finished report.

4. Organize the material within each of these groups in a logical order, possibly in second- and third-order groupings.

5. Arrange these major organized sections in a logical sequence.

6. Make a working outline for the body of your report.

7. Lay out from the working outline the main and subordinate headings for your finished report.

Stage III. A Period for Writing.

Write rapidly as much as possible at one sitting. Aim to get the whole story told, to reach the end; do not be concerned, for the time, being, about defects of phrasing and crudities of expression (pages 9 and 10).

(Note that the logical order of composition given below bears no relation to the order of parts in the report as finally assembled.)

1. Introduction (pages 35 to 63).

    a. State the subject; stress its value, or other important features, to arouse interest.

    b. Indicate the purpose of the report.

    c. Summarize briefly the results, the conclusions, the recommendations.

    d. Announce the plan of the report.

If the introduction becomes longer than a page or two, you should transfer the summary to the preliminary section—the first main section following the introduction (pages 53 to 56).

These are some special problems you will meet in preparing your introduction: How much of an analysis of the situation with which the report deals do you need (page 50)? How fully should you elaborate the requirements of design (page 51)? How extensively should you review the basic theory (page 52)? How much in detail should you announce your plan (page 52)? Should you include results and recommendations (pages 52 to 53)?

2. Body (pages 111 to 114).

    a. Describe the equipment you used.

    b. Tell what procedures you followed.

    c. Give the detailed results.

    d. Analyze these results.

Follow the outline of headings you have prepared in Stage II. If this outline does not work, revise it, make a new outline, and start over, but do not muddle through by changing the plan as the writing progresses.

3. Terminal Section (pages 104 to 110).

    a. Summarize the discussion.

    b. Draw conclusions as appear warranted.

    c. Make recommendations based on your discussion and conclusions.

    d. Close with emphasis on the final impression you desire to leave with your reader.

If you have made the summary of results or conclusions in the introduction or in a preliminary section, you may omit it from the terminal section, or you may restate it more fully in the light of the subsequent discussion.

4. Synopsis or Abstract (pages 115 to 117).

    a. Condense the entire report into a substantial paragraph or two.

    b. Make sure that the conception of the whole proposition is still clear and agrees with your thesis sentence.

5. Prepare the Table of Contents (pages 117 to 118).

    a. Copy the main and subordinate headings from the entire report.

    b. Check for inconsistencies in the structural design.

    c. List tables, figures, and other illustrative material.

    d. Indicate the paging and check on its accuracy.

6. Appendix and Bibliography.

    a. Material for these two parts of the report should be accumulated during the period of organization and writing.

        (1) Pertinent material too bulky or too detailed to be used in the text should be laid aside for the appendix.

        (2) Bibliographical references used as a source of material or which furnish supplementary or supporting data should be noted.

    b. The final assembling, checking, and arranging of both appendix and bibliography may be made when the rough draft is completed or after the text is in its final form.

Stage IV. A Period for Criticism and Revision.

When you have completed the rough draft, lay it aside for a day or so, if possible, until you can criticize it objectively as though it were the work of another (pages 233 to 236).

1. Make a general examination of the report as a whole (page 234).

    a. Check the balance and proportion of parts.
    b. Verify the soundness of the structural pattern.
    c. Discover any obvious cause of possible confusion.

2. Consider the title, table of contents, introduction and synopsis in relation to each other (page 235, Number 1).

    a. Make sure these parts are in agreement.
    b. Study the introduction carefully; determine whether you have stated the subject, purpose, and plan clearly.

3. Analyze the terminal section (page 235, Number 2).

    a. Check its agreement with the introduction.
    b. Discover any evidence that you have confused objectives or limits of the project.
    c. Consider whether you have reenforced the proper points of emphasis.

4. Check the system of headings (page 235, Number 3).

    a. Have you used headings consistently?
    b. Do they agree with the table of contents and with the plan outlined in the introduction?

5. Examine the text.

    a. Have you marked clearly the transitions from one topic to another?
    b. Are paragraphs too long? Too short?
    c. Is there coherence within the paragraph system?
    d. Is the sentence structure clear and grammatical?
    e. Is the choice of words, and their order, effective?

6. Finally, consider whether the report as a whole accomplishes what it is expected to do.

a. Does it fulfill the requirements of a report as defined on pages 3 to 5?

b. Does it accomplish the purpose of the report as emphasized on page 6?

Read your text aloud. Listen for repetition in sentences, words, or phrases. Watch for sentences that are either too short and abrupt or too long and complicated. Consider if your text reads easily and smoothly.

If possible, before preparing the final draft, submit the report to a person qualified to give constructive criticism.

Check the final draft for typographical errors.

PART V

MANUAL FOR CLASS USE

The course outlined consists of 30 class periods of one hour each, to be held twice a week for 15 weeks. This approximates a semester university course. If additional time is available, it can always be used to advantage, and, if less time, the assignments may be adjusted to local conditions. The course wastes no time on details of form. It deals primarily with basic principles and procedures involved in the writing and criticizing of technical reports. These fundamentals are covered briefly in the first six periods, to be followed by practice in writing reports which are to be criticized by the instructor and revised after consultation with him over personal difficulties.

For convenience of both instructor and student, the manual has been presented in two parts: the first distinctly for the instructor, the second the schedule of assignments with such illustrative material as would seem useful to the student.

For the Instructor

Each instructor should consider carefully the special needs of his class as a whole and the time available for the course and should either simplify or amplify the syllabus outlined to meet those needs. Individual difficulties, he will find, are best dealt with in personal conferences. Such conferences should be an integral part of his program of instruction; they are indispensable.

PERIOD I. INTRODUCTION TO THE COURSE.

Before meeting your class have well in mind Chapters IV and V. Open your introductory talk by reading to the class the last paragraph, page 23, and the first paragraph, page 36. In your own words point out that any introductory talk like this should make clear the character and limits of the subject matter to be covered in the course, the objective you have in mind—what you hope to accomplish for your students—and, finally, quite definitely, the plan you intend to follow in the course. In this way, you will be answering the three questions that lie more or less consciously in the mind of every student: What will the course cover in the semester? What will it accomplish for me? What plan will the instructor follow?

Then read the last paragraph, page 23, and the first paragraph, page 36. Here are three important principles which apply to introductions in general. Note that they are quite fully treated in Chapters IV and V, which you recommend them to read.

Consistent with these important principles as applied to introductions, you are going to answer their three questions which are consciously, or subconsciously, in their minds. You will tell them your plans for the 16 weeks you will be working together and what you hope to accomplish. This should assure the cooperation which is indispensable for the success of the course.

1. *The Purpose of the Course.* Preface, pages vii and viii.

> *a.* To inspire a keener and more intelligent interest in report writing.
>
> *b.* To give greater assurance, based on a better understanding of the mental processes and the practical procedures involved in producing a well-organized report.
>
> *c.* To stimulate intelligent self-criticism.

2. *The General Plan.* Preface, page viii.

   a. The development of a few indispensable, fundamental principles.
   b. The illustration of these principles.
   c. The demonstration of how to apply these principles; specifically, the demonstration of a simple procedure for preparing a report.
   d. The formulation of a program of critical procedure which the student may apply to his own work.

3. *The Detailed Plan.*

   a. The first six periods will be devoted to an examination and discussion of the text with a view to discovering the fundamental principles and procedures involved in the preparation of a report. This survey will make available at once the basic material that will be applicable to the preparation of the reports to be written in the course.
   b. The course will include the preparation of two reports. The first will be produced by slow stages synchronized with study of the basic text. Later the second report will be written rapidly and under the pressure usual in practice. The choice of a project for the first report will need to be made by each student during the first three weeks, while he is getting the over-all view of the basic theory of report writing.
   c. The two assigned reports will be criticized by the instructor and revised by the student.
   d. Consultation periods will be arranged for each member of the class. These consultation periods will give opportunity for discussing and correcting individual difficulties.

4. *Assignment.* Get acquainted with this text—its author, his background and experience with reports, his point of view. What qualifies him to generalize as he has on the writing of technical reports?

PERIOD II. TWO IMPORTANT DEFINITIONS; FINDING A USABLE SUBJECT.

1. *Two Important Definitions.* Read to the class: Preface, page vii, lines 9 to 15. Acknowledgments, page x, lines 14 to 19. Synopsis, page xiii.

Discuss the characteristics of a report which these passages suggest. How does a report differ from any other form of exposition (see Chapter I, pages 5 and 6)?

2. *Finding a Usable Subject.* Base your talk on the text, pages 315 to 322. Illustrate fully from your own experience.

3. *Assignment.* Read Chapters II to IV. Written Assignment I is due at the next period (see pages 315 to 322).

PERIOD III. PROCEDURES IN THE DEVELOPMENT OF A REPORT.

1. Review the definition of a report; its fundamental characteristics. Emphasize the importance of having a clear understanding of the unifying purpose of the report, and all the requirements for use which it must satisfy, before trying to write.

2. *Procedures in the Development of a Report.*

 a. The four periods in the development of a report, Chapter II.
 b. Two tests of progress in the preliminary study of one's material: the thesis sentence and the outline plan, Chapter III.
 c. Three ways to help the reader: the introduction, pages 23 to 24; order in the presentation of the body of the report, pages 24 to 27; a terminal section, page 27.
 d. Two final tests of performance: synopsis, or abstract, pages 115 to 118; a table of contents, pages 118 to 121, Chapter XV.

3. *Assignment.* Pages 320 to 322 due at Period VII. Read for the next period, Chapters V, VI, and XIII. Primary Functions of the Introduction, and the Terminal Section.

PERIOD IV. THE INTRODUCTION AND CONCLUSION.

1. Recall the three ways by which the reader may be kept aware of the precise subject, the necessary limitations, and underlying purpose of the report and of the plan for presentation. Two of these aids to the reader will be discussed—the Introduction and the Conclusion.

2. *The Introduction.*

 a. The primary functions of the introduction, Chapter V (note especially pages 28 to 29, and page 35, lines 15 to 18).

 (1) To make clear the precise subject.
 (2) To indicate the writer's purpose, his attitude or intent with reference to the subject.
 (3) To outline the proposed plan of presentation.

b. Variations of these three functions in both expository papers and in reports (pages 36 to 41).

c. The important first focus of attention, Chapter VI.

d. Some special problems in introductions to reports, Chapter VII. How much of an analysis of the situation or project is needed (pages 50 to 51)?

3. *The Terminal Section.*

a. The primary functions of the terminal section, Chapter XIII.

b. Requirements for a terminal section, pages 104 to 105.

c. Classification of objective, pages 106 to 110.

4. *Assignment.* Read for next period Chapters VIII to X.

PERIOD V. THE PARAGRAPH AS EVIDENCE OF DESIGN.

1. Recall briefly the two ways, already discussed, for keeping the reader aware of the subject, the purpose, and the plan for the report.

2. *The Paragraph as Evidence of Design.*

a. Why do we have paragraphs? How would you like to read a report of 50 pages—a highly technical report, for example —if it were cast in a solid piece, a text without any paragraph indentations? Even if you could perform such a feat without letting your attention wander, how would you feel at the end of such a task? What does this suggest as to the psychology of the paragraph (Chapter VIII, pages 64 to 70)?

b. What determines the length of the paragraph? Of what use are the indentations in the text (Chapter VIII, page 65)?

c. How are the paragraphs related to the outline plan (Chapter IX)?

d. What means have been developed in practice for keeping the paragraph system coherent and indicating the relation of part to part as one progresses through the text (Chapter X)?

3. Demonstrate on the blackboard the graphs on page 73.

4. *Assignment.* Study carefully Chapters XI and XII.

PERIOD VI. SECTIONAL HEADINGS AS EVIDENCE OF DESIGN.

1. Recall briefly the discussion of the paragraph as evidence of design. Stress the importance of the paragraph system in facilitating communication between writer and reader.

2. *Sectional Headings as Evidence of Design.*

    a. Explain how sectional headings assist the paragraph system (pages 86 and 87).

    b. Demonstrate how the system of headings represents the structural plan of the report and indicates the relation of main and subordinate units of the plan.

    c. Study the illustrative examples (pages 87 to 94). If possible, substitute reports written at your institution, or of special interest, to the class. Develop on the blackboard the outline of headings of one such report.

3. *Special Paragraphs as Evidence of Design.*

    a. Explain the use of topic, concluding, and transitional paragraphs (pages 95 to 97).

    b. Discuss theory: use charts (pages 95 to 97).

    c. Study examples (pages 98 to 103).

    d. Refer to Annotated Reports (pages 162 to 187), or better, to local examples.

4. *Assignment.* Study the Annotated Reports on pages 188 to 230. Select the subject for the report you will write; this selection should be made before Period VII, one week from today. This report must be on a subject which is not too confidential to be discussed in class. It should be one that can be treated adequately in a report not much longer than 10 to 15 typed pages. Suggest that you will be in your office and glad to consult with any who have difficulty in finding a suitable subject.

PERIOD VII. DRAFTING THE THESIS SENTENCE.

1. *Selection of Project.* Recall that the class is now to apply the theories discussed to the preparation of their reports. This will be done, as was explained, by slow stages, with critical comment at each stage. Discuss the projects on which the class plan to write. The following questions may disclose whether the subject is wisely chosen or whether it should be abandoned and another selected.

    a. Is the subject of such a confidential nature that it could not be discussed freely in class?

    b. Is sufficient material for proper development of the subject^ʳ readily obtainable?

    c. Can the subject be treated completely and adequately in a report not much longer than 10 or 15 typed pages? (Reports longer than this are difficult to discuss in class and throw too heavy a load on the instructor.)

    d. Has the student a definite purpose in mind in writing the report? For whom is it to be written? How will it be used? What will be accomplished by writing it?

Arrange for consultation with any who have difficulty in selecting a topic.

2. *Preparation of a Bibliography.* Suggest the use of a card system for references accumulated during the progress of study.

In some cases it may be advisable to devote an entire period or more to detailed instructions on the preparation of a bibliography and on the use of libraries and of library indices.

Review Chapters II and III. Emphasize that the thesis sentence is a useful means of determining how clearly and simply one sees his subject as a whole. Examine, with the class, examples of the thesis sentence on pages 19 to 22.

3. *Assignment.* For next period, prepare a thesis sentence for your first long report.

Period VIII. Making the Plan.

1. *The Thesis Sentence.* Collect the thesis sentences prepared by the class; discuss any difficulties the students have had in preparing their sentences; clear up any points that are not well understood. Explain that you will return the thesis sentences at the next period after you have had opportunity to examine them.

2. *The Outline Plan.* The outline plan is a test of the writer's mastery of the details of his material and of his discovery of a plan of presentation. Emphasize the need for careful planning (page 9).

Demonstrate the use of a card system for analyzing material and getting it in order (pages 15 to 18). Use an actual example. Stress the fact that the ease with which cards can be manipulated makes their use preferable to the use of sheets of paper, since these tend to freeze the analysis prematurely.

3. *Assignment.* For next period, prepare a plan for your first long report. This plan will, of course, be subject to revision as the details of the report are worked out. See pages 15 to 18.

NOTE TO INSTRUCTOR: In preparation for the next period, the instructor should study the thesis sentences carefully and mark them for correction. Certain representative thesis sentences should be selected for discussion, some which illustrate good points and some which show defects to be avoided. These may, to an advantage, be mimeographed and distributed to the class. The instructor should be prepared to summarize the good and bad points discovered during this examination of the work of the class.

PERIOD IX. WAYS TO HELP THE READER.

1. *The Thesis Sentence.* This sentence is a test of progress in the study of subject material. It is a formulation of the writer's conception of his subject and usually also suggests the purpose he has in mind. It is concrete evidence of how clearly and simply the writer sees his subject. Sometimes it indicates, also, in a general way, the points to be included in the report.

Be sure the class understands that this sentence is purely a working device and is not likely to appear in the completed text of the report (pages 12 to 13).

Discuss and criticize several thesis sentences selected from those written by members. Put the sentences to be studied on the blackboard, project them on a screen, or, best of all, mimeograph them for distribution. Ask the following questions in each case: Does the sentence give a sharply defined idea of the subject of the proposed report? Does it suggest the limits, the scale and scope of treatment? Does it indicate the writer's objective?

Return the thesis sentences. They are to be revised in light of the discussion and returned at next period.

2. *Three Ways to Help the Reader.* Emphasize the obligation of the writer to help the reader get the facts easily and without confusion (page 23, second paragraph).

> *a.* The *introduction* as a preliminary view of the subject matter, of the writer's purpose, and of his proposed method of presentation.
> *b.* The explicit *pattern* of the report, with emphasis on the component units and their relation to each other.
> *c.* The *terminal summary* with emphasis on the results of the discussion.

Study, with the class, the graphical analysis made on pages 25 to 26. Direct attention to the reports on pages 162 to 217, and suggest study of the report on pages 188 to 217, with special reference to the three ways for helping the reader.

3. Collect the outline plans for Report 1. These will be criticized and returned one week from today. Arrange for personal consultation with any who are having difficulties they wish to discuss with you.

4. *Assignment.* Read carefully Chapters V and VI in preparation for the discussion at the next period. Review Chapter IV and examine the introductions to reports on pages 57 to 63.

PERIOD X. FUNCTIONS OF THE INTRODUCTION.

1. *Three Primary Functions of the Introduction,* Chapter V.

    a. Comment on subject (pages 35 to 38).
        (1) In popular exposition:
            (*a*) Emphasis on value to reader.
            (*b*) Definition of terms.
            (*c*) Relation to cognate subjects.
        (2) In reports:
            (*a*) Comment on scope of treatment.
            (*b*) Limits of investigation or contents.
    b. Comment on motive (pages 35 to 40).
        (1) Use by a specific reader or class of readers.
        (2) Point of view.
    c. Announcement of plan (pages 40 to 41).
        (1) Detailed statement.
        (2) General lines of treatment.

Analyze briefly the introductory functions of the four reports on pages 164 to 226 and discuss the way the three functions are exemplified.

2. *First Focus of Attention.* Discuss Chapter VI, noting the following points of importance:

    a. Need for directness in establishing contact between the reader and the subject (page 42, lines 8 to 20).
    b. Importance of initial sentences (pages 42 to 43).
    c. The immediate answer to the question in the reader's mind (page 44, second paragraph).

Study the introduction to the report on pages 45 to 46.

3. *Assignment.* Prepare an informal statement of what you consider should be the content and the functions of the introduction to your report (pages 336 to 337). These statements will be written but not handed in. Reread Chapter VII in preparation for discussion at the next period. See pages 50 to 63.

PERIOD XI. SPECIAL PROBLEMS IN INTRODUCTIONS.

1. *Outline Plans.* Emphasize that these plans are not to be regarded as final. They should be thoroughly tested as designs for a structure to be built with the materials available. It will save much rewriting and revision later if the design is such that it cannot be torn down. Defects in the structural pattern can be more easily detected in this schematic setup than in the developed text. Time spent in perfecting the plan will be saved later on.

Discuss selected outline plans chosen from those handed in by members of the class at Period IX. Stimulate general discussion and develop a spirit of cooperation by encouraging constructive criticism from members of the group. Discussion may be encouraged by having the outline written on the blackboard or projected on a screen. Refer also to outlines on pages 19 to 22.

Return outlines to the class for correction and revision.

2. *Special Problems of Introduction* (Chapter VII).

a. How much of an analysis of the situation or problem to be treated is required (page 50)?

b. How fully should the requirements for a design be given (page 51)?
How should they be presented if they are in the form of detailed specifications (page 51)?

c. How much needs to be said of the proposed method of treatment (page 52)?

d. How fully should the results be stated in the introduction? How is such an inclusion of results in the introduction related to the terminal section (pages 52 and 53)?

e. How can some of these elements be elaborated at length without apparently throwing the introduction out of balance (pages 53 to 56)?

Study, with the class, some of the examples of introductions illustrating these problems (pages 57 to 63). Suggest that they study the rest of these examples before they draft their own introductions.

3. *Assignment.* A first draft of the introduction to your report will be due at the next period. This introduction is apt to be quite tenta-

tive; final decision regarding the limits of the subject, special features, definitions, and other preliminary information frequently cannot be made until the rough draft of the body of the report is written. See pages 38 to 41.

Read Chapter VIII in preparation for discussion at the next period.

PERIOD XII. THE PARAGRAPH AS EVIDENCE OF DESIGN.

1. *The Importance of the Paragraph.*

  a. Why do we need paragraphs (pages 64 to 65)?
  b. What determines the length of a paragraph (pages 65 to 66)?
  c. How can a writer use the paragraph to mark the beginning and ending of paragraph units?

2. *The Psychology of the Paragraph.*

  a. There is a limit to the period of concentrated attention (pages 66 to 70) natural to each reader.
  b. This differs with the character of the reader.
  c. It differs also with the character of the subject matter.
  d. To meet these psychological conditions, the skillful writer will plan to present his subject matter in units not too taxing for his reader. He will provide pauses where he and the reader stop to recover from the strain of concentrated attention.
  e. The attention of the reader must be caught and focused sharply as soon as possible on each component unit. This is done by the topic sentence which provides initial emphasis.
  f. Each unit must contain a coherent, logical sequence of ideas permitting no break in the current of thought.
  g. Often a final emphasis on the topic is used to mark the end of the paragraph unit.

3. The definition of the paragraph (page 70). Read the concluding paragraph, page 70.

4. Collect the first drafts of the introductions due this period. They will be discussed and returned at the next period.

5. *Assignment.* Read Chapter IX and be prepared to discuss it at the next period.

PERIOD XIII. RELATION OF THE PARAGRAPH TO THE PLAN.

1. Discuss the drafts of introductions due at this period.

 a. Have the points of importance discussed in Period X been satisfactorily covered?

 b. Have all of the special problems discussed in Period XI been met and adequately handled?

Return drafts for revision; answer questions regarding corrections; summarize good points and faults that you have noted.

2. *Relation of Paragraph to Plan*, Chapter IX. A paragraph is an attempt to adjust the amount of material delivered to the limits of the reader's attention; the relation of the paragraph to the plan depends on the scale on which the plan is to be developed.

Demonstrate the progressive effect of increasing the scale of development of the plan on page 73. Stress the importance of a forecast as to the approximate scale on which a plan is to be developed. Emphasize the advantage of making a tentative apportionment of the material to the paragraph units in advance of actual writing. The writer learns in this way to use paragraphs effectively as an evidence of a preconceived plan; he also establishes the habit of previsioning the scale of development.

Study the notation on the outline plan, page 73. Study the distribution of subject matter to the paragraph units in the report, pages 189 to 217. Annotate the Table of Contents on the board with suggestions from the class; for example: Introduction (4 paragraphs), Procedure (5 paragraphs, 1 of introduction), Legal Aspects (7 paragraphs).

3. *Assignment.* Consider the scale on which the outline of your report will be developed (10 pages, or 15 to 20). Then make a tentative scheme for paragraphing, as illustrated on page 76. See pages 304 to 305 (not written).

Study Chapter X for discussion at the next period.

PERIOD XIV. TRANSITIONAL DEVICES.

1. *Coherence within the Paragraph System*, Chapter X. Summarize, with the help of the class, the transitional means listed in the chapter, writing on the blackboard as the points are made.

 a. Initial topic sentence.

 b. Initial topic sentence, plus final emphasis in the concluding sentence.

 c. Transition words or phrases in the topic sentence.

 d. Transition phrases, clauses, or sentences preceding the topic sentence.

 e. Transition words, phrases, or clauses in the final sentence of the paragraph with reference to the following paragraph.

 f. Transition paragraphs.

Review the illustrative examples, pages 24 to 27, and the article on pages 28 to 34. Study some of the examples on pages 81 to 83.

 2. *Assignment.* Study the remaining examples on pages 268 to 276. Read Chapter XI and bring in a sketch of the headings for your reports for discussion at the next period.

PERIOD XV. SECTIONAL HEADINGS.

 1. *Headings as Evidence of Design*, Chapter XI. Go over the introductory text of the chapter carefully. Emphasize the following points.

  a. The sectional headings are supplementary to the orderly, coherent paragraph scheme with its usual means of marking the component units distinctly (page 87, first paragraph).

  b. The system suggested on pages 87 to 88 has three qualifications to recommend it.

   (1) It represents the structural plan of the report.

   (2) It indicates the relation of main and subordinate units in that plan.

   (3) It is flexible enough to allow a sensible use.

Examine with the class the examples on pages 88 to 94.

 2. *Criticism of Headings.* Examine critically and discuss as many of the sketched headings the class has brought in as possible. Have the headings put on the blackboard, or projected on a screen, and get class to discuss how adequately they mark, and show relationship of, the units of the report.

 3. *Assignment.* Read Chapter XII and be prepared to discuss it. Decide on subject of your second report, on which work will begin in three weeks.

PERIOD XVI. SPECIAL PARAGRAPHS.

 1. *Special Types of Paragraph*, Chapter XII. Emphasize the importance of these three pages of text and discuss them thoroughly. Study

carefully with the class the illustrative material on pages 98 to 103. Supplement this material with examples from other professional reports you may have available, using, if possible, not only good examples, but also reports which you can show would be improved by the use of special paragraphs.

2. *Use of Manual and Card.* Explain "Summary of Basic Principles" and the reminder card. Show that, although there has been discussion of some topics that are listed under "Step IV—Criticize," this has been done to ensure sound planning; that, in the main, progress has been made by slow stages through "Step I—Study" and most of "Step II—Plan," and that the class will soon be engaged in "Step III—Write."

Suggest that frequent reference to the reminder card, and rereading of the references listed in the manual for each step, will keep one conscious of the pattern to be followed and will impress the basic principles more firmly on his memory.

3. *Assignment.* Study Chapter XIII carefully. Come prepared to discuss any questions you may have about the content, the functions, and the importance of the Terminal Section. Read also Chapter XIV.

PERIOD XVII. THE TERMINAL SECTION.

1. *Functions and Content of the Terminal Section*, Chapter XIII. Cover pages 104 to 106 thoroughly, especially the second paragraph, page 104. Summarize, with the help of the class, the requirements for an effective terminal section, as follows:

a. It must add definitely to the value of the report.
b. It should develop no new material but should only reinforce the conclusions or recommendations already made evident.
c. It must give the effect of a completed performance.
d. It should agree on all vital points with the introduction.

Study with the class the classification of objectives, pages 106 to 107, and the illustrative examples, pages 107 to 110. If possible, add examples from local reports. If there is time, examine the terminal sections on pages 187, 215, 219, and 226. Read, first, the introduction of the report and then the terminal section; consider how well they agree and balance one with the other.

2. *The Rough Draft*, Chapter XIV. Discuss briefly those high lights of the chapter which apply to the class. Stress the advisability of

rapid writing, which should now be possible because of the careful planning. Urge the class to avoid interrupting the writing process for critical examination of their work.

3. *Assignment.* Write the rough draft of the second report. The class, if they have not already done so, should read Chapter XV before writing the draft.

PERIOD XVIII. THE ROUGH DRAFT; TWO TESTS OF PERFORMANCE.

1. Review the important points of Chapter XIV; emphasize especially the last two paragraphs.

2. Criticize the rough drafts due at this period. Call for free discussion of problems encountered in the preparation of the rough draft. Have two or three rough drafts read and criticized as to coherence and logical progress from topic to topic. At this stage, errors of grammar or details of diction need not be considered. Be sure that each member who has had difficulty has an opportunity to report and discuss it; get a solution from the class, if possible. Arrange for private consultation with any who desire it.

These consultations afford an important opportunity to give help where it is needed. It may be advisable to devote another period to a continuation of the discussion if the class seems to need it.

3. *Two Tests of Performance*, Chapter XV. Discuss the synopsis as a test of the writer's grasp of the subject as a whole. Examine some of the synopses on pages 119 to 121 and those prefacing the illustrative reports, pages 167 and following. The table of contents as a record of the design which the report finally took may represent radical changes in the original pattern. Use illustrative material.

4. *Assignment.* See pages 342 to 344. Apply the two tests of performance to your own report. Bring to the next period the title page, synopsis, and table of contents. The first report is due one week from today. At the next period be prepared to discuss questions concerned with final preparation of this report. Bring to class the rough draft, see pages 340 to 341. For details of form and style consult pages 135 to 161.

PERIOD XIX. STYLING THE REPORT.

1. *Discussion of Details.* Allow time for full discussion of all questions the class may ask regarding the details of their reports. Give as full directions as you think necessary regarding format. Refer to pages 135 to 161; call attention to any details there which differ from

practice; and outline such requirements as are set up by local conditions in the special field of your students. Suggest full use of the "Summary of Basic Principles" and of the reminder card.

2. *Assignment.* The completed reports are due at the next period. As many as possible should turn their reports in at that time, so that you may have a chance to study them carefully; but be sure that no one does a hasty, careless job. If some members require more time, have them set a date for completion.

Announce that a second report will now be started and will be due four weeks from this time. Ask the class, therefore, to bring to the next period the subject, thesis sentence, and outline plan for the second report.

NOTE TO INSTRUCTOR: If the regular work load of your students is such that the preparation of these heavy assignments seem impracticable, a longer time than usual should be allowed before the next class meeting is held.

PERIOD XX. THE FINISHED REPORT.

1. *Report 1 is due at this time.* These reports should be returned as soon as you have studied them. The class periods for the next month will be devoted largely to crticism of reports, as covered by Part III, by Step IV of the reminder card, and by the "Summary of Basic Principles."

2. Discuss the title, synopsis, and plan for the second report. Review as much of Periods II and VII as seems necessary. Call on several members of the class to read the titles of their report, explain their plan for presenting their subject matter, and read their thesis sentences; ask others for critical comment.

Emphasize the importance of the thesis sentence; have several written on the blackboard for criticism and general discussion.

3. *Assignment.* Remind the class that the finished second report will be due three weeks from today; schedule personal inerviews with those who wish to discuss this report with you. Plan to return the corrected plans for the second report as soon as possible, either in consultation hours or at the next class period.

Complete your examination of the finished reports as soon as possible. They should be ready to be returned not later than Period XXV; the sooner they are returned, the more helpful your suggestions for correction will be to the students in the preparation of their second reports. In the meantime you will be able to use, as illustrative material, points you discover during your study of the reports.

Refer to pages 45 to 49 for suggestions you may find helpful in marking the manuscripts. Periods XXII to XXIV of the course outline call for the application of the successive steps of the process of criticism to one of these reports. You should select this report carefully, so that it will be a satisfactory basis for discussion, illustrating both good and bad points. The discussion will be more profitable if the selected report is mimeographed or otherwise duplicated, so that each member of the class may have a copy for reference.

PERIOD XXI. PROGRAM OF CRITICAL PROCEDURE.

1. Comment on the six parts of Step IV on the reminder card and on the six parts of Stage IV in the "Summary of Basic Principles"; urge a study of the references to the text. Show how you will apply these principles to the criticism of the first reports submitted at the last meeting for your examination.

2. *Assignment.* The second report, now in preparation, is due two weeks from the next period. Be sure you have your outlines with the instructor's suggestions.

Study Clinic One with the illustrative examples, pages 237 to 253.

NOTE TO INSTRUCTOR: From now on you should fit your class discussions of reports as much as possible to the pattern set up in Stage IV of the "Summary of Basic Principles," so that this pattern becomes well fixed in the minds of the class members. For the discussion of one of the finished reports at the next period, you should be prepared with notes on various points of the report which do or do not bear up well under the critical examination called for in parts *a, b,* and *c* of Stage IV. See assignment for Period XX.

PERIOD XXII. CLINIC ONE—STUDIES OF INTRODUCTIONS.

1. *General Examination of a First Report.* Review Stage IV, part 1 in the "Summary of Basic Principles." Apply this procedure for general examination to one of the reports submitted for your criticism. Use the blackboard freely, project parts of the report on a screen, or use mimeographed copies. So far as possible, use material from class reports which you have studied. The class will be more keenly interested in your comments on their own reports than in a discussion of the reports in the text.

2. *Study of the Introduction.*

    a. Reduce the statement of the critical procedures given on pages 237 to 238 to the briefest possible form, as follows:

(1) Check the statement of subject, purpose, and plan.

(2) Study the initial emphasis of the opening sentence or of the first paragraph.

(3) If a preliminary section is used, consider if it is justified.

(4) Read the entire introduction aloud to see if it reads smoothly and coherently.

b. Discuss the clinical examples, pages 240 to 253, which cover the following cases:

(1) Subject not fully stated.

(2) Initial focus of attention misleading.

(3) Lack of coherence between sentences.

(4) Statement of purpose defective.

(5) Statement of plan too detailed or out of place.

Return first reports which you have corrected and which you no longer need for discussion. Urge careful study of the corrections and suggest consultation with you regarding points that are not clearly understood.

3. *Assignment.* Study pages 254 to 256 and read the examples on pages 257 to 264. Make notes of questions you wish to ask at the next period.

PERIOD XXIII. CLINIC TWO—STUDIES IN REORGANIZATION.

1. Examine the introduction and terminal section of the same first report studied at the last period. Refer to "Basic Principles," and review Step IV, parts 2 and 3.

2. Examine the system of headings in this same report, as suggested: pages 254 to 256.

a. Are both main and subordinate headings in alignment?

b. Does any section exhibit only one heading for a subordinate order?

c. Are more headings used than are needed?

d. Are the headings worded exactly as they are in the table of contents and in the introduction?

e. Is the plan set up in the table of contents and in the introduction represented exactly by the heading system?

f. Does the plan indicated by the headings need any revision?

g. Is there any evidence of unaccountable proportioning of unit sections?

3. Discuss examples on pages 257 to 264.

    a. Confusion of title with first main heading.
    b. Use of a superfluous heading.
    c. Unaccountable proportioning of parts.
    d. Lack of agreement as to plan.

4. Supplement the text material with cases taken from class reports. Return the first reports studied which you no longer need for discussion.

5. *Assignment.* Study pages 265 to 267 and examine the examples on pages 268 to 277. The second report will be due three periods from today.

PERIOD XXIV. CLINIC THREE—STUDIES IN COHERENCE.

1. Stress the importance of the first two paragraphs, pages 265 to 267, as justifying reports in which but little text is required.

2. *The Critical Procedure.*

    a. Study the introductory, transitional, and concluding text of all units, both main and subordinate, to see if these units are sufficiently marked as components of the whole.
    b. Study all transitional means employed to indicate the relation of component parts to each other and to the subject as a whole.
    c. Test: If the headings were entirely omitted, would the text be coherent and the relation of parts be clear?

3. *Defects Found by This Procedure in the Clinical Studies,* pages 268 to 277.

    a. Lack of introductory text at the begining of a section.
    b. Misplacing of the introductory text of a section.
    c. Labeling of the introductory text of a section as if it were one of the component units of the section.
    d. Omission of a needed, and logical, subordinate heading.
    e. Unnecessary elaboration of transitional text.
    f. Repetition of one transitional device until it becomes mechanical.

PERIOD XXV. CRITICISM OF FIRST REPORTS.

1. *Directions for Revision.* Emphasize the importance of careful revision. Urge the full use of all points of criticism you have noted.

All possible corrections should appear either on the blank page facing the page to which they refer, or on an inserted page facing the text. The exceptions are, of course, defects in punctuation, which should be marked in red ink in the text. The elimination of an incorrect paragraph indentation or the addition of an indentation should be indicated in the margin in red ink.

2. *Summary of Defects Noted.* Summarize the principal defects you have observed in the reports you have read, illustrating with examples from the reports. Encourage class discussion.

3. *Assignment.* The completed second report is due at the next period. Check carefully the corrections made in your first report and avoid making the same mistakes in this second report.

NOTE: If possible, the students might well be given an extra week for the completion of the second report. The week could be devoted to personal conferences scheduled for all students desiring to discuss either your criticism of their first reports or points of difficulty they may be having in the preparation of the second report.

PERIOD XXVI. STUDY OF SECOND REPORTS.

1. Criticize the second report. Have the class exchange reports and each prepare a written critique of the report he is to examine. This should be signed and handed in at the end of the hour.

2. The procedure outlined in "Basic Principles" as Stage IV should be followed.

   a. Examine title, synopsis, table of contents, and introduction. Are they in agreement as to subject, purpose, and plan?

   b. Read the terminal section. Is it in agreement with the introduction as to underlying objectives?

   c. Check the headings. Do they agree with the table of contents as to wording and with the introduction as to plan?

   d. Read the transitional text introducing main and subordinate units. Are they adequate? Are they varied enough to avoid appearing mechanical?

   e. Check format—margins, placing of illustrative material on page, footnotes, use of appendices, etc. Are they such as to give the greatest amount of help to the reader?

Circulate among the members of the class and direct their work. Discuss with individual students points that are disclosed as they study the reports assigned them. At the end of the period, have the reports returned to you, making sure that the notes for correction bear the name of the member who made the criticism.

PERIOD XXVII. THE ENGLISH OF THE REPORT.

1. Discuss Chapter XVII, "The English of the Report" emphasizing particularly the following points:

> *a.* The success or failure of a report depends largely on the thoroughness with which the preparatory processes have been performed.
> *b.* English is an important medium of communication that may be used, but it is not the only medium available.

Discuss the use of English as a medium for communicating ideas, using questions similar to the following: What is meant by the vague term "English"? What does a critic mean when he says, "Your English is poor"? Is the language you use in writing a report fundamentally different from that which you use in communicating your ideas orally? If you know your subject thoroughly and are anxious to make your listener understand it as you do, are you not able to give him a clear convincing oral account of it? Why do you find it more difficult to give the same account in writing?

Why do British engineers and scientists discourage the use of graphical means of demonstration in their reports and insist that the text alone should be sufficient? Why, on the other hand, do American engineers and scientists resort so largely to graphs, figures, and various ingenious devices of demonstration, at times almost completely eliminating text?

2. Summarize the discussion and draw the following conclusions:

> *a.* The handicap of a person who thinks he can't write is usually a fear that he will make mistakes or express himself badly. The way to remove this drag is to develop confidence through mastery of and enthusiasm for one's subject. If the writer concentrates on his subject and keeps in mind for whom he is writing, he should gain facility and assurance.
> *b.* If a person speaks simple English with normal facility, he should be able to use the same English naturally in writing.
> *c.* It is true, of course, that written style will reflect characteristic speech habits. If a person wishes, therefore, to improve

his writing, he should cultivate the speech befitting his profession, midway between pedantic discourse and loose shoptalk. The point at which to begin better writing is in the cultivation of better speech habits.

PERIOD XXVIII. CRITICISM OF SECOND REPORTS.

1. Discuss the second reports. Summarize the principal defects you have noted, using selected reports to illustrate the points. Conduct a discussion similar to the one held in Period XXV. Emphasize especially any violations noted of the principles discussed at the last period.

Return the second reports. Arrange for consultations.

2. *Assignment.* Give instructions for revision of the corrected reports and make arrangements for their return to you. The students are to bring their second reports to class at the next period. Ask them to make note of questions they would like to have answered and discussed.

PERIOD XXIX. DISCUSSION OF SECOND REPORTS.

1. This period should be devoted to the free class discussion of the second reports. Let the class lead by posing the questions they wish answered. At the close of the session summarize for them the results of this question-and-answer period.

2. Announce that at the next, and last, period of the course, the work of the 15 weeks will be summarized.

PERIOD XXX. SUMMARY OF COURSE.

1. Urge frequent rereading of the text and the habitual use of the reminder card, which is a brief version of the manual. When a student is about to write a report, he should check his performance against the card; if uncertain about the statement on the card, he should consult the manual for a brief explanation or the text for a more detailed one.

2. Make arrangements for consultation regarding individual difficulties. Offer your services for any assistance they may need in the preparation of future reports. Suggest that they always have the text available for reference. Make arrangements for return of any reports that you still have for correction.

3. *Summary.* Gather up in some clear, simple way the fundamental things you wish them to remember as they proceed with their report writing.

    a. Emphasize:
        (1) Classification and organization as a sound basis for the writing of all reports.
        (2) The objective of a report as a shaping factor in determining the structural design.
        (3) The need for taking the point of view of the prospective reader in considering the requirements for a satisfactory report.
    b. Sum up in a way the class will remember:
        (1) Before you begin to write, be sure that you know precisely *what* you are going to do, and *why*, and *how*.
        (2) Keep these three things clearly in mind all the time you are writing.
        (3) When you have finished, check to be sure you have nowhere become confused as to what, and why, and how.

Close with emphasis on the necessity for continually improving the quality of reports. Recall the final sentence, "The final injunction . . . is that every report be so designed as to serve all the uses to which it may be put, and always to the full satisfaction of all concerned."

For the Student

The first critical, and most immediate, problem for a student in a course in report writing is finding something to write about. If you can find a subject that will warrant a large investment of your time and effort, will stir your genuine enthusiasm, and enlist your best energies, you will experience the satisfaction of creating something reasonably original and worth while. In actual practice, you will, of course, never meet this problem. Your assignments will be given you in no uncertain terms by those who require your report. If you are research men or women enrolled in a training course in report writing, your research projects will furnish you rich material for your practice reports. But in an academic course you will naturally have to provide a usable subject for yourself. You may accomplish this most successfully by correlating your course assignments with some of the things you are most interested in—past experience, present activities, plans for the future.

If you have had work in even the most elementary forms of engineering, or forestry, or architecture, or in any field of technology, you can capitalize on such experience in a course like this, to good effect. This is, perhaps, the most useful correlation because it will force you to depend less on reference books or other bibliographical material and more on your own ideas. These may, at present, seem to you confused and difficult, but the experience of putting them in order and marshaling them for some specific use may be very valuable to you. Another correlation might be made with your plans for your future. If, after graduation, you hope to go into certain professional work, you may be better prepared for it if you have written a report dealing with some of the problems you are likely to meet.

ASSIGNMENT I

Write your instructor a letter telling him something of your background and your special interests. Recall the definition of the report given in Chapter I. Make your letter fundamentally a report by giving your instructor what he must know about you if he is to advise you intelligently in your choice of a subject for the two long-form reports in this course. If you are a student you should include a statement of your present courses in engineering or other fields of technology. If you are already in research or other professional work, you should present a clear, simple statement of that work with special emphasis on the phases of it that might furnish you with usable subject matter for your course reports. It may be well also to include an account of any experience you have had outside school—summer work in a factory, on the road, in the forestry service. You should certainly mention any hobbies and avocational interests that you would like to write about.

If you write your letter definitely to tell your instructor what he needs to know about you, you will be illustrating one of the fundamental principles of report writing—"Give him what he wants and must have."

Your instructor will no doubt judge your letter, aside from its content, largely on the basis of how well it accords with the generally accepted conventions for professional letters. The note on pages 317 to 319 will be helpful to you in reviewing what you probably already know about letter forms. [Sample letters written by students in this course in the past are given on the following pages. They show how these students met the requirements of this assignment. A few brief comments on the generally accepted conventions of professional letters may bring together, in convenient form, points to which the student may refer in the preparation of his letters. It should be remembered that professional letters differ—sometimes quite radically—from business letters.

609 Hill Street[1]
Ann Arbor, Michigan
September 30, 19__

Professor J. R. Nelson[2]
Room 9, University Hall
University of Michigan
Ann Arbor, Michigan

Subject:[3] Assignment I, Report
of Experience and Per-
sonal Interests

Dear Sir:[4]

At[5] present I am enrolled as a student of the Aeronautical Engineering Department here at the University
and am specializing in the structural and design aspect
of this profession.

I have been fortunate in that for the summer months
of the past three years I have had employment with the
Sikorsky Aircraft Corporation, Division of United Aircraft Corporation. Thus I have been able to add to my
store of theoretical knowledge some of the practical considerations confronting the designer and manufacturer of
aircraft. It is my desire to obtain employment with this
company after I have finished my schooling here, both for
personal reasons and obvious technical and practical
advantages.

During the last eight years, I have been interested
in the production of model airplanes. I have built several models, and, while I have not been successful in
winning any awards for craftsmanship, I feel that I have
obtained quite a large amount of theoretical and practical knowledge from my experimentation along this line.

I feel, therefore, that it would be most profitable
to me to choose the subject matter for my reports from
the wealth of aeronautical knowledge that is at present
available.

Very truly yours,[6]

Signature[7]
Name typed.[8]

---

[1] The heading contains the exact, complete mailing address of the writer of the
letter and the date. It is displayed in a single-spaced block, so placed that the
extreme right-hand point is in line with the right-hand margin. In the "un-
punctuated" form, which is now usual in typed letters, only the comma separating the name of the town from the name of the state and the comma separating

the day of the month from the year are retained; in other words, the punctuation is omitted at the end of the lines, unless in case of an abbreviation, but is retained within the lines to separate the component units. If letterhead is used, it absorbs everything except the date.

[2] The "introduction," so-called, contains the name and exact mailing address of the persons or group of persons to whom the letter is written. It is displayed, single-spaced and blocked in line with the left-hand margin. The space between the heading and the introduction may be varied in order to get the text, as a whole, centered on the page, but it must not be less than two spaces. The introduction is punctuated uniformly with the heading: that is, the punctuation is omitted at the ends of the lines, except for abbreviations, but is retained within the lines.

The question of abbreviations in both the heading and the introduction calls for a word of comment. In business letters, of course, abbreviations are freely used in both these units, but in professional letters of a formal sort one should abbreviate as little as possible. Concession will sometimes need to be made, in the interests of making a blocked display, in the case of a city and state that happen to have long names, as, for example, Los Angeles, California, or Philadelphia, Pennsylvania. As has been noted, all abbreviations whenever they occur must be marked with a period.

[3] The display of "subject," in a block under the heading and two spaces below the introduction, is not used in all types of professional letters, but it is gaining favor as a convenience and timesaver for those who must handle large numbers of letters. The punctuation is uniform with that of the heading and introduction.

[4] The so-called "salutation" is displayed at the left-hand margin, two spaces below the last line of subject, or if this unit is omitted, as is often the case, two spaces below the introduction. The colon is used following the "Dear Sir." "Gentlemen," never "Dear Sirs," is to be used in addressing more than one individual.

[5] The body of the letter begins two spaces below the salutation and at the point that sets the paragraph indentation for the entire letter. Five or six spaces is acceptable spacing, though six to nine are often used on 8″ x 11″ paper.

The blocked paragraph has come to be much preferred to the more conservative indented paragraph in both business and professional letters. Such paragraphs are single-spaced, with double spacing between paragraphs. In reports, however, and in letters of transmittal of reports, the blocked paragraph does not seem, to the author of this book, to lend itself to so effective a display of the sectional headings as does the indented paragraph, which has, therefore, been specified and demonstrated for use in his classes in report writing. The student or young practitioner should be warned that, if in this or other details of form or usage, he finds his instructor or his office supervisor in disagreement with the author of this book, he should follow the specifications of those to whom he is responsible. He should always remember one of the basic principles of this book, that the writer of a report should give his client what he wants in the form in which he wants it.

[6] The "complimentary close," divested of its ancient and now obsolete expressions of hope and trust (hoping, trusting that, etc.) is now displayed in line with

the blocked heading. Note carefully the capitalization of the first word and the use of the small letter for the beginning of all other words. The comma at the end of the line is now often omitted. Such an omission is, of course, consistent with the omission of punctuation in the heading, and introduction, but the author prefers the conservative usage, which retains the comma because it separates the substantive, "yours," from its appositive, the name of the writer of the letter. The rule that an appositive must be so separated from the noun to which it is in apposition seems to supersede the claim of consistency.

[7] The "signature" is, of course, pen-written.

[8] It is, and always should be, followed in the line below with the typed version of the signature. Anyone who has read many letters will appreciate how illegible signatures may become.

ASSIGNMENT II

DECIDING ON A SUBJECT

Decide on a subject for your first report, which is to be a formal, long-form report. Be sure it is something you are vitally interested in developing. Be sure it is limited enough so that it can be fully and adequately treated in the compass of a single report of 10 to 15 or 20 typewritten pages. Be especially sure that you have a definite purpose or objective in writing it, that you know exactly what it is expected to do. Review Chapter I and the introductory chapter in Part IV.

Analyze carefully the conditions under which it is to be written and the requirements for its satisfactory use.

1. If you are using an assignment made in some one of your courses, inform yourself as to what is wanted, and by what standards the report will be judged.

2. If possible, even in the case of a course assignment, set up a hypothetical situation that might arise in engineering practice requiring such a report as you propose to write. Be sure you are clear as to who wants it, how he will use it, why he asks you for it, and what his preferences and prejudices are.

Write your instructor a coherent, detailed statement of the problem or situation you propose to use for your first report. Possibly you may wish to recall to him why you are especially interested in presenting the subject you have chosen. Above all things, make clear to yourself and to him what use will be made of the report and what the requirements for such use must be.

4215 South Oak Street
Detroit, Michigan
October 31, 19__

Professor J. R. Nelson
University of Michigan
Ann Arbor, Michigan

Subject: Deciding on a
Subject

Dear Professor Nelson:

In selecting as a subject for my report ''Underground Distribution as Compared with Overhead Distribution for Residential Areas,'' I have in mind answering the question that is so often asked: Why doesn't The Detroit Edison Company put all its lines underground and thereby improve the appearance of our streets and alleys? This question frequently comes from the people who are only generally interested in the matter of public improvements. It also comes from individuals who wish poles and wires removed from their own property and its vicinity, developers of high-class real-estate projects ask for all-underground distribution, or municipalities request lines to be removed from their streets.

My intention is to discuss in this report the factors that necessitate the greater cost of underground as compared with overhead distribution and the offsetting advantages. I will also describe some of the different types of underground installation and mention some possibilities of future development that may have an effect on the situation. In general, my purpose will be to summarize our ideas on underground distribution for residential areas and define its present status as a usable form of distribution with some speculation on future prospects.

My report will be written for the information of our chief engineer, Mr. J. W. Parker. It should be of value to him as a condensation and summarization of the subject. It is possible that he may wish to pass the report to other company executives for their information. It will be sufficiently nontechnical for that purpose but would not be suitable for general distribution to outsiders who know nothing of the power business.

As to Mr. Parker's personal preferences in regard to reports, I believe that he likes them to be as brief as is feasible to cover the subject fully, to contain no more technical data than necessary to bring out the purpose in mind, and to proceed logically from given premises, through a comprehensive discussion to definite conclusions.

Yours very truly,

Signature
Name typed.

Professor J. R. Nelson
East Engineering Building
Ann Arbor, Michigan

                    Subject: Assignment II, Deciding
                        on a Subject

Dear Professor Nelson:

You may recall that I am planning to prepare my
first report on an inspection trip I made recently to the
Peninsular Paper Company in Ypsilanti. In order to make
the conditions under which I write it seem somewhat similar to those I might meet in practice, I have assumed
that the Midwest Printing and Publishing Company of
Chicago, publishers of advertising pamphlets and cata-
logues, greeting cards, and similar products requiring
cover grade papers are considering the construction or
purchase of a small paper mill equipped for the production and surfacing of colored cover papers.

Since most of the makers of fine colored cover have
developed their own secret formulas, especially as to
dye mixes and sizing, over a long period of years, and
because a mill capable of supplying the demands of the
Midwest Company would necessarily have a greater full-
time capacity than they could consume, the company would
prefer buying up one of the smaller mills producing the
desired type and quality of paper and already having
established markets.

Accordingly, Mr. H. C. Fairmont, President of the
Midwest Company, has asked me, as an employee familiar
with both the papermaking industry and the needs of the
company, to visit the mills of the Peninsular Paper Company at Ypsilanti, Mich., for the purpose of preparing a
somewhat nontechnical report for the use of the department heads and Board of Directors in determining the
advisability of the investment. It was further specified
that only such details as production facilities and capacity, nature and quality of product, storage and transportation facilities, together with a general account and
description of the plant need be included in the report
proper. In my report, I shall recommend the purchase of
this plant.

                            Very truly yours,

                                Signature
                                Name typed.

ASSIGNMENT III

EXAMINING THE SOURCES OF MATERIAL

Consider carefully and critically the sources of information you have available for your first report. Your instructor must be convinced, either that your experience has been sufficient to qualify you to write such a report without supplementary reading, or that you can secure the necessary bibliographical material to prepare yourself for your task. Write him an informal progress report telling him what you have done thus far to check on your available sources.

In the interest of making your letter complete and independent of your previous correspondence, it will be well to recall briefly at the outset the project you have taken and the conditions you have assumed. You should not lose sight of the fact that your report of progress should remove any doubt in your instructor's mind that you are now in a position to go ahead with your report so far as material is concerned. Keep reinforcing the ideal for every report that it has a definite task to perform, a definite objective to accomplish. Your report may take one of the following forms:

1. A letter giving him a detailed account other than bibliography, of your original sources of information—personal experience, personal interviews, personal research—such as will convince him that you do not need to do any reading.

2. A similar letter regarding original sources with a brief list of supplementary reading incorporated.

3. A tentative bibliography set up in proper form with an accompanying letter of transmittal. It is understood that this bibliography is not in final form and that you have not as yet examined or read in detail all the items you list. It represents merely what you find available in the library.

914 Hill Street
Ann Arbor, Michigan
October 18, 19__

Professor J. R. Nelson
University of Michigan
Ann Arbor, Michigan

Subject: Assignment III, Examining
the Sources of Material

Dear Sir:

For my report on the installation of Republic flow-meters in the Crystal Flake Salt Company, I shall depend for a source of imformation almost entirely upon my personal experiences. During the two years following my graduation from high school, I did the flowmeter maintenance work in the salt factory at Saint Clair, Mich. Through this work, I learned how these meters operated and how and where they were installed. I was also called upon to make the steam and power reports for the factory; and all of these reports were made from the meter readings. In this way, I learned of the importance of meters for the economical operation of the plant.

While at this factory I became acquainted with R. C. Ascher, the sales and service manager for Republic flow-meters in the State of Michigan. Last Sunday I called him in Detroit, and he promised to send me advertising literature and any other material that he thought would be necessary for such a report as I intend to make. As yet I have not heard from him; but when I do, I am certain my material will be adequate for the report.

Very truly yours,

Signature
Name typed.

714 East University Avenue
Ann Arbor, Michigan
October 15, 19__

Professor J. R. Nelson
Professor of English
University of Michigan
Ann Arbor, Michigan

Subject: Assignment III, Examining
the Sources of Material

Dear Professor Nelson:

On October 8, I wrote to you concerning my first
report which deals with radio—control apparatus.

The material for this report is to be gathered
largely from practical experience and experimental work.
Although I have read many magazine articles dealing with
radio control, the devices set forth in these articles
have either the inherent disadvantage of being able to
control only one thing at a time, of which the well—known
selector type system of remote control is a good example,
or they gave flexibility at the expense of becoming very
complicated.

The device on which my report is based is one of my
own design and is much more simple than those set forth
in the articles, and at the same time it is very flexible. Any number of operations may be controlled by it.

I have already drawn up the plans; the device itself
is now being constructed. I shall use schematic and
wiring diagrams, dimensions, photographs, and characteristic curves for illustrating the report.

I feel that through my personal work and reading I
have ample material for this report and that I have a
thorough understanding of the subject.

Very truly yours,

Signature
Name typed.

412 Thompson Street
Ann Arbor, Michigan
October 17, 19___

Professor J. R. Nelson
College of Engineering
Ann Arbor, Michigan

Subject: Assignment III, Examining
the Sources of Material

Dear Professor Nelson:

This is in reference to the subject about which I
have chosen to write for English Six, namely, ''The Advantages in the Use of the Podbielniak Standard Precision
Low-temperature Fractional Distillation Column over the
Use of the Regular Low-type Temperature Fractional Distillation Column.''

Inasmuch as the bulk of this subject matter will
necessarily have to come from my own experience in operating both of the above-mentioned columns, it will be
rather difficult to submit other than a very short list
of bibliography. Furthermore, in view of the fact that
the development of such equipment is a recent one, carried out by one man only, the published articles are few
in number.

However, the following will serve to give a résumé
of the development and use of the above-mentioned equipment. They are:

Podbielniak, Walter J, Low-temperature Distillation
Apparatus, Industrial Engineering Chemistry, analytical
edition, 3:2:177, April, 1931.

Podbielniak, Walter J, Standardization of Podbielniak Low-temperature Fractional Distillation Columns,
Industrial Engineering Chemistry, 4:5:219, November,
1933.

Also, I might add, that the material in the above
references is fresh in my mind so that all that remains
to be done is to organize it and begin writing the
report.

Very truly yours,

Signature
Name typed.

326

Professor J. R. Nelson
Room 9, University Hall
Ann Arbor, Michigan

Subject: Assignment III, Examining
the Sources of Information

Dear Professor Nelson:

The subject of my report is the preliminary mechanical design for a cargo vessel to be built especially for the transportation of standard less-than-carload containers. In obtaining material for my report I have had to rely largely upon suggestions from Professor H. C. Adams and my personal experience in this line which consists of a summer's work as a shipfitter's helper for the N. Y. Shipbuilding Company of Camden, N. J. This knowledge has been supplemented by inspection trips through other shipyards, and by a preliminary course in naval architecture in the university. For the bulk of my information and criticism, however, I shall have to rely upon Professor Adams.

The general characteristics of the ship will be of conventional design, so that little time need be spent in delineating these features. All necessary information for this can be found in the ''Shipbuilding Cyclopedia,'' published by Simmons-Boardman of New York. Most of my time will therefore be spent on the special features of the boat. For this work, I must develop my own ideas, and those of Professor Adams, based as much as possible upon already existing equipment.

Additional information on general design for various types of vessels may be found in the following references:

Karl, Alexander, The Design of Merchant Ships and Cost Estimating, p. 307. Simmons-Boardman Publishing Company, N. Y., 1930.

Walton, Thomas, Steel Ships, p. 332, Charles Griffin & Co., Ltd., London, 1918.

Very truly yours,

Signature
Name typed.

ASSIGNMENT IV

FORMULATING A THESIS SENTENCE

Having worked with your report material until you see quite definitely its limits and possibilities and the scope of your proposition, and having definitely settled in your own mind the purpose of your report, try to set up your proposition in a single, comprehensive sentence. This thesis sentence is not necessarily one that you will use in the text of your report; it is merely an attempt to crystallize in concrete form your conception of your entire subject, unified and motivated by a definite purpose. It is an embryonic sentence that suggests the whole—a working sketch that will serve to keep you within definite limits and moving toward a definite end. Review Chapter III, pages 12 to 22.

It will also help you at this point in your consideration of your material to give the report a brief but significant title. Note examples of title display and thesis sentences. Transmit the title and thesis sentence to your instructor in a letter in which you may make any comment you wish or ask any questions you need to ask.

THE DETROIT EDISON COMPANY

General Offices
2000 Second Avenue

Detroit, Michigan

November 7, 19__

Professor J. R. Nelson
1025 Service Building

Subject: Assignment IV, Formulating
a Thesis Sentence

Dear Professor Nelson:

For Assignment IV in your English composition
course, I have prepared the following sentence which
states the proposition of my report to be entitled ''A
Study of Methods of Controlling Voltage to Industrial
Customers.''

An analysis of voltage drops to industrial customers
supplied from class C, or industrial type, substations
shows that regulators in the individual lines at the sub-
station are not necessary and that group regulation of
lines by 5-per-cent bus regulators, which is the least
expensive method of regulation, will provide satisfactory
voltage for the customers.

Yours very truly,

Signature
Name typed.

ASSIGNMENT V

MAKING A PLAN FOR THE REPORT

Make an analysis and classification of your material. Follow the directions given in Chapter III. Examine especially the examples pages 19 to 22. Submit this preliminary design for your report with a separate letter of transmittal, making such comment as is necessary. It should be understood that this plan for your report is unlikely to be in its final form. You must expect to revise it at various points before you use it in writing your report. You are submitting it to your instructor for his criticism. If there are points in its structure of which you are uncertain, call his attention to them in your letter and ask his advice regarding them. Display the title, the thesis sentence, and the plan on the same sheet. Note the examples on pages 331, 332, and 334.

                                        2000 Second Avenue
                                        Detroit, Michigan
                                        November 14, 19__

Professor J. R. Nelson
The Detroit Edison Company
Detroit, Michigan

                            Subject: Assignment V, Making a
                                     Plan for the Report

Dear Professor Nelson:

    In fulfillment of Assignment V in your English com-
position course, I am sending you herewith an outline
plan of my proposed report on ''Underground Distribution
as Compared with Overhead Distribution for Residential
Areas.''

                            Yours very truly,

                                  Signature
                                  Name typed.

UNDERGROUND DISTRIBUTION AS COMPARED

WITH OVERHEAD DISTRIBUTION FOR RESIDENTIAL AREAS

Thesis Sentence: Although underground distribution cannot
at present be considered for general use in residential
areas on account of its cost being much greater than that
of overhead distribution, in certain specific cases additional expenditure for improved appearance can be justified and for these cases some new ideas in underground
construction, overhead construction, and combinations of
the two are being developed in addition to the types of
underground construction now available.

PLAN

I. Introduction
    a. Scope of report
    b. Demand for underground distribution
    c. Analysis of objections to overhead lines
II. General Comparison of Overhead and Underground
    Distribution

    a. Advantages of overhead distribution

        1. Economy
        2. Flexibility
        3. Maintenance of service
        4. Simplicity

    b. Advantages of underground distribution

        1. Appearance
        2. Reduction of outages
        3. Voltage regulation

    c. Comparison of cost of overhead and underground
       distribution

        1. Similar layouts
        2. Layouts for comparable service

III. Available Designs

    a. All underground

        1. Radial
        2. Loops, duplicate feeds, and other special
           arrangements
        3. Multiple-feed networks

<u>b</u>. Part underground and part overhead

    1. Small sections of underground tapped off
       overhead lines
    2. Underground primaries with overhead trans-
       formers and secondaries
    3. Underground primaries and transformers
       with overhead secondaries
    4. Overhead multiple-feed networks

<u>c</u>. Possible improvements in overhead construction

IV. Summary

    <u>a</u>. Present situation
    <u>b</u>. Prospect for future developments

ASSIGNMENT VI

SETTING UP A WORKING SKETCH WITH THE HEADINGS

The topic headings must correspond exactly with the units in your outline plan. They are displayed, however, in somewhat different relations. It will be well to review Chapter XI, pages 86 to 94. Study also pages 334 and 335 till you understand the relation of the heading system to the outline plan.

Prepare a working sketch of headings for your report. This will serve to fix more and more definitely in your mind the pattern of the report before you plunge into the confusing details of your subject. Be sure you understand how to show the relation of main headings to subordinate headings.

```
                                        2000 Second Avenue
                                        Detroit, Michigan
                                        November 14, 19__

Professor J. R. Nelson
2000 Second Avenue
Detroit, Michigan

                Subject: Assignment VI, Setting up a Working
                         Sketch with the Headings

Dear Professor Nelson:

        In accordance with Assignment VI in Engineering
Report Writing, I am submitting, on the attached pages,
a sketch of the topic headings for my report, on ''An
Installation of 120-Kilovolt Cable on The Detroit Edison
System.'' As it is based on the outline plan which I have
already made, I am submitting also a copy of that
outline.

                                        Yours very truly,

                                             Signature
                                        Name typed.
```

AN INSTALLATION OF 120-KV CABLE
ON THE DETROIT EDISON SYSTEM

Thesis Sentence: Since the necessity may arise not only of placing underground certain portions of existing overhead 120-kv tie lines, but also of making initial installations of all underground 120-kv cable between stations, a plan is provided covering the design, construction and installation features of the cable, conduit and cable accessories.

PLAN

I. Introduction

II. Cable

    a. Conductor

    b. Insulation

    c. Sheath

    d. Specification

III. Joints

    a. Straight and Stop Type

    b. Oil Reservoirs and Accessories

IV. Terminals

V. Conduit

    a. Number of Circuits per Run

    b. Separation of Circuits

    c. Size, Kind, and Number of Ducts

    d. Length of Section

VI. Manholes

    a. Design

    b. Accommodation for Oil Reservoirs, etc.

VII. Protective Features

    a. Elimination of Sheath Currents

    b. Oil Pressures Dependent upon Ground Profile

    c. Necessity of Lightning Arrester Protection

VIII. Summary

GBMc/
11-14-32

TOPIC HEADINGS

CABLE

<u>Conductor.</u>

<u>Insulation.</u>

<u>Sheath.</u>

<u>Specification.</u>

JOINTS

<u>Straight and Stop Type.</u>

<u>Oil Reservoirs and Accessories.</u>

TERMINALS

CONDUIT

<u>Number of Circuits per Run.</u>

<u>Separation of Circuits.</u>

<u>Size, Kind, and Number of Ducts.</u>

<u>Length of Section.</u>

MANHOLES

<u>Design.</u>

<u>Accommodation for Oil Reservoirs and Accessories.</u>

PROTECTIVE FEATURES

<u>Elimination of Sheath Currents.</u>

<u>Lightning Protection.</u>

<u>Alarms on Oil-feed System.</u>

SUMMARY

NOTE: If the student has any uncertainty as to the relation of the system of sectional headings to the outline plan, he should compare carefully the sketch of headings with the outline on which it is based. He will note that they are identical, except that no heading is used for the introduction and that the type of the headings and their points of display on the page differ from those in the outline.

ASSIGNMENT VII

PLANNING THE INTRODUCTION

Reread carefully Chapters IV to VI and VII. Study especially Chapter V. Write your instructor a discussion of what you think your introduction should contain if it is to satisfy the requirements of those who will use it. Study the two sample letters, pages 336, 337.

2000 Second Avenue
Detroit, Michigan
November 21, 19__

Professor J. R. Nelson
1023 Service Building

Subject: Assignment VII, Planning
the Introduction

Dear Professor Nelson:

This letter, written in accordance with Assignment VII of your course, states what I believe the introduction to my report should contain. The title of the report is ''A Study of Methods of Controlling Voltage to Industrial Customers.''

The report will be written primarily to Mr. Parker. I do not have to arouse his interest in the subject as he has questioned me regarding apparent inconsistencies in our practices of handling it. Therefore, I plan to catch his interest in the report by stating early in the introduction that its purpose is to analyze these inconsistencies, to give data showing where voltage losses occur, and to recommend what appears to me to be the best method of obtaining the desired results. It will be desirable that the introduction include a history of our practices, which have changed considerably, and that the reasons for these changes be stated.

The introduction will have to state the boundaries of the report. In effect, this will be emphasizing information already given in the title, that the report deals with voltage control of industrial customers only. For your information the permissible voltage range for different classes of customers differs. Perhaps ordinarily the limits of the report should be stated first in the introduction. However, in this case, I believe it would be strategic, because of Mr. Parker's known interest, to cover first the phase stated in the previous paragraph.

The introduction will conclude with a statement of the data on which the report is based and the order in which it will be presented.

Yours very truly,

Signature
Name typed.

420 East Ann Street
Ann Arbor, Michigan
November 21, 19___

Professor J. R. Nelson
Room 7, East Hall
Ann Arbor, Michigan

Subject: Assignment VII, Planning
the Introduction

Dear Professor Nelson:

In compliance with Assignment VIII of your course in English, ''Report Writing,'' I shall discuss briefly the material which I intend to include in the introduction to my proposed report on ''Underground Distribution as Compared with Overhead Distribution for Residential Areas.''

The general character of my report will be more informative than argumentative. Its major purpose is to present, in a concise, summarized form, pertinent facts concerning the subject, which in themselves are not particularly new. Any conclusions which may be drawn will be relatively unimportant compared with the display of the facts themselves. This, naturally, is a determining factor in the composition of my introduction.

The matter of ''interest'' or ''value'' need not be stressed since the intended reader is well aware of the main reason for distribution lines. The limits of the report will be quite clearly defined, however. It is proposed to summarize definitely and concisely the advantages and disadvantages of underground distribution as compared with overhead distribution and to discuss various types of construction, underground, overhead, and combined underground and overhead, which are available. It is not intended to go into any great detail in describing designs, materials, or methods of construction but to give the essential features only. The plan of the report is quite simple. In my outline submitted under Assignment IV, I divided the introduction into three parts, namely, ''Scope of Report,'' ''Demand for Underground Distribution,'' and ''Objections to Overhead Distribution.'' The first of these parts is really the introduction and will include the material discussed in this letter. The other two parts are also of an introductory nature; so I included them with the introduction. In them I intend to include a brief statement of the sources and magnitude of the demand for underground distribution and a short analysis of the factors which give rise to objections to overhead lines.

Yours very truly,

Signature
Name typed.

ASSIGNMENT VIII

WRITING THE INTRODUCTION

Submit the first draft of your introduction to your instructor for his criticism. Use a separate letter of transmittal. In case you intend to include a brief summary of results or findings or a general statement of conclusions and are, naturally, at this stage not ready to summarize these details in final form, merely indicate their place in the introduction. Study carefully the sample introductions on pages 57 to 63 and Clinic One, pages 237 to 253.

```
                                        Room 619
                                        2000 Second Avenue
                                        Detroit, Michigan
                                        November 28, 19__

Professor J. R. Nelson
Room 1023
2000 Second Avenue
Detroit, Michigan

Dear Professor Nelson:

        In compliance with Assignment VIII of the course in
Engineering Report Writing, I am sending you the proposed
introduction for my report on ''An Installation of 120-Kv
Cable on The Detroit Edison System.''

                                        Yours truly,

                                        Signature
GBMc/MW                                 Name typed.
```

AN INSTALLATION OF 120-KV CABLE
ON THE DETROIT EDISON SYSTEM

Because of the possible human hazard in densely populated districts particularly where apartment buildings may be constructed near Detroit Edison 120-kv overhead transmission lines, the need may arise at any time for replacing the overhead conductors with underground cable.

In the event of such a contingency, the use of cable, operating at the same voltage as the 120-kv overhead line, and connected direct thereto, is recommended, thus resulting in the elimination of costly step-down terminal apparatus, in simpler operation, and in a reduction of line voltage drops. Justification for the adoption by The Detroit Edison Company of such high voltage cable, operating at a voltage five times that of its present highest voltage cable, is found in the quite satisfactory experience for more than five years of the Chicago and New York utilities in the operation of over 75 miles of cable at 132 kv.

The original scope of this report, which, according to the first paragraph, implies that the proposed 120-kv cable is to serve only as underground dips in existing 120-kv overhead lines, might be enlarged to include also the possible need of 120-kv cable lines entirely underground from station to station.

In anticipation of the necessity of a 120-kv cable installation and in view of its proven feasibility, a plan is provided covering the design, construction, and installation features of the 120-kv cable, conduit, and cable accessories.

ASSIGNMENT IX

WRITING THE ROUGH DRAFT

Prepare a rough draft of your report. Reread Chapter XIV, pages 111 to 114. Concentrate on your subject matter. Write rapidly and with the idea of getting it all said according to your plan. Make a careful list of questions you would like to have answered before putting it in final form.

The following directions will put in explicit form a few practical suggestions for the revision of your first draft:

One should take the attitude that if he does not find the defects in his report someone else will and that it is far better for him to eliminate them than to leave them to mar and discredit his performance. Review Part III on "The Criticism of the Report."

1. Lay your first draft aside a few days till you can regard it objectively.

2. Take the point of view of those for whom the report is written. Exactly what do they want? Why do they want it. What use will they make of the report?

3. Examine the report in order to check up on the material. Is it complete? Will it fully satisfy the reader? Is it accurate? Check every detail, especially figures and computations.

4. Read the introduction carefully as a unit independent of the text. Does it give a complete, self-contained statement of your subject or proposition, your purpose, your conclusions or your recommendations, your plan for presenting the details of your subject matter? Be sure it does not depend on either title or letter of transmittal for its meaning, assuming no collateral information on the part of the reader.

5. Now consider whether the terminal section agrees with the introduction as to the proposition, the purpose, the plan, and the conclusions or recommendations.

If you have placed your summary of conclusions immediately after the introduction, you must regard it as an integral part of the preliminaries to the report.

6. Take a general view of the main body of your report. Do the headings used mark a pattern that checks perfectly with any statement of plan given your introduction? Do your headings indicate the relations of main and subordinate units consistently? Do you

discover any unaccountable proportioning of parts? Is there any point at which the text depends too much on the headings? Check your headings carefully against your table of contents, if you are using one.

You are trying to make sure that from first to last, you have kept clearly in mind what you set out to do and what your original plan for doing it was, to discover any points at which you became confused as to your proposition or lost your sense of direction or perspective or proportion.

7. Read your report aloud, slowly, deliberately; listen for repeated words, for repeated sentence forms, for repetitions of the same transitional devices. If you stumble over awkward, involved sentences, be sure your reader will not have the same difficulty. Make your text read smoothly and coherently.

8. Study the articulation of the parts; especially note your topic and transitional text at the beginning of the various sections. Be careful, while marking the necessary relationships at these critical points, not to make your transitional text too obvious or too mechanical.

9. Check your paragraphing.

Read your paper by skimming the topic sentences only, and thus see if these sentences are functioning properly. If you have several short, fragmentary paragraphs in succession, see if you cannot fuse them together into a single coherent unit with an appropriate topic sentence.

If you find a paragraph that is too long and taxing, analyze it into subordinate, component units and provide each with the proper topic sentence.

ASSIGNMENT X

Testing the Rough Draft

In Chapter XV two final tests were given which one may apply to his rough draft to determine how successfully he has accomplished what he set out to do. Reread this chapter, examine the illustrative material, and apply these tests to your own rough draft. Submit your title sheet, synopsis, and table of contents.

Review pages 119 to 121, 165 to 169, 188 to 193.

The table of contents, while it is invaluable as a final checkup of the structural soundness of a report, is not to be displayed in a final setup of many reports. It would be superfluous in very brief reports, in standardized forms, as in test and progress reports, or in reports requiring only a simple plan of organization.

AN INSTALLATION OF 120–KILOVOLT CABLE

on

THE DETROIT EDISON SYSTEM

Prepared By

Electrical System

December 31, 19___   Written by G. B. MoCabe

SYNOPSIS

The report that follows reviews briefly the conditions
that may, in the near future, necessitate not only the
placing underground of certain portions of the existing
120-kv tie lines but the making of initial installations
of all underground 120-kv cables between stations. It
purposes to present a complete and detailed plan for the
design of such installations. It covers the design and
construction of the cables and conduits and their accessories, as well as the protective features which are
important considerations in such a design.

TABLE OF CONTENTS

Introduction

Preliminary Considerations

Cable

    Conductor
    Insulation
    Sheath
    Specification

Joints

    Straight and Stop Type
    Oil Reservoirs and Accessories

Terminals

Conduit

    Number of Circuits per Run
    Separation of Circuits
    Size, Kind, and Number of Ducts
    Length of Section

Manholes

    Design
    Accommodation for Oil Reservoirs and Accessories

Protective Features

    Elimination of Sheath Currents
    Lightning Protection
    Alarms on Oil-feed System

Summary

The Reminder Card

The reminder card has been found useful for ready reference by those who have had the basic training presented in this book. In practice one often has little time or opportunity to refer to his text. This card will serve to recall the fundamental procedures and ultimately make them habitual.

The highly concentrated texts displayed below may be copied or cut out and pasted on a substantial card and kept always at hand where you can use them. They are a "vest-pocket" edition. Unfortunately, in these days, vests are not worn. A rear trousers pocket or a billfold will do as well. When you have an office of your own, tuck the card under the glass on your desk.

THE REMINDER CARD

STEP 1. PREPARE.
1. Collect material.
2. Check details.
3. Decide on the purpose of report.
   Who will read it?
   Why does he want it?
   What does he require?
   How will he use it?
4. Draft a thesis sentence.

STEP II. MAKE A PLAN.
1. Classify your material.
2. Make an outline.
3. Make a sketch of headings and subheadings.

STEP III. WRITE.
1. Introduction: state subject, purpose, plan; summarize results, conclusions.
2. Body: describe equipment; procedure, results.

3. Terminal Section: summarize findings; make recommendations; give final emphasis.
4. Abstract or Synopsis: condense report to a paragraph or two.
5. Prepare table of contents.
6. Assemble and organize appendix and bibliography.

STEP IV. CRITICIZE.
1. Examine report as a whole: the plan; the proportioning of parts.
2. Check agreement of title, table of contents, introduction and abstract or synopsis.
3. Check agreement of terminal section and the introduction.
4. Check agreement of headings with table of contents.
5. Check proportion of unit parts.
6. Examine details of text: transitions from topic to topic, part to part, sentence structure, wording.

As a final test read text aloud, preferably to some one with a critical ear.

In Retrospect

Consistently with the theory of terminal sections laid down in this book, it is important now at the end to lift the really essential thesis from the welter of detail and set it up in a final form easy to remember. The emphasis on the need of classification and organization of material as a basis for writing has been so constant throughout the discussion that it is not apt to be lost. The recognition of the shaping and determining effect of the objective on the structural characteristics of a report, also, is likely to be remembered when many details of its applications are forgotten. The insistence that the writer take the reader's point of view and prepare the report to meet his requirements has been reiterated till it has become a commonplace. Perhaps all these indispensable ideals may best be kept in mind by recalling the definition of the report as a document prepared for a designated reader or group of readers who need it for certain definite uses. The final injunction, based on this definition, is that every report be so designed as to serve all the uses to which it may be put, and always to the full satisfaction of all concerned.

Index

The index will be found to have many important uses. Like the dictionary, it does not make interesting reading, but it does assemble under the listed topics material which one finds scattered throughout the text. If the teacher discovers that a student has difficulty in the delicate matter of transitions, for example, one of the last arts to be mastered by the beginner, he may advise him to study all the passages in the text listed in the index under "Transitional devices." Any writer who becomes aware of his own difficulties may follow this same suggestion. The index thus becomes a supplementary source of assignments for study. It also affords a convenient way of locating some passage that one recalls from a cursory reading of the book; it is much more expeditious to use the index than to thumb one's way vaguely through the text.

Index

351